Islands,
Capes,
and
Sounds

Photograph by David Rolfe

Islands, Capes, and Sounds

The North Carolina Coast

by Thomas J. Schoenbaum

JOHN F. BLAIR, PUBLISHER
Winston-Salem, North Carolina

COPYRIGHT 1982 BY THOMAS J. SCHOENBAUM

Library of Congress Catalog Card Number 81-21557
ISBN 0-89587-059-2

Design by Virginia Ingram
Printed in the United States of America

Third Printing, 1992

LIBRARY OF CONGRESS CATALOGING IN PUBLICATION DATA

Schoenbaum, Thomas J.

Islands, capes, and sounds.

Bibliography: p.
Includes index.
1. Coasts—North Carolina. 2. Islands—North Carolina.
3. Sounds—(Geomorphology)—North Carolina. 4. Natural history—North Carolina. 5. North Carolina—Description and travel—1982-   . 6. Coastal zone management—
North Carolina. I. Title.
F260.S34   975.6   81-21557
ISBN 0-89587-059-2   AACR2

For Luke

Preface

THIS BOOK IS A DESCRIPTION OF THE COASTAL HERITAGE OF North Carolina, a guide for those who wish to know her coast, and the story of how man is dealing with North Carolina's coastal resources. My method is largely subjective and impressionistic, at times eschewing scientific objectivity in favor of exploring the implications of the history and natural processes of the coast for decisions that will determine the future of the region.

Coastal resource management must take into account more than legal doctrines and the predictions and projections of government planners. The human and natural history of the North Carolina seacoast is extremely rich and complex. It provides the essential background and the inescapable context for making management decisions. I offer here a humanistic exploration of the coastal heritage of North Carolina and suggestions on how that heritage should be preserved.

I am grateful for the reception accorded to this book, which has merited an updated new edition.

During the last several years, development has proceeded apace on the North Carolina coast—but so has care and preservation of coastal resources. Areas of environmental concern have been designated, estuarine reserves have been established, and a beach access program is being maintained. Complex issues remain, but they are now being addressed by a state management program that is the most interesting and innovative in the nation.

Contents

Illustrations

Introduction

MY INVOLVEMENT WITH THE NORTH CAROLINA COAST BE-
gan in 1969, shortly after I joined the law faculty of the University of North Carolina at Chapel Hill. When I was assigned a
course on environmental law, I sought out people in state government and the universities who were dealing with environmental
problems. I discovered a deep concern about what was happening to the coastal environment.

The 1960s were a time of accelerated change on the coast.
Land values skyrocketed and new roads and bridges opened up
previously inaccessible places. Encouraged by local politicians,
developers hastened to cash in on the boom. Where the natural
environment got in the way, it was simply removed. Marshes
were dredged and filled, dunelands were flattened, and forests
were cut. The object of all this was to get as close to the water as
possible. The possibility of a major storm or a hurricane was
rarely mentioned. The Army Corps of Engineers could be
counted on to provide the necessary protection. As for the destruction of the natural environment, this was of concern only to
bird watchers.

The more I learned about what was happening on the coast,
the more I agreed with those people who expressed alarm at the
unrestrained development taking place. I had come to North
Carolina from Chicago, where going to the beach meant putting
your towel down alongside those of several thousand other
people at the foot of Oak Street on the shore of Lake Michigan.
There was no sense of solitude in this experience, and nothing
at all was left of the natural world except for the dead fish floating belly-up in the water. To be sure, there are beautiful areas of

the Lake Michigan shore, but few of them are open to the public. While in high school, my friends and I used to climb fences and sneak onto the private beaches, but I soon lost my nerve for that sort of thing. Thereafter, to get to a relatively unspoiled beach I had to drive forty miles to the Indiana Dunes National Seashore, a grandiose name for a patch of shore wrested from the steel companies after years of effort.

I remember well the words of the late Illinois senator Paul Douglas, who was in the forefront of fighting for the park: "When I was in my twenties, I wanted to save the world; when I was in my thirties, I wanted to save the nation. In my forties, I wanted to save Illinois. Now all I want to do is save the Indiana dunes." By that measure, he was a success.

Getting to know the North Carolina coast was a unique experience for me. It was not love at first sight. In winter, the Outer Banks can be a cold and forbidding place. Even in summer, to be caught on an island as a sudden storm approaches can be terrifying. But I soon realized that these elements were part of the reason for my growing fascination with the area. It was a place stripped to the most fundamental and powerful natural forces: the tides, the wind, the waves, sun and rain, day and night—reminders of the cyclical nature of the world and of life. I also became aware of the great variety of living things that enrich the coastal environment. And I got to know some of the people who lived in the area, people who seemed remarkably satisfied with where they lived.

I saw that the coast is mile after mile of open sandy beach, the smell of marsh and sea, colors that change with the season and the weather, and—above all—a place of order and solitude. But I realized that this environment is a fragile one. Through misuse we could destroy the very values that make the coast such a special place.

In the early 1970s I became involved in an effort to create new laws to "manage" the North Carolina coast. "Manage" is a word that attracts few admirers. In this context it usually means government regulation, and that is thought of as bad. But such a judgment oversimplifies things. By 1970 the North Carolina coast was already extensively managed by government. Federal and state agencies were heavily involved in constructing bridges and roads, in attracting new industry, in moving millions of cubic feet of sand and other material around from place to place every year. The question of management involved not *whether* but *how*. Moreover, good management can mean getting rid of government programs (popularly called deregulation) as well as creating them. As we shall see, this is especially true for coastal management.

As I studied the management techniques of the past, I decided that the most fundamental error we had made was to carry out programs without understanding what was really going on, how the natural systems worked. I was convinced that we needed to know the ecology and geology of the area before we could adopt policies for solving the problems. We have to work with the natural forces of the coastal environment, not against them, if we are to succeed.

I sought out marine biologists, geologists, and oceanographers to educate myself on the complexities of how coastal systems work. I was surprised to learn that much of our knowledge about the coast has come from the work of scientists during only the last ten or fifteen years. This revolution in thinking is still not generally known beyond a small number of scientists actively working in the field. Because of the great importance of these new findings, especially for policy choices and the resolution of controversies, we cannot afford to allow them to remain buried in obscure scientific reports.

I also came to realize that making intelligent decisions about the future of the coastal area should not be attempted without an intimate knowledge of the history and culture of the people of the area. I owe this insight primarily to Professor William S. Powell, who in his book *North Carolina: A Bicentennial History* points out in some detail how physical geography has played an important role in determining the history of North Carolina, especially the coastal section of the state.

The present book, then, attempts to synthesize and relate, in a form accessible to the general reader, several disparate fields of knowledge—politics, law, geology, ecology, and history. The reader will find that Part I locates the problem in its context by describing in broad-brush terms the natural and human history of the North Carolina coast. Part II treats each of the regions of the North Carolina coast as I have somewhat arbitrarily chosen to identify them. The emphasis here is on the major events and controversies that define the area. Part III deals with the political and legal decisions that have shaped and continue to shape the future of the coast. Finally, in an Appendix, I have compiled a selective list of some of the most interesting sites and activities to be enjoyed by the traveler. The structure of the book rests on the assumption that the scientific and historical contexts need to be brought to bear upon our perception of what we want this lovely and interesting area to become. The issues and conflicts that arise over the future use of coastal resources will not be resolved next year or even in the next twenty years. Like the coast itself, the problems we face are constantly changing but will always be with us.

This book is neither a conventional travelogue nor a tract on some specialized aspect of the North Carolina coast. Such impersonal and restricted approaches to knowledge obscure the essential nature of the object in question. As the novelist Walker Percy points out, "Every explorer names his island Formosa, beautiful. To him it is beautiful because, being first, he has access to it and can see it for what it is. But to no one else is it ever as beautiful—except the rare man who manages to recover it, who knows that it has to be recovered."* We can know something only by reclaiming it from prepackaged ideas and scientific abstractions. This requires an integrative view of the different qualities of the object. That is the method of this book.

Several persons provided significant help in solving some of the problems encountered in earlier drafts of this manuscript. Orrin Pilkey gave me some excellent help and encouragement about how to handle the geological materials. John Orth provided suggestions on organization. David Owens gave me helpful comments on the coastal zone management sections. George McDaniel has been a superb editor and has helped immensely with the work of organizing this complex subject.

*"The Loss of the Creature" in *The Message in the Bottle*, (New York: Farrar, Straus and Giroux, 1975), p. 46.

I

Background

1

Natural Systems and Human Policies

THE ATLANTIC COAST SWEEPS BOLDLY DOWN FROM THE Virginia capes in a series of graceful arcs. This edge of land is a thin ribbon of sand islands separated from the mainland by shallow bays and sounds. The northern half of this ribbon of islands is called the Outer Banks. The first long arc reaches far out to sea, finally falling away to the west to form historic Cape Hatteras, whose offshore shoals are called the "graveyard of the Atlantic." The second arc trends southwesterly, comprising, among others, the island of Ocracoke, once a haven for pirates, and culminating in Cape Lookout, a dagger point of sand marking the southern boundary of the Outer Banks. Thereafter the islands hug the coastal mainland but jut out again at Cape Fear, the ominous name given by early explorers to the third and last of North Carolina's perilous capes.

This long, thin chain of sand is the preeminent feature of the North Carolina coast. Geologists call its components *barrier is-lands* because they block the high-energy waves and storm surges of the ocean, protecting the coastal mainland. Barrier islands are common features of most of the low-lying coastlines of the world, yet no two of them are alike. They differ depending on latitude, shape, vegetation, and their position with respect to the prevailing winds and waves. The east and Gulf coasts of the United States have the best-evolved chain of barrier islands in the world, and North Carolina is blessed with more than three hundred miles of them, including the greatest extent of relatively undisturbed sections left along the east coast.

Despite the individual variations, there are certain character-istics that barrier islands tend to have in common. To observe these basic features, it is necessary to choose an island that has not yet been severely altered by man. There, on the sand beach (what geologists refer to as the *berm*), over which the tide ebbs and flows, is a world in motion. The surf is frequently filled with small fish less than an inch long. Blue crabs scavenge on the bottom. Just seaward of low tide live flounder, sand dollars, sea cucumbers, and several species of clams and shellfish. A "pop-ping" sound can sometimes be heard coming from the water above these small animals; this is a turbulence signaling the pres-ence of a school of bluefish or menhaden. Porpoises can often be seen alternately riding above the waves and plunging beneath the surface. Gulls, terns, and skimmers wheel and hover over-head.

On the exposed beach of the intertidal zone, the area between high and low tide levels, there is no visible vegetation, although microscopic plants and animals live beneath the surface of the sand. Looking closely, one can see a myriad of small, barely no-ticeable eruptions in the sand as the surf runs down from the beach after rolling up on the shore. These are mole crabs filter-ing small pieces of organic matter called *detritus* and various mi-croscopic organisms suspended in the waves. Another common filter-feeder here is the small coquina clam, no two of which seem to be exactly the same color. Several types of worms and other creatures live in the sand as well. These also live on detritus. More than a dozen species of shorebirds, including sandpipers and plovers, may be found running just in front of the waves, feeding on small animals.

On the dry-sand part of the beach, above the reach of high tide, are the round burrows of the ghost crab. Here also is the first vegetation—hardy, salt-tolerant grasses such as sea rocket, sea oats, and a spiky hay known as *Spartina patens*. This grassland tends to be very sparse since it is constantly being buried by the moving sands. From time to time, some sand will become trapped behind these plants and a dune will form. If the prevailing winds blow directly across the beach, high dunes may build up, covered with sea oats and *Spartina*, interspersed with blowouts and richly vegetated swales. If the prevailing winds blow the sand down or off the beach, the dunes will be low and temporary, often lasting only until the next storm waves, which may overwash much of the island, creating flat terraces that are barren or only sparsely vegetated. On protected flatlands behind the dunes there will be a denser grassland community with such species as broom sedge, wild lettuce, goldenrod, rush, and pennywort.

Farther away from the sea, where there is some shelter from the salt spray, shifting sand, and storm waves, grow shrubs and small trees. Shaped by the wind and sea, these have an appearance different from those of mainland forests. Broad-leafed, evergreen shrubs such as wax myrtle and silverling first invade the grassland, forming a protective fringe, back of which may be yaupon, red cedars, live oaks, and a few loblolly pines. The mature maritime forest community, found only on undisturbed portions of the larger islands, is a spectacular tangle of these and other woodland species festooned with vines and Spanish moss. Since anything that grows above the invisible line of protection afforded by the dunes will be damaged by salt spray, the tops of the trees have a "pruned" and gnarled appearance.

Freshwater marshes are often found in the interior of a maritime forest since a thin layer of fresh water, which geologists call a *lens*, is just under the sand of a barrier island, reaching the

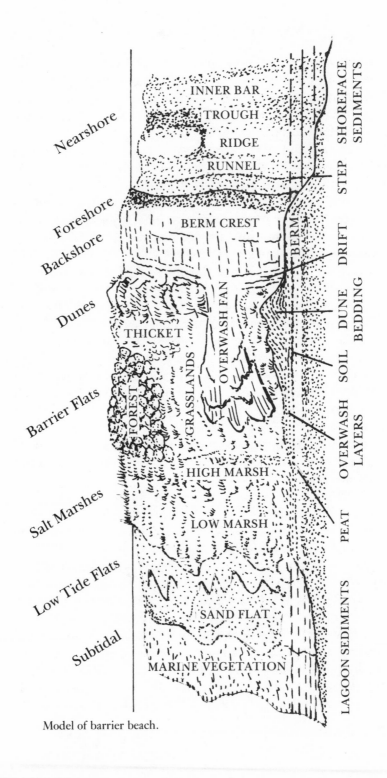

Model of barrier beach.

surface at low points. Plants growing here include cattails, arrowheads, black needlerushes, and marsh mallows. A variety of birds, including redwings, grackles, bitterns, rails, herons, and egrets, live in the marshes as well.

The maritime forest ends on the far side of the island, where the land slopes down to meet the waters of a lagoon or sound. Here in the shallows is the salt marsh. Higher terraces, flooded only by wind and spring tides, are covered with *Spartina* and *Juncus* grasses. Lower areas of the marsh that are flooded by the daily tides are dominated by a denser and taller plant, *Spartina alterniflora*, or saltwater cordgrass. Fiddler crabs can usually be found, their burrows aerating the soil of the marsh. Blue-green algae, diatoms, and other microscopic forms of life flourish. Rails, herons, egrets, and other water birds find shelter and food. The salt marsh produces an invisible but critical source of food, small pieces of organic material that are carried away by each tide, the critical source of nutrients for the rich life of a healthy estuarine system.

In the shelter of the barrier-island chain of the North Carolina coast are the lagoons, bays, and sounds of the estuaries. These are places partially cut off from the sea where fresh water coming down from the rivers meets salt water entering through the inlets. North Carolina has more than 2.2 million acres of these estuarine waters, more than any other state except Alaska and Louisiana.

In the southern half of the North Carolina coast, rivers are short, sometimes with both source and mouth in the same coastal county. Only the Cape Fear, which rises in the piedmont section of the state, has an extensive drainage basin. This part of the coast is a series of small estuaries connected by narrow lagoons with inlets located opposite the mouths of rivers. Strong tidal action and the high salinity of the shallow water provide ideal conditions for extensive salt-marsh complexes, sometimes covering virtually the entire area of the lagoon between island and mainland.

North of Cape Lookout, behind the Outer Banks, a very different type of estuary occurs. A huge, shallow basin, the Pamlico-Albemarle-Currituck Sound complex, covers more than two million acres of a "drowned" portion of the North Carolina coastal plain. Several rivers, including the Chowan, Roanoke, Pamlico, and Neuse, and numerous creeks feed enormous quantities of fresh water into the area, which mix with salt water supplied through the inlets. Tidal action is virtually absent from most of the area, and the salinity of the water is low because the inlets are relatively few; north of Cape Hatteras only Oregon Inlet breaks the Outer Banks barrier. Anyone who has gone boating in these sounds is aware that they are very shallow, ranging from a few inches deep in the numerous shoals to a maximum of seven feet in Currituck Sound and twenty-four feet in Pamlico Sound. Many small islands in the sounds provide nesting sites for rookeries of herons, ibises, brown pelicans, gulls, and terns.

Currituck Sound is a lovely, clear, almost freshwater lagoon behind Currituck Banks, which stretch up to the Virginia line. Numerous islands and freshwater marshlands of saw grass, giant cordgrass, and cattail provide shelter for wintering flocks of ducks, swans, and geese. The largemouth bass fishing attracts sportsmen from all over the country.

Much of the fringing shore of the deeply indented Pamlico and Albemarle sounds nearer the inlets is covered by irregularly flooded, brackish-water marsh species, especially black needlerush. These are rooted in a tough, erosion-resistant, peaty soil. Farther inland, along river floodplains at the mouths of the Roanoke, Chowan, and Pamlico rivers, there is a wild and spectacular shoreline of cypress trees with elongated "knees" and trunks submerged in three to five feet of water. This is the fringe of the dense swamp forests of those areas. Along the Chowan River estuary are high bank and bluff shorelines of hard clay that have been worn away by the action of the water.

This estuarine system is second in size on the east coast of the United States only to the Chesapeake Bay. Its protected waters, with abundant organic material available from the marshland grasses, is an important fishery resource. Shrimp, oysters, blue crabs, hard clams, and bay scallops are harvested by North Carolina fishermen, and finfish such as menhaden, alewives, spot, mullet, striped bass, and sea trout are caught as well. The estuary also acts as a nursery for the juvenile stages of many species of open-ocean fish. Fishery biologists estimate that sixty-five percent of the fish and shellfish taken along the North Carolina coast depend at some time in their life cycles on marsh plant nutrients and the estuary. In addition, ducks and geese winter here by the hundreds of thousands.

The peninsulas and fingers of land between the estuarine rivers of North Carolina are extensive floodplains where the water table often reaches the surface of the soft, peaty land. Here can be found extensive swamp forests of cypress and tupelo gum trees such as the Great Dismal Swamp on the border between North Carolina and Virginia. These swamps in their natural state are virtually always flooded. Higher, irregularly flooded areas are dominated by a hardwood swamp forest of water oaks, sweet gum, river birch, and sycamore.

Two additional interesting coastal environments occur in North Carolina. The Indians used the term *pocosin*, meaning bog on a hill, to refer to extensive bogs rising slightly in elevation toward the center, covered with dense evergreen shrubs such as sweet bay and fetterbush combined with scattered clumps of pond pine. These interesting areas may be seen in the "Carolina bays," large, peat-filled, elliptical depressions that some people think were formed by meteorites, as well as in low flatland regions and sandy depressions between ridges. These shrub-bogs are almost impenetrable. There is a story that once a U.S. Marine drill sergeant gave two groups of his best men the task of hiking eight miles through a pocosin in the Croatan National Forest near Morehead City. One team made it in thirty-six hours, while the other gave up after three days and had to be lifted out by helicopter.

Closely related to the pocosin is the pine savannah, characterized by gently sloping sand ridges and poorly drained flatlands. Pond pine, longleaf pine, and scattered evergreen shrubs grow amid a continuous ground cover of grasses. The area is kept open by being highly susceptible to fire. A rich wildflower and plant community flourishes, which includes the exotic, insect-eating pitcher plant and Venus flytrap as well as goldenrod, orchids, sunflowers, and asters.

All of these distinctive coastal environments are produced by the interaction of the land with water—the sea, rivers, swamps, bogs, and estuaries. In this confrontation, it is the water that always wins. The land here is yielding sand, clay, and other sedimentary material eroded from the Appalachians and deposited by rivers in geologically recent times. The nearest naturally occurring hard rock is at the "fall line" (where the piedmont begins), many miles to the west. It may not seem like it on a still, warm summer's day, but the coastal area is *in motion*, at the mercy of the relentless waters.

We know that the level of the sea has stood both much higher and much lower than it is today. On satellite photographs of the North Carolina coast one can easily make out a thin, low ridge line that is the western boundary of Dismal Swamp, stretching south to the west of Edenton and Plymouth and cutting through the Pamlico peninsula to Newport in Carteret County. This is the remnant of an ancient coastline marking the edge of the sea perhaps 100,000 years ago. Geologists have named this line the "Suffolk Scarp," and other such "scarps" exist even further to the west on the coastal plain. These high sea levels are thought to have existed during warm periods in the earth's history.

During the "ice ages," when glaciers locked up much of the earth's water, sea level was much lower than at present. About 18,000 years ago, during the last ice age, the sea stood perhaps as much as 400 feet below its present level. The North Carolina coast looked very different from the way it does now. Dense northern forests of spruce and fir, intermixed with cold, freshwater bogs and marshes, covered the land, and rivers like the Neuse and the Cape Fear occupied deep channels, which are now "drowned" topographic features of the continental shelf.

A general warming of the earth's climate then caused the glaciers to melt. Sea level rose rapidly for about 13,000 years, then slowed, reaching a point near its present level approximately 5,000 years ago. The northern forests were replaced, first by beech and maple, then by oak and hickory, with pines occupying sandy ridges and those areas within the hardwood forest frequently swept by fire.

The banks and barrier islands of the North Carolina coast were probably formed during this last period of sea-level rise.

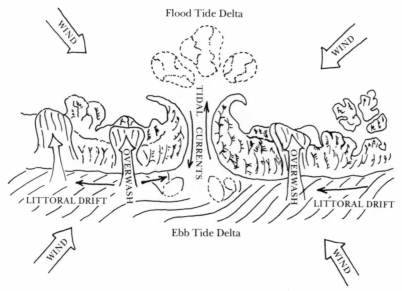

Flood Tide Delta

WIND WIND

TIDAL CURRENTS

OVERWASH OVERWASH

LITTORAL DRIFT LITTORAL DRIFT

Ebb Tide Delta

WIND WIND

Mechanisms of sand transport on barrier beaches.

According to the late Dr. John Hoyt of the University of Georgia, when the sea reached its lowest point, a high ridge of sand dunes on the mainland beach was formed by the action of the waves breaking on the shore and by winds blowing seaward over the beach. As sea level rose, this beach ridge was breached and the low-lying area behind became flooded by the sea, creating shallow sounds and lagoons. The former dune ridges thus became a series of islands parallel to the mainland coast.

But remarkably, as the level of the sea continued to climb, the barrier islands were not covered by the rising waters. Complex geologic processes enabled the islands both to maintain their elevation above the sea and to "migrate" as a unit by moving their front edge backward in response to the rising waters.

Dr. Paul Godfrey of the University of Massachusetts has shown that wind-driven dune migration and a process called *overwash* are the major ways these islands retreat from the sea and grow toward the land. Overwash occurs when storm winds and tides breach the dune line, moving sand back across the island in a pattern called an *overwash fan*. This is not a destructive process but rather helps the island to *roll over upon itself* and grow landward. After the storms have subsided, the rapid colonization of the area by beach grasses results in new dune formation to maintain the island's elevation.

A continuous supply of sand for this process is available from sediment carried down from the rivers or deposited on the beach by fair-weather ocean waves. The inlets and lagoons behind the islands also act as sand traps which build up the back sides of these islands. Sand held in suspension by the waves is first moved into an inlet in immense quantities by flood-tide currents. In the slack lagoonal waters it settles out and is not carried back out by the ebb-tide current. The tidal delta that typically forms behind an inlet is also part of the process of island-building. When the inlet shoals up, dune formation adds a new island link to the system.

Inlets are among the most interesting areas of change on the North Carolina coast. Permanent inlets exist only in the southern half of the coast at the mouths of rivers. Even there, the channels are constantly changing in response to the action of the waves, winds, and tides. On the Outer Banks, inlets are only temporary, formed by the surge of storm waves across the bar. We know from historical records and old maps that more than two dozen inlets have existed at various times on the Outer Banks, although only six are still open. The inlets on the Outer Banks seem to go through a natural cycle of birth, change, and death. Whether this takes two hundred years or a few weeks is determined by factors we do not yet fully understand. Inlets may also change position, migrating along a barrier island shoreline if the accretion rate is greater on one side than the other. Inlets are essential to the functioning of the coastal system since they allow an exchange of water, nutrients, and small organisms between the estuaries and the sea.

The naturally occurring dynamics of the barrier islands of the North Carolina coast have allowed them to survive the rise in sea level and migrate as much as fifty miles landward as the sea has flooded what was the coastal area of 18,000 years ago. During the last 5,000 years migration has slowed because the rate in the rise of sea level has declined. Nevertheless, sea level continues to rise today at the rate of about one foot per century, causing

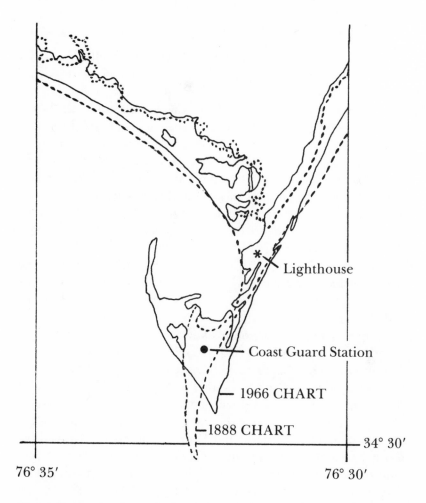

Lighthouse

Coast Guard Station

1966 CHART

1888 CHART

34° 30'

76° 35'

76° 30'

Charts showing the changes in the shape and orientation of Cape Lookout from 1888 to 1965.

shoreline retreat of 50 to 200 feet a century over most of the North Carolina coast.

In certain areas of the Outer Banks from Currituck to Shackleford Banks, remnants of tree stumps are exposed in the surf at low tide. Beneath a layer of sand on the dunes of these islands is a layer of peat deposit. This is evidence that overwash and island migration landward are still occurring in many areas and that perhaps less than several hundred years ago, lands that are now submerged were covered with trees and vegetation.

The barrier islands are in motion laterally as well. Practically everyone who has been to the beach has experienced the reason why. After a half hour in the water, the bather returns to the shore only to find that he has drifted many yards down the beach from the point at which he entered the water. He has been carried along gradually by the waves, which although appearing to strike the beach directly, actually roll up at an angle determined by the prevailing winds. The force that carries the bather also transports great quantities of sand and sediment parallel to the coast, eroding some areas and depositing material in others. This phenomenon is called *littoral drift* by geologists. By comparing the shoreline shown on old maps with the present shoreline, we can see that this process has changed the configuration of the coastline dramatically even in the last thirty to forty years. For example, Shackleford Banks has grown a half mile on its western end during this time.

The estuarine area of sounds and lagoons behind the barrier islands is also affected by rising sea level and the action of winds and waves. The mainland side of Currituck Sound is being scoured back by the north winds that blow down the length of the sound during winter storms. Recent studies by Stan Riggs of East Carolina University show that the erosion rate of most of the shoreline of Albemarle and Pamlico sounds is two to three feet per year and is even higher where protective shoreline vegetation has been removed. Islands in the sounds are subject to severe erosion, and several have disappeared entirely. In the 1700s, Batts Grave Island was situated off Drummond Point at the mouth of the Yeopim River and was large enough for houses and orchards. Today only a few stumps of trees are visible above the waters of Albemarle Sound.

We have learned a great deal about the ecology and geology of these natural coastal systems. But what science cannot tell us is the answer to the question of what policies we should adopt for the management and use of this region. This judgment is a political one depending on human values. Basically, the choice for the future is whether development should be fostered to transform these environments, creating new urban areas, resorts, and industrial centers, or whether development should be allowed to proceed in such a way as to take into account the limitations of the natural environmental forces.

My own preference is for a policy of respecting the limits imposed by natural environments. In the future these coastal resources should be used only for purposes that are consistent with the long-term functioning of the barrier islands, estuaries, and coastal wetlands. The rest of this book is in part an attempt to explain the whys and hows of this proposal.

The major arguments for protection of this area can be briefly stated. First, these barrier-island and estuarine ecosystems are among the richest and most interesting in the world. Because of the wide variety of habitats and the availability of food, plant and animal species are both more numerous and more diverse than on land environments. Many threatened or endangered species, such as the bald eagle, the peregrine falcon, and the loggerhead turtle are present here. Since it is a highly specialized environment, many species of plants and animals are found nowhere else.

The rich flora and fauna of the coastal environment are more than just an aesthetic asset. Sport and commercial fishing, hunting, and water recreation are all multimillion-dollar industries in eastern North Carolina. They depend directly upon the continued productivity of the natural systems. Environmental degradation threatens food supplies and jobs. The livelihood of those who sell related supplies and services to hunters, fishermen, and vacationers is also affected.

In recent years scientists have compiled data that have revolutionized our conceptions of the value of coastal wetlands. The argument that these areas are unproductive "wastelands" has been thoroughly refuted. A tidal marsh produces vegetation that is essential for fisheries, provides habitat for wildlife, acts as a storm buffer, and reduces sediment in adjacent waters. Its value as a food source alone is comparable to that of our most productive agricultural areas.

A second reason for appreciating, and therefore preserving, the natural environments of the North Carolina coast is a historical one. It has to do with the intimate role the environments have played in the development of North Carolina and the nation. The characteristics of the coast determined the course of exploration and settlement. They influenced the life-styles and culture of the inhabitants. Settlement sites and building techniques were a direct result of man's interaction with the coastal environment. As a theatre of action during the Civil War, the coastal environment shaped the strategy of both sides and the course of individual battles and skirmishes. Social patterns, occupations, and language were also profoundly affected by environmental factors. Preserving the integrity of the coast can help us understand these events and give us a greater appreciation of our past. It will also allow us to highlight and preserve the remaining physical evidence, the range of buildings, fortifications, and physical sites that reflect our culture and history.

A third ground for protection is that this is what most of the people who live there want. In spite of some voices to the contrary, every time soundings of public opinion have been taken, the results have shown that people value the way things are and that they realize they live in a very special place. They appreciate living in small towns or rural communities with ready access to fishing, hunting, and other recreational opportunities. The residents of the North Carolina coast will accept a preservation policy as long as it is not imposed by government without their full participation, and if it is applied sensibly and equitably.

One point needs to be made about the choices involved. "Preservation" must not be taken in this case to mean merely preventing the damage done by overdevelopment, resource depletion, and pollution. It also implies a certain humility toward natural threats, and the realization that the coast must, to some extent, be let alone. In the long run, given the power of geologic evolution, this is the only policy that can succeed. The tremendous forces at work on the coast—sea-level rise and island migration—cannot be effectively resisted. The hurricanes and other storms we know will someday come cannot be ignored. Man-made attempts to transform these environments can only be costly stopgap exercises in self-deception. Our only real choice is to align our activities and the management of coastal resources to the realities of the natural world. In doing so we can benefit in ways that are better and more economical than our futile attempts to impose our will upon the sea.

2

This "Goodliest" Land

To a surprising degree, the environments of the North Carolina coast have been decisive in shaping the character of its people, their settlements, and their way of life. Coastal Carolinians have never been like the Dutch—engaged in a continuous battle with the sea for possession of the land. Rather, they have adopted a different approach, taking what the sea, marshes, and sounds offered them and paying tribute by accepting the powerful natural forces of their world.

The unique combination of Outer Banks coastline, extensive but shallow estuaries, vast and impenetrable inland swamps, and river bottomland forest explains in large measure why North Carolina developed as a colony and a state in a different fashion from that of her neighbors to the north and south. These physical features shaped the lives of the early Indian inhabitants, the voyages of discovery, the settlements of the European colonists, and the course of the American Civil War. They determined the location of present-day cities and towns as well as the occupations and social relationships of the people. Even in this day of

Activities in an Indian village as depicted by John White, 1587. (*Courtesy of Division of Archives and History, Raleigh, N.C.*)

industrialization and mechanization, they continue to play a major role in the way people live and work.

For at least 10,000 years, man has been living with the changing conditions of the North Carolina coast. The area was one of the last places in North America reached by the peoples that crossed over to the American continent on the land bridge across the Bering Sea. But very little is known about the first Indian inhabitants of the land. We find their spear points and hunting axes and conclude that they were wandering hunters and fishermen. We also know that about 3,000 years ago the introduction of agriculture and ceramics allowed the Indians to lead a more sedentary way of life.

Algonkian Indians were living in the coastal area of North Carolina when English colonists arrived in the sixteenth century. They had been there at least since about A.D. 1000 and were the southernmost of the many Algonkian-speaking tribes who inhabited the middle- and north-Atlantic seaboard at this time. They were ethnically and linguistically related to the Indians of the Powhatan Confederation encountered by the Jamestown colonists in Virginia in 1607.

Interestingly, the Algonkian lands coincided almost exactly with the estuarine area of North Carolina. To the west lived an Iroquoian people, the Tuscarora, and tribes of Siouan stock lived south of the Neuse River. The Algonkians lived on the shores of the rivers and sounds, raising beans, maize, gourds, and tobacco, hunting waterfowl and other game, spearing and trapping fish, and gathering oysters and shellfish. There was no state and no private ownership of land; power was concentrated in the hands of certain chiefs and priests called *weroances*. The Algonkians worshiped forces in nature, and their most important religious ceremony was the corn dance around a circle of poles to celebrate the harvest. Their dead were buried in common graves after the bodies had been dried by fire in a wooden temple. John White, the governor of the second Roanoke colony, vividly depicted the daily life of these Indians in a series of watercolors now in the British Museum. In these paintings, he showed their villages, each a cluster of huts built out of bent saplings and reeds, often surrounded by a defensive palisade.

The Indians must have had a healthy respect for the natural forces of the Outer Banks. For the most part the islands were used only by hunting and fishing parties. The only Indian town on the banks was Croatoan on Hatteras Island. Most towns were located far inland on protected areas alongside rivers or sounds.

The Algonkian tribes are now gone from coastal North Carolina, driven out or exterminated by early white settlers, but many place names are derived from them. The Yeopim River north of Albemarle Sound gets its name from Weapemeoc, the name of the tribe living in this area at the time of the Roanoke colony. The Chowan River was the center of the territory of the Chowanoc tribe, and until the eighteenth century the Roanoke River was known as the Moratoc, after the Algonkian-speaking Indians who lived on its banks. Roanoke Island was the home of the Roanoke Indians, who greeted the English in 1584. Hatteras Island is named for Hatteras Indians, a tribe living on the Outer Banks, and the name of the Neuse River comes from the Neusiok people, who lived along it. Pamlico is a derivation of the Indian name Pomouik, and the Core Banks are named for the Coree Indians.

Other than place names, the most vivid reminders of the longtime Indian presence on the North Carolina coast are the large mounds of shells in places where tribal groups must have gathered for feasting and celebration for many hundreds of years. One such mound, on Harkers Island, measured more than one hundred yards in diameter and ten feet thick at the center until it was trucked away for road-building material. In addition, bones from Indian burial grounds are sometimes found after being exposed by shoreline erosion.

In the sixteenth century these coastal Indians encountered European man. Two more different cultures can hardly be imagined. The Europeans were in the midst of a great era of discovery and exploration motivated by acquisitiveness, mercantilism, and the pursuit of economic advantage. Spain was the leader in this quest, having explored the Caribbean area and established permanent settlements in Hispaniola, Puerto Rico, Jamaica, Cuba, and at scattered points along the mainland of South America. By 1519, the Spanish were ready to embark on their major exploits—the conquests of the Indians of mainland Mexico, Yucatan, and South America.

The coast of eastern North America was an unexplored borderland, largely ignored by the Spanish. Almost certainly, however, Spanish settlers sailed up the coast on reconnaissance voyages. The first recorded trip, in 1520, was mounted by Lucas Vásquez de Ayllón, a legal official in Hispaniola, who sent ships under Francisco Gordillo and Pedro de Quexós to the Bahamas, apparently with the purpose of capturing Indian slaves for the labor-short Spanish colony. Failing there, in 1521 the expedition sailed up the mainland coast, perhaps reaching North Carolina.

In 1523, Ayllón received a patent authorizing him to found a colony in this region. In July, 1526, he set out with 500 men and 6 ships loaded with provisions and about 80 horses. Entering the mouth of a river he called the Jordán, almost certainly the Cape Fear, his flagship ran aground. Ayllón was looking for a land the Indians referred to as "Chicora," but he gave up when his Indian guides deserted. The party of colonists decided to move south to a river they called the Gualdape, present Winyah Bay below Georgetown, South Carolina. It was necessary for part of the group to travel overland with the horses, and they utilized an Indian path that ran down the coast, much of which followed the route of present Highway 17 through Supply and Shallotte, North Carolina, and Myrtle Beach, South Carolina. The colony they established, San Miguel de Gualdape, the first Spanish town in North America, was abandoned after Ayllón fell sick and died on October 18. Only one ship and some 150 survivors returned safely to Hispaniola. One result of this ill-fated attempt at colonization was that many early maps dubbed the Carolina coast the "Tiera de Ayllón."

The eastern shore of North America became the focus of attention for the European maritime powers at the time of Ayllón's venture. In 1513 a Spanish expedition under Vasco Núñez de Balboa had established that in Central America a relatively narrow isthmus separated the Gulf of Mexico and the Pacific Ocean. In 1522 the Magellan–Del Cano voyage around the world showed that there was a passage through the southern part of South America to the riches of the Spice Islands of the East.

These events excited everyone interested in commerce. Almost nothing was known of the eastern coast of North America. If a passage existed to the south, as Magellan's voyage had proved, a far less difficult way to the East might exist through North America.

France, Spain, and England immediately started preparing to send ships to explore eastern North America and to find the Northwest Passage. France was first in the attempt. Giovanni da Verrazzano, an Italian in the service of France, set out in *La Dauphine* on January 17, 1524. After being thrown off course by a storm, he wrote that he "discovered a new land, never before seen by any man either ancient or modern." Historians believe that this landfall was on the Carolina coast south of Cape Fear. At first Verrazzano turned southward to look for a harbor, but fearing he would run into the Spanish, he returned to the north. At one point he saw people gathered on the shore and would have landed except that there was no harbor. A boat with twenty-five men was sent out, but it could not safely land on the open beach. One man swam ashore to give the natives some trinkets. Afterwards he had trouble getting back to the boat through the waves that crashed onto the shore. The Indians rescued him, warmed him by a fire, and carried him out past the breaking waves where he could swim back to the waiting boat. Verrazzano seems to have admired the Indian peoples he saw, and he remarked about the "sweet savours" of what he called the laurel and cedars growing on the islands.

When Verrazzano saw the open waters of Pamlico Sound across the Outer Banks, probably in the vicinity of Ocracoke, he was convinced that he had found the "oriental sea" that was the way to "China, India and Cathay."* He called this point Annunciata. He was unable to find a way through the banks to test this theory, however, and so continued north. Verrazzano's next an-

---

*It may seem somewhat ridiculous today that Verrazzano took Pamlico Sound to be the Pacific Ocean, but it is nevertheless a surprisingly broad expanse of water. I first realized this while flying in a small plane from Raleigh to Ocracoke. After leaving the mainland, out over Pamlico Sound flying east, I had the impression of flying over the Atlantic. For what seemed like a very long period, we were completely out of the sight of land. Finally Ocracoke appeared, looking like some mid-ocean mirage.

chorage was at a place on the Outer Banks where a stand of tall trees grew. This place, which historians believe was Nags Head Woods near Kitty Hawk, he named Arcadia. Here the exploring party rested for three days, kidnapping an Indian child to take back to Europe with them. They then continued northward along the coast as far as Newfoundland before returning to France.

Later voyages by Estévan Gomez, a Portuguese in the service of Spain, in 1524–25 and by the Englishman John Rut in 1527 turned up no passage across North America, and most people were evidently very skeptical since there was no follow-up to Verrazzano's exploration. For the next 150 years, however, the myth persisted that a great western sea extended into the middle of the North American continent.

For many years after Verrazzano's voyage, the Europeans largely ignored the coast of North Carolina, and the Indians had no contact with them except for an occasional Spanish or French sailing vessel wrecked on the shoals of the Outer Banks. Interest in the southeastern coast picked up in the latter half of the century, however, as Spain—which first laid claim to the area—twice attempted unsuccessfully to establish colonies in the Chesapeake Bay region. The first attempt, led by Fray Pablo de San Pedro in 1566, failed because the expedition could not locate the bay entrance. The party did by chance land on Currituck Banks, however, where they erected a wooden cross claiming the area for Spain. They discovered Currituck Sound and named it the River San Bartolomé. The second colony, established in 1570 as a Jesuit mission on the York River, collapsed when the priests were killed by Indians on February 9, 1571.

Though these attempts failed, they marked the beginning of real European interest in North America. A group of influential Englishmen were unwilling to let the Spanish proceed to colonize the eastern coast of North America unchallenged. One of these was Sir Humphrey Gilbert, who dreamed of establishing a great landed estate in the area. He obtained a patent from the English Crown allowing him to establish a settlement anywhere he chose. He decided to try the region called Norumbega, an ill-defined place somewhere on the New England coast, but he was lost at sea returning from an unsuccessful attempt to found a colony in 1583.

As relations between England and Spain worsened, Gilbert's idea was turned into a nationalist cause by men such as Richard Hakluyt the younger, who wrote an influential bit of propaganda in 1582 called *Divers Voyages Touching the Discovery of America.* When Walter Raleigh, Gilbert's half-brother, took over the patent in 1584, it was with the idea of establishing a military base just beyond the pale of Spanish influence so that privateers could harass Spanish shipping. Raleigh also hoped to explore the interior to search for gold or the fabled passage to the Pacific. The North Carolina coast appeared ideal for this venture since Spanish ships coming from the Indies made the crossing to Spain by sailing up the coast to Cape Hatteras to pick up the Gulf Stream for the voyage east.

A reconnaissance expedition was sent in 1584 under Philip Amadas and Arthur Barlow. They made landfall at Core Banks between Cape Lookout and Cape Hatteras and, sailing north, found an inlet through Bodie Island (north of present Oregon Inlet, which did not exist at the time). This was the inlet later called Port Ferdinando, which has since closed. Entering, they found Roanoke Island and soon encountered Granganimeo, the brother of Wingina (or Pemisepan, as he called himself), chief of the Roanoke Indians. The English were taken to the Roanoke village, a fortified town of nine houses, where they inquired about the surrounding country and observed how the people lived.

After about six weeks, Amadas and Barlow sailed for home with two Indians on board, Wanchese and Manteo. Raleigh used them to mount a propaganda campaign for a second voyage, and the report of Barlow and Amadas touts the mildness of the climate and the friendliness of the Indians, describing them as "living after the manner of the golden age." Raleigh hushed up the fact that Amadas, exploring Chesapeake Bay on the way back to England, ran into hostile Indians. He also shrewdly named the area "Virginia" in honor of the queen.

After this promotional work, Raleigh had little trouble in arranging an attempt to found a colony, and Sir Richard Grenville sailed from Plymouth harbor on April 9, 1585, with 600 men and 7 ships, including the flagship, a 160-ton galleon named the *Tiger*. As they approached the Carolina coast, the *Tiger*'s journal records that they were almost wrecked on the shoals off Cape Lookout. Even worse trouble was encountered as they tried to sail through one of the inlets into Pamlico Sound. The *Tiger* ran aground and was almost lost. She was floated off, but the supplies in her hold were a total loss. Finally arriving at Roanoke Island, Grenville negotiated an agreement with Wingina to allow the building of a fort, and he returned to England, leaving the soldier Ralph Lane in command of about 100 men.

Lane spent the winter building fortifications and exploring the rivers, the sounds, and Chesapeake Bay. He saw Secotan, an Indian village on the Pamlico River, and rowed up the Roanoke River to check out rumors of the precious metals of the Tuscarora tribe, the Iroquoian group of Indians who at this time functioned as traders to the coastal tribes of materials found only in the mountains. Lane also went up the Chowan River and traveled overland to the Chesapeake Bay. Two of his men, Thomas Hariot and John White, investigated the horticulture and customs of the Indians as well as the fish, mammals, and birds of the region. As noted previously, John White made watercolors of the Indians and their villages. This was a time of peace and happiness for the explorers, and Lane declared the region "the goodliest and most pleasing territory of the world."

The Indians helped the soldiers get through the winter, giving them corn and supplies, but by May, 1586, friction had developed. Lane attacked Dasemunkepeuc, the mainland Roanoke village, and killed Wingina. When Sir Francis Drake happened to call at the Roanoke colony on his way from destroying the Spanish settlement at St. Augustine in Florida, Lane and his men, fearing the Indians' revenge, asked to be taken back to England, and Drake complied.

Meanwhile, Sir Richard Grenville, returning to Roanoke that summer with supplies and more men, found the fort deserted. He arranged for eighteen of his men to remain while he again returned to England. These unlucky eighteen were all either killed or driven out by the now hostile Indians and were never heard from again.

Despite this adversity, John White and a few others convinced

Raleigh that another attempt at settlement should be made. They knew that the Roanoke Island settlement had failed, and so they planned to take their families this time to the shore of the Chesapeake. On May 8, 1587, White and 110 people sailed in the *Lion*, under the Portuguese master Simon Ferdinando, and in two other ships.

White, who was to rule the colony as governor, intended to sail to Roanoke Island, pick up the men left there, and go on to the Chesapeake Bay. During the voyage, however, he quarreled with Ferdinando, who was more interested in privateering operations against the Spanish than in helping to found a colony. When the colonists reached Roanoke, they found the fort deserted, but Ferdinando refused to go to Chesapeake; he wanted to take the *Lion* and get on with his privateering. Since the colony was deserted, there were no stores for the coming winter. It was agreed that White should take one of the other ships and sail to England for supplies, leaving the others there for the winter. Just before White left, his daughter gave birth to a child, Virginia Dare, born August 18, 1587, the first child of English parents born in America. The departure must have been terribly sad, both for White and for those left behind.

Because of hostilities between England and Spain, White was unable to return to the Roanoke colony until after the defeat of the Spanish Armada in 1588. When he did return, aboard a privateering vessel, he found the colony deserted, but there was no sign of the Maltese cross, the agreed-upon distress signal. Instead, White and his party found carved into trees the words "CRO" and "CROATOAN." This meant to White that the settlers had gone to live with Manteo in the village of Croatoan, on present Hatteras Island. But the captain of the privateering ship refused to look further for the colonists, and White returned to England with a heavy heart.

The mystery of the "Lost Colony" is unsolved today. Some scholars maintain that the colonists were killed by Indians or lost at sea. Others believe, as did White, that they went to live with the Indians on Hatteras, or even that they moved to the Chesapeake region as originally planned and were killed by Indians just before the founding of the Jamestown Colony in 1607.

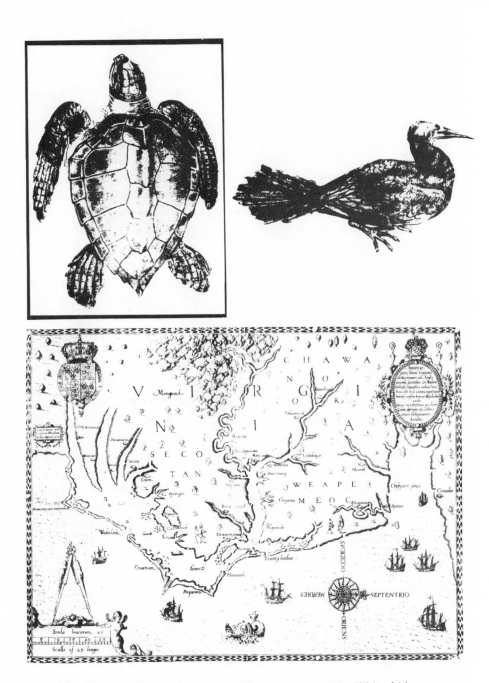

The White-DeBry map of the North Carolina coast, 1590; John White faithfully drew the animals and birds of the region. (*Courtesy of Division of Archives and History, Raleigh, N.C.*)

The tragic story of the first explorations and settlement of the North Carolina coast tells us a lot about the characteristics of this area. The barrier-island coastline, despite its rare beauty, is inhospitable and dangerous to approach from the sea. The inlets are navigable only for small vessels with experienced pilots. Even the protected bays and sounds present difficulties. They are too shallow for most craft except where a channel is kept open by constant dredging. It is no wonder that no major port city ever developed on the North Carolina coast, either in colonial times or since, in marked contrast with the other eastern seaboard states.

Another attribute of the region is that areas naturally suited for human settlement are limited. By the sixteenth century, the Indians obviously had discovered and were already using most of the available sites. The English, in choosing a place for a colony, were smart enough not to settle on the barrier islands. Roanoke Island was a good site except that a relatively large population of Indians was already there, inevitably leading to trouble. The Europeans eventually drove out the Indians, of course, but that happened much later. And it is interesting to discover that they chose to found their principal towns at places where the Indians had also lived. Bad memories of the "Lost Colony" prevented any further attempt to settle North Carolina from the sea.

The region was mostly settled from the *inside out* by people coming down from other colonies to the north. They followed the river valleys leading to the coastal sounds. The first people to arrive in this way came in the second half of the seventeenth century from the Virginia colony that had been established at Jamestown in the Chesapeake region in 1607. Through grants from the English Crown in 1663 and 1665, North Carolina became a private proprietary colony owned by eight English noblemen. In the early eighteenth century the principal towns of the coast—Bath, Edenton, New Bern, and Wilmington—were founded by people who came to North Carolina from or through more settled colonial regions. From 1729 to the Revolution, during which period North Carolina was a royal colony under the direct rule of the English Crown, settlers streamed down the

Great Philadelphia Wagon Road into the piedmont, by-passing the inhospitable coast.

Until almost the middle of the twentieth century, coastal North Carolina was a homogeneous, isolated area, thinly populated primarily by descendants of people, black and white, who had arrived in the eighteenth century. On the Outer Banks, the same family names predominated throughout the period—Gaskins, Bragg, Etheridge, Daniel, Twiford, Baum, Midgett, Wade, Austin, and O'Neal, to mention a few. Many people retained the distinct English accent and expressions of their forebears, as well as customs such as the celebration of "Old Christmas" on the night of January 5. They used the land as subsistence farmers, hunters, and fishermen. They manned the lifesaving stations and tended the lighthouses on Smith Island, Cape Lookout, Ocracoke, Cape Hatteras, Bodie Island, and Currituck Banks. "Fishing and lifesaving, those were the two activities on the Outer Banks," says Aycock Brown of Dare County, a colorful character in his ever-present banana-boat hat, protecting him from the sun during his more than thirty years on the Outer Banks. "If you retired from one you did the other in the old days." Outsiders congregated at a few coastal resorts such as Nags Head, Morehead City, and Wrightsville Beach, and a few wealthy people established gun clubs to hunt the abundant waterfowl in Currituck Sound, but for the most part the "bankers" and other coastal residents had the area to themselves. Much of the region was still the wilderness that the Indians knew.

All this has changed abruptly during the past thirty-five years or so. Suddenly the unique resources of the North Carolina coastal area were "discovered." Recreation and tourism exploded, and barrier islands were subdivided for second-home developments, motels, and condominiums. Business corporations increasingly located new plants in the region. New shopping centers, fast-food restaurants, and stores were built. Military bases and airports were established by the Department of Defense. New highways were constructed, and bridges were built to formerly inaccessible places on the Outer Banks. A nuclear power plant was built and more were planned to utilize the abundant water of the sounds. Oil and gas companies explored the area for possible energy resources, for sites for refineries, and for oil and gas storage terminals. Mining became an important industry as vast phosphorus resources were discovered. Port facilities were expanded at Wilmington and at Morehead City. Timber companies exploited the rich forests, and hundreds of thousands of acres of the swamp forests and pocosins were cleared, ditched, and drained by large agribusiness companies to raise corn and soybeans. The coastal area of North Carolina had entered upon a new era that was a sharp departure from the relative isolation and independence of the past.

Increased navigation and pleasure boating meant that the government had to undertake a massive and continuous program of dredging in order to keep channels open through the shallow inlets, sounds, and lagoons. Inlets that shoaled up or closed became hazards to navigation, so government assumed the job of opening and "stabilizing" them. The natural processes of barrier island movement and change became "beach erosion" once these areas were developed, and private property owners cried out for protection against it. As one beach cottage owner said, "I know that the state cannot prevent beach erosion, but they can come up with funding or some plan to slow it."

These activities made life better for greater numbers of coastal residents. They had better jobs and more money than ever before. Yet many people were concerned about the effects of rapid development. The barrier-island dunes were bulldozed and developed, often with the unintended effect of increasing erosion. Marshes were drained and filled, decreasing the productivity of the estuarine-based fishery. Pollution and its potential hazard to public health required the closing of more than one-third of the estuarine waters to shellfishing. The once-abundant wildlife decreased, and water birds such as terns, skimmers, and gulls were driven off the beaches and had to find nesting sites on spoil islands made by man's dredging activities. It was simply a case of too many people trying to use the same resource.

The degradation of the nation's coastal areas began to be recognized as a national problem in the 1960s. In the decade of the '70s, both the national and state governments acted to attempt to preserve and protect the heritage and natural resources of the coastal region. Many people felt that it was necessary to *manage* the development, growth, and resources of the area. This was considered governmental intervention and was opposed by many coastal residents of North Carolina, who resented interference with their traditional freedom and independence.

The policy of management of coastal resources was first directed toward preserving the marshlands and the associated estuarine waters. Dredging and filling in these areas was prohibited without a permit from the federal and state governments. Laws were also passed to attempt to control pollution in the estuaries. Two national seashores, at Cape Hatteras and Cape Lookout, were established by the National Park Service. A federal law, the Coastal Zone Management Act of 1972, was passed by Congress to provide financial support to states that established comprehensive programs to manage coastal resources.

The State of North Carolina paralleled and supplemented the federal initiatives by enacting the Coastal Area Management Act of 1974. This law created the North Carolina coastal area as an administrative unit consisting of twenty counties that border the Atlantic Ocean and the bays and sounds. These counties were required to adopt and implement land-use guidelines to plan the further development as well as conservation of lands and waters within their borders. The governing board of each locality was required to consult the citizenry, to gather data about economic and population trends, and to make decisions on what they wanted their community to be like in the future. The state and local governments also designated certain categories of specially protected lands and waters that cannot be developed except by special permit. These "areas of environmental concern," as they are called, can include coastal wetlands, estuarine waters, renewable resource areas such as public water supplies and prime forestry land, fragile or historic areas, and certain natural areas, public trust lands, and natural hazard areas such as sand dunes, the ocean and estuarine shorelands, floodways, and floodplains.

Although this process was completed in 1978 and a state plan to guide development was formulated to safeguard the natural and historical values of the North Carolina coastal area, considerable doubt still remains about the ability of government to implement the plans that have been laid. Each region of the coast stands at a significant crossroads. The choice is clear: either the area will be overwhelmed by the kind of rapid, intense, and wasteful development that has devastated many coastal areas in the northeast and in southern Florida, or future growth will be channeled, respecting and safeguarding the traditional natural and historical resources and way of life. This is not to say that the region should try to return to the past or reject the modern world. It is a question of accommodating the modern world to traditional values and the natural forces that have made the area what it is. If we disregard these, the price will inevitably be paid not only in a decreased quality of life but also in direct economic terms. And the task is too great for government alone.

In the last analysis, the pride of coastal residents in their region and heritage and their attitudes toward themselves and their land will determine whether the unique beauty of the North Carolina coastal region will be preserved.

II

The Regions

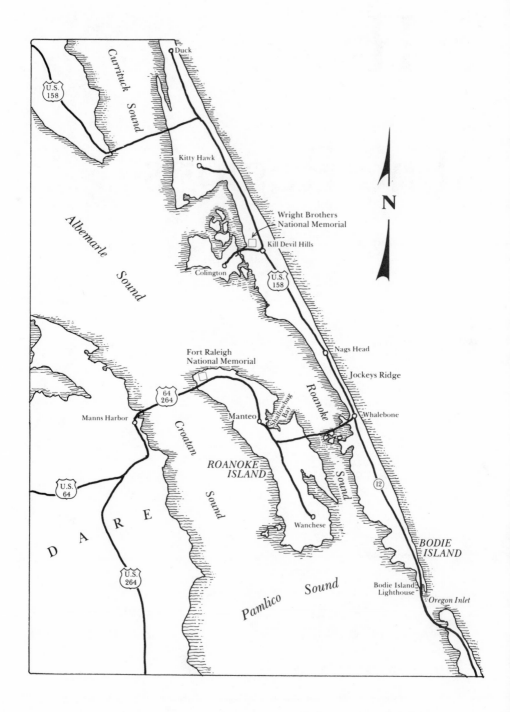

3

Roanoke Island and the Dare Beaches

For gentle illusion, historical romance, and the beauty of sand, surf, and sky, Dare County is the place. Roanoke Island is a verdant twelve-mile-long Atlantis that refused to be lost, situated between the mainland and the Outer Banks at the junction of four sounds. From the island, the highway crosses over Roanoke Sound to the banks, reaching them precisely at the point where the historic old Roanoke Inlet cut through before it closed in the early nineteenth century. The highway's eastern terminus, at the beach, is known as Whalebone Junction. A short distance south begins Cape Hatteras National Seashore, the Outer Banks preserved. To the north lies the most heavily developed part of the banks, mile after mile of motels, shopping centers, gift shops, beach cottages, water slides, and restaurants. For the discriminating, there are suburban-style subdivisions of expensive and exclusive homes. Vacationland Dare, as the tourist brochures proclaim, is indeed the "compleat" beach resort.

Yet Dare is not just another beach resort. There is a feeling about the place that is different from that of Myrtle Beach, Ocean City, and other watering holes. I find it hard to express the reason. Maybe I am captivated by the names of the towns: Nags Head, Kill Devil Hills, and Kitty Hawk. Farther north on the Dare Banks is the old village with the improbable name of Duck. But I think my fondness for the Dare Banks is that it hasn't quite given up its soul. Despite all the new prefabricated buildings and strip development, the older Dare traditions are still there under the surface. It is sometimes difficult, however, to distinguish them.

Take Roanoke Island, for instance. As the site of the first English attempts to settle North America, this island has a secure place in history. Today an area near the sites of the original settlements is designated a national historic site and is administered by the National Park Service. At the visitors' center, the story of the abortive colony is recounted and artifacts of the time are displayed. We are told that despite extensive exploration of the area by archeologists, the actual settlement sites have never been found. What should be emphasized, but isn't, is that these sites have probably eroded into the sound, although the location of Ralph Lane's 1585 fort has been discovered and partially restored for the benefit of visitors.

In addition to being the site of the sixteenth-century English attempts at settlement, Roanoke Island was also the scene of the pivotal battle for the North Carolina coast during the Civil War. Since, as we have seen, it is located at the conjunction of four sounds—Pamlico to the south, Albemarle to the north, Croatan on the west, and Roanoke on the east—Roanoke Island was the key to the control by Union forces of the entire North Carolina coast. The Confederates, although they knew the Federal approach would be from the south, chose to fortify the northern end of the island because it was easier. The southern end was then largely marshland, which in the 1860s extended almost to the mainland shore. The Confederates constructed three turf forts on the northwest shore, Fort Huger somewhere near the terminus of the present bridge across Croatan Sound, and forts Blanchard and Bartow several hundred yards to the south. Di-

rectly across the sound on the mainland shore was a small battery known as Fort Forrest. The sites of these forts have now
been eroded away. On the eastern side of the island, a two-gun
battery was put up at the head of Shallowbag Bay, protecting
against a passage through Roanoke Sound. In addition, a barrier
of piles and sunken vessels was formed across the northern end
of Croatan Sound. Brigadier General Henry A. Wise of Virginia, who was belatedly put in charge of the defense of Roanoke
Island, realized that the defenses were weak, but before he had
time to correct the situation, the Federals, under General Ambrose Burnside, were under way.

Already in control of the Outer Banks, the Union expedition
under Burnside, with 80 ships and 13,000 men, began crossing
over the bar at Hatteras Inlet into Pamlico Sound in January,
1862. For a time it looked as if the winter storms might wreck
the venture. For two weeks the ships were delayed by heavy
seas, and several were lost crossing the shallow swash into Pamlico Sound. But by February 7, Federal gunboats had passed
unopposed up Croatan Sound through the Roanoke marshes
channel and were in position in front of the Confederate line of
sunken ships and pilings.

The Confederate position was weak. General Wise had been
taken ill with an attack of pleurisy and was confined to bed in his
headquarters at Nags Head. The naval defense was seven small
gunboats under Commodore Lynch, which someone had nicknamed the "mosquito fleet." General Wise, using somewhat
stronger language, called the fleet "perfectly imbecile." The Federal gunboats traded fire with the mosquito fleet and Fort Bartow
on shore. The mosquito fleet got the worst of the fight. One
ship, the *Curlew*, was hit and grounded directly in front of Fort
Forrest, which could no longer fire upon the Federals. The rest
of the fleet soon exhausted its ammunition and retired.

Meanwhile the Union troop transports were coming up
through the channel. Aided by a slave boy named Thomas R.
Robinson, who was familiar with the area, the troops successfully made an amphibious landing at Ashby's Harbor, in the
middle of the western side of the island, three miles south of
Fort Bartow. From there they advanced through the swamps to

the north-south road in the center of the island. After heavy fighting, Union forces overwhelmed the hastily erected Confederate redoubt across the road, and outflanked, the Confederates were forced to surrender. The victory exposed all the remaining North Carolina coastal towns to eventual Union domination.

The exploits of the sixteenth-century colonists still live after a fashion for tourists on Roanoke Island. At the Waterside Theatre near the Fort Raleigh historic site, summer productions of Paul Green's symphonic drama *The Lost Colony* are given, dramatizing and romanticizing the venture. Nearby too are the Elizabethan Gardens, which face Roanoke Sound. Formal gardens, reminiscent of Elizabethan England, are arranged in an attractive setting. The historical theme is maintained by a nude statue of an adult Virginia Dare, in the "best" classical style, although she most likely never got past infancy. Despite the somewhat illusory link with history, a walk through the garden is a delightful experience, especially in early April when the flowering dogwoods, azaleas, and tulips show off the North Carolina spring.

There are two towns on Roanoke Island, Manteo and Wanchese, named after the two "friendly" Indians taken to England in 1584 by Amadas and Barlow. Manteo, originally a fishing village and agricultural community incorporated as the county seat in 1873, is now the major service center of the area and the residence of the islanders who disdain "living on the beach." The town fathers and merchants have combined to create a pleasant put-on for visitors, renovating the business district to reflect an Elizabethan decor. Restaurants, motels, coffee shops, and an old-fashioned ice cream parlor offer a friendly hospitality. The waterfront is the site of a park with a rather comical statue of Sir Walter Raleigh. One who desires a respite from the Elizabethan theme can repair to the Christmas Shop, at the south end of town, where the holiday is maintained all year.

Beneath the posturing, glimpses of old Manteo can still be seen as well. Fishing trawlers still tie up at the waterfront docks at Shallowbag Bay. There are several simple, frame churches that have been used since the early part of the century. Some of the gable-roof, frame farm and town houses survive, reminders of a simpler, less affluent past. Despite the new prosperity of the resort and tourist business, Manteo is still primarily a closely knit society of families who have for generations made their living from the resources of the island and the surrounding waters. People in Manteo wonder how they can preserve the best aspects of their past. As Mayor John Wilson IV puts it, "We're very rapidly developing, and we realize that if we don't concern ourselves with the future we're going to lose the identity that made us unique."

Wanchese, on the southern end of the island, is facing even more important changes than Manteo. For many years Wanchese has been a small, bustling fishing village with its picturesque harbor crowded with trawlers. Over 21 million pounds of fish are landed each year. Much of the catch is sold right off the dock for local consumption. A large portion is also packed in ice, boxed, and shipped by truck to northern markets. Wanchese fishermen are small, independent operators who generally own their own boats and gear and spend long, hard hours on the water. They tend to do things in the old, time-tested way, although in recent years many have invested in modern equipment such as hydraulic and electric pot-pullers and net-winders.

People may tell you that Wanchese fishermen are hard to get to know and that as a rule they don't like outsiders. But when they extend their friendship, it is very special. A few years ago, a Wanchese fisherman came to see me for some legal advice after his boat had been run down by a Greek freighter off Oregon Inlet. I helped him as best I could and refused his offer to pay me. A few weeks later he drove two hundred and fifty miles to deliver a trunk-load of seafood to my home. We have since spent many pleasant hours talking together, and I know I have a standing invitation to visit his home.

An unusual series of events has determined that Wanchese is to be transformed into a modern commercial seafood center through a large infusion of federal and state funds. This decision is an outgrowth of the effort since the 1940s to obtain congressional authorization for a project to stabilize Oregon Inlet. The large amount of money needed for inlet stabilization could not be justified if it were to serve existing fleets on Roanoke Island and elsewhere alone, so the Wanchese Harbor Development

Project, as it is called, was proposed. The idea was to construct the harbor facilities necessary to create a seafood industrial park that would accommodate large-scale commercial seafood handling and processing. This new facility would, it was thought, provide a boon for Roanoke Island fishermen and justify economically the stabilization of Oregon Inlet.

In the late 1970s, the State of North Carolina, with considerable help from federal grants, went ahead with the development of Wanchese harbor. By the end of the decade, more than $7.2 million of public money had been spent to enlarge and deepen the basin and to construct bulkhead and dock work. Much more remains to be done, including the construction of new roads, an electric system, and water and sewage treatment facilities. After that is accomplished, the seafood industrial park itself must be financed and developed. For this purpose the state has created the North Carolina Seafood Industrial Park Authority, a public body with eleven members. No one can now predict how many more millions of dollars in public money this will cost or whether it will be successful. It has already been very costly in environmental terms—a large area of marsh has been filled. Can all this new development be accommodated on an eroding island that is more than fifty percent marshland? What will it mean for the lives of the people on Roanoke Island? Will the island become an urban area that will have to be protected by a circle of bulkheads? Could the money be better spent to improve the lot of the individual fisherman and the resources on which he depends?

Ironically, while the Wanchese Harbor Development Project has gone ahead, the Oregon Inlet stabilization proposal has become more controversial. There is considerable doubt that Oregon Inlet can be successfully stabilized and concern about the adverse consequences to the Cape Hatteras National Seashore if the attempt is made (see Chapter 8). It is certain, however, that without inlet stabilization, the Wanchese project cannot succeed. We are thus caught in a circular trap, forced to justify the inlet stabilization in order to save the Wanchese project.

Similar questions are facing the Dare County Outer Banks, which, like Roanoke Island, are a blend of tradition and modern

Wanchese harbor on Roanoke Island. (*Courtesy of N.C. Travel and Tourism Division*)

changes. It is instructive to consider the history of these resort towns and the way human settlement patterns developed on the Outer Banks. Nowadays, the focal point of these resorts is the oceanfront. The land closest to the beach is the most densely developed and the most valuable. This is a very recent trend on the banks. All of these areas were originally settled as *sound-side* communities. Even the early resorts were not built on the beach.

An early settlement attempt was on Colington Island, where Sir John Colleton, one of the original Lords Proprietors of Carolina, established a plantation in 1664. Like the early Roanoke Island settlements, it failed, but a few hardy people chose to live on the banks through the entire colonial period, raising cattle, scavenging for the cargo of wrecked ships that washed up on the beach, and extracting oil and whalebone from whales that beached or washed up on the shore. They had their homes in the thick woodland that grew on the shore near the sound. This environment provided shelter, building material, fuel, and fresh water. Colington evolved into a fishing community, which it remains today, although in recent years several residential and vacation-home subdivisions have been constructed on the island.

By the early years of the eighteenth century, the area of the banks at the end of Albemarle Sound became known as Nags Head, although no one knows exactly why. The favorite explanation is that it was the habit of the local people to drive a pony with a lantern around its neck up and down the beach at night in order to lure unsuspecting ships to founder on the shore. A more likely reason for the name is that some homesick Englishman noticed a resemblance to a place on the coast of England with that name. In any case, the name "Nags Head" appears on a map of the North Carolina coast drawn by James Wimble in 1738.

The first summer resort development on the banks occurred in the area now known as Old Nags Head, to the southwest of the huge sand dune known as Jockey's Ridge. Today this is a cluster of beach cottages overlooking Albemarle Sound. Beginning in the 1830s, prosperous planter families from the Albemarle region began spending time here in late summer after their crops were in. They arrived by boat, bringing their entire household including many slaves, equipment, and horses. They bought land and built houses overlooking the waters of the sound and on the sand hills. A lively social life evolved, and by 1840 a hotel had been constructed that became very popular among visitors to the banks. A rail track and boardwalk gave access to the ocean beach, and a dock a half-mile long was built out into the sound to make it easier for arriving packet steamers from Elizabeth City and the other cities and towns of the Albemarle. The Civil War ended this first period of resort life. The Nags Head Hotel was headquarters for Confederate General Wise during the battle of Roanoke Island and was burned by his troops before they evacuated the banks to keep it from falling into Union hands. No trace of antebellum Nags Head remains today.

A few years after the Civil War, people again started vacationing at Nags Head, and another hotel was built. Until it burned in 1900, the new Nags Head Hotel offered to its guests good food, drink, and dancing every night. Additional cottages were built as well. The visitor today can still find examples of this early settlement. The Fearing House, probably constructed just after the Civil War, still stands in Old Nags Head, now adorned by placards bearing the names of ships.

The first structures on the beach were built in the nineteenth century by the U.S. Lifesaving Service, the forerunner of the U.S. Coast Guard. So many ships were running aground on the offshore bars that the service established a series of lifesaving stations at intervals of about seven miles along the banks. Each of these frame, weatherbeaten structures housed a crew whose job it was to patrol the beach and upon finding a ship in distress, to fire a line to the survivors or to launch small boats into the surf to pick up the passengers and crew. By the 1870s, stations had been established at Caffey's Inlet, Kill Devil Hills, Kitty Hawk, and Nags Head. Because of modern navigational aids, the need for their services ceased by the time of the Second World War, but many of the old structures remain, enhancing the beauty of the Dare Banks. They are shingled buildings with gable or hip roofs, now often converted into beach cottages.

The Nags Head Beach Cottage Row historic district, a line of starkly beautiful gray-brown shingle and weatherboard beach houses, stretches for almost a mile along the oceanfront. These houses were built in the early twentieth century when the original sound-side vacation-home development first expanded along the oceanfront. They have had to be moved back away from the ocean several times to cope with the constant erosion. With their wraparound porches, gable or hip roofs, and porch benches, these two-story buildings on wooden pilings have influenced later construction designs by their beauty and functionalism. They contrast sharply with the newer steel structures, which tend to be intrusive and somewhat flashy. The first hotels built on the beach were of a similar character. The only traditional hotel now remaining is the First Colony Inn in Nags Head, built in 1932. It is covered with wooden shingles with double-decker porches that completely surround the H-shaped structure. The hip roof with dormers is a particularly striking feature.

Another old community on the banks to the north of Nags Head is the village of Kitty Hawk. Settled as a sound-side community, it expanded onto five miles of beach frontage in the mid-twentieth century. Originally, however, Kitty Hawk was a small farming and fishing village, which had been inhabited since the eighteenth century. The name apparently comes from the Indian word "Chickahauk," which appears on eighteenth-century maps of the area.

Kitty Hawk is believed to be Verrazzano's "Arcadia," and it has been etched in history as the site of man's first powered flight in 1903. Orville and Wilbur Wright, bicycle makers from Dayton, Ohio, chose Kitty Hawk as the site of their flying experiments because of the large stretches of open, sandy duneland and their belief that the winds of the banks blew at a relatively constant rate for most of the time. From 1900 to 1903, the Wright Brothers spent several weeks each year on the banks, living in a tent or among the "Kitty Hawkers," conducting glider and flying experiments.

The bankers and the two men from Ohio got along quite well. The brothers were regarded as mild eccentrics, and their activities were closely watched by everyone. The Wrights remarked that people were friendly and neighborly, but thought that living conditions were less than ideal. They were amazed at how little the people of the banks lived on without any particular sense of

The Fearing House in Old Nags Head. (*Courtesy of Division of Archives and History, Raleigh, N.C.*)

Traditional Nags Head beach cottage. (*Courtesy of Division of Archives and History, Raleigh, N.C.*)

privation. Fish and game were abundant, and the Wrights commented several times about the number of bald eagles in the area, now long since gone. Wilbur Wright complained that although Kitty Hawk was a fishing village, there was no place to buy fish. The only way to get them was to catch them yourself. These are telling clues to the way the bankers lived in this difficult environment.

The Wrights worked at a camp they set up just to the north of the Kill Devil Hills, which is now the name of an incorporated beach-resort town between Nags Head and Kitty Hawk. Legend holds that the name is derived from a load of bad rum called "Kill Devil" carried by a ship that once wrecked nearby. In the Wrights' day, the only building on the beach was the lifesaving station. Their camp was four miles from the nearest town, Kitty Hawk.

The Wright brothers' achievement was remarkable. Using knowledge compiled from their wind-tunnel experiments and glider trials on the sand hills, they designed a glider-type aircraft, built a four-cylinder gasoline engine to power it, and invented a propeller to pull it through the air. On December 17, 1903, they were finally successful in flying a heavier-than-air craft under power for the first time in history.

Today the site of the first flight is surrounded by the roads, motels, and commercial establishments of the modern beach resort. The largest of the sand dunes, Big Kill Devil Hill, has been stabilized, fertilized, and planted with grass by the National Park Service. A large white pylon on top, the Wright Memorial, commemorates the first flight. In the visitor center there is a replica of the airplane flown by the brothers and information about their work on the banks. A large boulder now marks the spot where the first flight left the ground. One wonders whether the Wrights would even recognize the place.

Despite the extensive development of the Dare beaches, significant natural features of the banks do remain. The most noticeable of these is the 110-foot-high sand dune known as Jockey's Ridge. This huge, unvegetated dune is like some ancient pyramid that can be seen from miles away, from either the ocean or the sound side of the banks. Residents and visitors alike enjoy

The Wright Memorial stands atop Big Kill Devil Hill and commemorates the "first" flight in 1903. (*Courtesy of Division of Archives and History, Raleigh, N.C.*)

The Wright Memorial. (*Courtesy of N.C. Travel and Tourism Division*)

climbing to the summit to gain a bird's-eye view of the islands and surrounding ocean and sound or to watch a spectacular sunrise or sunset. This pastime was popular as long ago as the eighteenth century, and no doubt by the Indians before that. There is a saying that "the lady who may accompany you to its summit if not already your wife, shortly will be." A piece of doggerel has been composed about a disappointed lover who climbed the ridge ready to throw himself off:

> But when he came near
> Beholding how steep
> The sides did appear
> And the bottom how deep;
> Though his suit was rejected
> He sadly reflected
> That a lover forsaken
> A new love may get,
> But a neck that's been broken
> Can never be set.

Jockey's Ridge is actually the highest and most impressive of a series of moving sand dunes on the Currituck and Dare banks. To the south were the so-called Seven Sisters, now largely obliterated, while to the north are Run Hill, the Round-about Hills, Scraggly Oak Hill, Graveyard Hill, and the Kill Devil Hills. Most of these have been tamed, stabilized with the planting of grass or cut into by developers.

The same fate seemed to await the majestic Jockey's Ridge. Residences and condominiums were constructed at the base of the ridge. Bulldozers began to grade and remove more and more of the dune. Then one day in the summer of 1973, Carolista Baum decided to act. Hearing a bulldozer in operation, she stood in its path until the operator stopped tearing away the dune. Afterwards, the indefatigable Carolista circulated petitions, organized an association called "People to Preserve Jockey's Ridge," and solicited contributions from across the state. Her efforts spurred the state government into action, and in 1975 $500,000 was appropriated by the North Carolina General Assembly to create a state park. Additional funds came from the U.S. Bureau of Outdoor Recreation, and Jockey's Ridge State Park was born.

When acquisition of some remaining land is completed, there will be 416 acres of duneland for hiking and hang gliding, and the preservation of this landmark will be accomplished, even though ultimately it might be hard to confine the moving dune itself within the park limits.

Between Jockey's Ridge on the south and Run Hill on the north and bordering Albemarle Sound is a two-thousand-acre natural area known as Nags Head Woods. This is the last extensive forest on the island, and one of the places of early settlement by inhabitants of the banks seeking sheltered lands near the sound. Wandering through the woods today, a visitor is likely to come upon old family cemeteries under huge, three-hundred-year-old live oak trees.

The rich and beautiful maritime forest of Nags Head Woods covers the old dunes east of the extensive marshes that border the sound. With elevations rising to sixty feet, the land is thick with live oaks covered with Spanish moss, sweet gum, holly, hickory, beech, and loblolly pine. Between the dunes are numerous depressions filled with water to form freshwater ponds. Bird and animal life within the forest is varied and includes rare birds of prey such as the Cooper's hawk and the swallow-tailed kite. Much of the woods is privately owned and is being subdivided for development into residential lots. Through the efforts of the North Carolina Nature Conservancy, the state, and the Dare County garden clubs, several hundred acres of this important ecosystem are being preserved.

The evolution of the Dare Banks from an isolated community of fishermen and lifesaving stations into a major tourist resort can be traced directly to the construction of bridges and highways in the 1920s and '30s. Before that time, the lack of access, except by water, prevented major resort development. In 1928, a bridge was constructed between Roanoke Island and Nags Head, and in 1931 the Wright Memorial Bridge spanned Currituck Sound from the mainland of the Currituck peninsula to Kitty Hawk. An eighteen-mile oceanfront road was laid shortly thereafter to connect the two bridges. This opened up the waterfront lots along the beach for extensive tourist development. By 1937, a bridge was built connecting Roanoke Island with the mainland. The access problem that had retarded development was solved. Now tourists could easily drive their private cars onto the banks. Soon all the oceanfront property had been developed, and a bypass road (U.S. 158 Bypass) was constructed parallel to the beach road, opening up the interior of the island to development.

Since the end of World War II, the population of the Dare beaches has grown at an ever-increasing rate. By 1975, the resident population had reached 9000, an increase of 22 percent over the figure recorded just five years earlier. Seasonal visitors to the banks totaled 30,000. This rate of growth is expected to continue. By the year 2000, according to the Dare County Land Use Plan, the resident population will more than double to 20,000, and the seasonal population will be 74,000, with an additional 20,000 day-visitors to the banks.

If this is allowed to happen in the haphazard fashion of the past, the Dare Outer Banks will lose the distinctiveness of its heritage, and unmanageable environmental problems will result. The trend toward overdevelopment of these beach resorts must be reversed. Account should be taken of the very real constraints of the natural systems. Virtually the entire strand is receding at a moderate rate; a major hurricane could cause great destruction and might even cut a new inlet. The water supply and sewage treatment capacity is limited. Engineering solutions to these problems are costly and ineffective on barrier beach islands, incompatible with their fundamental character.

Because of this, new development should be controlled, phased, and guided away from delicate natural systems such as the beaches and marshlands. Remaining natural areas such as Nags Head Woods, Jockey's Ridge, and the Roanoke Island marshes must be given adequate protection and preserved. These measures will ensure the survival of the heritage of this remarkable section of the Outer Banks.

4

The Ancient Albemarle

MORE THAN THREE HUNDRED YEARS AGO, EUROPEAN COLO-
nists began to settle the lands north of Albemarle Sound. These
people, the first permanent European settlers in what is now
North Carolina, came from the Virginia colony to the north.
They traveled down the rivers that flow into the sound to find
new lands and choice sites for settlement. Thinking of themselves as Virginians on the frontier of the Jamestown colony,
they had no idea that their region would become the nucleus of
a new colony.

Events in London, not in Virginia, were responsible for the
birth of the new colony. Sir Walter Raleigh's grant was invali-
dated by the English Crown after it became clear that the Roanoke colony had failed. In 1606, King James I granted a new
charter to the Virginia Company, a group of private investors,
for a vast area which included all the lands between the Cape
Fear River and present-day Bangor, Maine. In 1609, after the
Jamestown colony had been established, the Virginia Company's
charter was amended to extend from about the present North
Carolina–South Carolina line north to the Delaware River. On
May 24, 1624, King Charles I, dissatisfied with internal dissen-

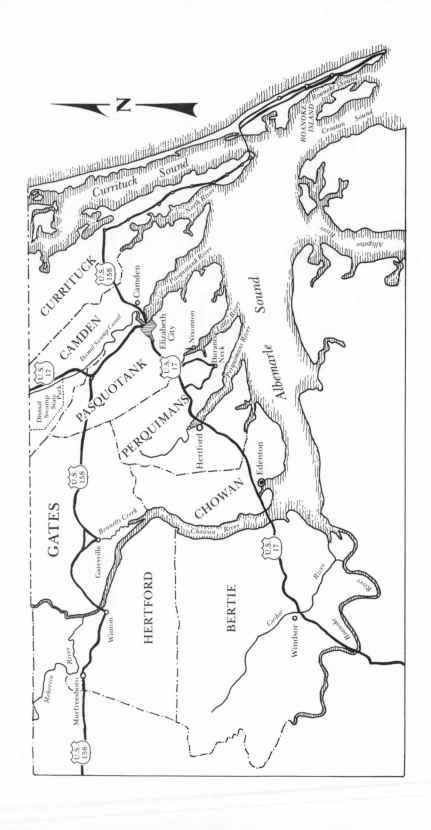

sion over the control of the Virginia Company, revoked the charter and proclaimed Virginia a royal domain.

In 1629, Charles began to implement his own colonial policy by making a proprietary grant to his attorney general, Sir Robert Heath, of the lands south of Albemarle Sound. Charles named this area "Carolina," after himself. Heath failed to use his grant and transferred it in 1632 to Henry Frederick Howard, Lord Maltravers. All plans for settlement of the tract were frustrated by the civil war in England and the beheading of King Charles in 1649.

After the restoration of the English monarchy in 1660, King Charles II undertook new policies of expansion and colonization in North America. In 1663, he made a proprietary grant of the Heath-Maltravers lands to eight noblemen who had remained loyal to the monarchy during the civil war, and the Heath grant was declared legally void. These new Lords Proprietors, as they were called, lost no time in getting still more land from the Crown. In 1665, they succeeded in extracting from the king an extension of their grant to include the lands north of Albemarle Sound to the present Virginia line as well as the area southward to Spanish Florida.

Except for sovereign duties owed to the king, the powers of the Lords Proprietors over the Colony of Carolina were supreme. They could pass laws and ordinances; create counties, towns, and other subdivisions of government; set up a judicial system; and even wage war. The people of the colony were considered to have the personal property rights guaranteed to all Englishmen and the right to consent to legislation. The Lords Proprietors divided their domain into three counties. The area north of Albemarle Sound was called the County of Albemarle after George Monck, the Duke of Albemarle and one of the Lords Proprietors.

By the time the County of Albemarle was formed, the area it encompassed had already been explored and thinly settled. Reconnaissance parties were sent out from Jamestown early in the seventeenth century, stimulated by rumors among the Virginia Indians that a few of the Roanoke Island colonists were living with friendly Indians in the Chowan River area. In 1610, Captain Samuel Argall traveled from Jamestown to the Chowan River valley, but what he found has not been recorded.

The first written report of an expedition into the Albemarle region is the voyage of John Pory, the secretary of the Virginia colony. In February, 1622, Pory explored the Chowan, finding "great forests of Pynes 15 or 16 myle broad and above 60 myle long, which will serve well for Masts and for Shipping, and for pitch and tarre, when we shall come to extend our plantations to those borders."

The "great forests of Pynes" referred not to the stands of loblolly pines one sees in the Albemarle today, but to the great longleaf pine forest that is estimated to have originally covered four million acres of the coastal plain. This resource was one of the first to be exploited on a large scale. England's mighty fleet of wooden ships produced a constant demand for masts and naval stores—tar, pitch, and turpentine. The longleaf pine was the source of such products. Millions of these trees were cut and burned for the tar that oozed out of the fiery remains. Resin for turpentine was extracted by chopping a deep hole into the base of the living tree. Other trees were cut for ship masts or for prized heart-pine lumber. North Carolina led the world in the production and exportation of naval stores during the colonial period and much of the nineteenth century. But by the end of this period, the great forests were gone, and only a few stands of longleaf pine remain today, primarily in the sandhills region of the state, on the southern border between the piedmont and the coastal plain.

By the middle of the seventeenth century, Virginia was actively encouraging settlement in the region. But first the Indians had to be dealt with. In 1646, Governor Sir William Berkeley sent a force under Major General William Bennett overland, while Colonel Thomas Dew and his men went down Currituck Sound. The object was apparently to impress the Indians with the military power of the Europeans.

Promotional tracts on the beauty and fertility of the new region began to appear in London and Virginia. One of these, published in 1650, was entitled, *Virgo Triumphans: or, Virginia Richly and Truly Valued; more especially the South Part thereof: viz. The fertile*

Carolana, and no less Excellent Isle of Roanoke, of Latitude from 31 *to* 37 *Degr., Relating the Means of Raysing Infinite Profits to the Adventurers and Planters.* Not surprisingly from the title, this pamphlet praised the Albemarle as an area "God and Nature had indulged with blessing incommunicable to any other Region."

Another midcentury exploration down the Chowan, Meherrin, and Roanoke river valleys by Edward Bland and Abraham Wood resulted in the publication in 1651 of *The Discovery of New Brittaine, 1650.* This book describes a land in which "Tobacco will grow larger and more in quantity. Sugar canes are supposed naturally to be there. . . . Tobacco Pipes have beene seene among these Indians tipt with Silver, and they wear Copper about their necks: They have two crops of Indian Corn yearely whereas Virginia hath but one." Another visitor about this same time was Francis Yeardley, who traveled down from Virginia, entered Currituck Inlet, and visited the remains of the Roanoke Island fort. Yeardley wrote a letter in 1654 describing Carolina as endowed with "a most fertile, gallant rich soil, flourishing in all the abundance of nature, especially in the rich mulberry and vine, a serene air, and temperate clime, and experimentally rich in precious minerals; and lastly I may say, parallel with my place for rich land, and stately timber of all sorts; a place indeed unacquainted with our Virginia's ripping frosts, no winter, or very little cold to be found there."

It is not known who was the first European settler to enter the Albemarle or when he arrived. According to legend, he was Nathaniel Batts, whose house was indicated on a 1657 map prepared by Nicholas Comberford, a London mapmaker. Batts apparently operated a trading post on the western shore of Albemarle Sound, on the neck of land between the mouth of the Roanoke River and that of Salmon Creek, as early as 1653. This area is now a part of Bertie County.

The earliest recorded patents of land were made by the Indians to individual settlers. On September 24, 1660, Nathaniel Batts received a deed signed with the mark of Kiscutanewhe, chief of the Yausapins, to the southwest shore of the Pasquotank River from Albemarle Sound to New Begun Creek. Another deed, dated March 1, 1661, from Kilcocanin, chief of the Yeopim, to George Durant, granted the lands between the Perquimans and Little rivers. This area is still known today as Durants Neck. Additional patents of land were obtained from the Virginia colony, so that by the time the County of Albemarle was created, a handful of people lived along the major rivers that flow into Albemarle Sound—the Chowan, Yeopim, Perquimans, Little, Pasquotank, and North rivers.

In 1664, organized government was established in the Albemarle with the appointment of William Drummond as governor of the county. An elected assembly of local landowners was also created, although its powers were largely advisory. The Lords Proprietors also attempted to attract additional settlers by reducing the annual quitrents for land to the level of those charged in Virginia. In 1669, they even gave the colony a sort of feudal government, the Fundamental Constitutions of Carolina.

This elaborate governmental structure was ill-suited to a frontier settlement of pioneer farmers and hunters with no town or fixed seat of government. The people resisted all authority, and one by one the appointed governors of the Lords Proprietors were either forced to resign, jailed, or banished.

The settlers especially resisted the attempt by the governors to enforce the British trade and navigation laws. Tobacco was the major agricultural product, and when England tried to tax its export to other colonies, evasion and smuggling became widespread. When Governor Thomas Miller tried to enforce the tobacco tax in 1677, an incident known as "Culpeper's Rebellion" resulted. A group of local farmers arrested Miller and appointed one of their own, John Culpeper, to lead the colony. Miller escaped jail and fled to England for help. Culpeper also went to London to present the local farmers' side of the story. He was tried for treason but obtained an acquittal when the Lords Proprietors determined that since there had been no regular government, he could not be guilty of insurrection.

Seth Sothel, one of the Proprietors, took over as governor in 1682, in the hope that direct rule would accomplish something. Sothel attempted to rule with an iron hand, jailing his political enemies and seizing their lands, and in 1689 the Assembly arrested him and banished him from the colony. Sothel was the last of the Albemarle governors. The Proprietors gave up trying to administer the county as a separate region, and the next appointee, Phillip Ludwell, was designated as governor of the "Province of Carolina that Lyes North and East of Cape Feare."

The people of the Albemarle had had enough, however, and were not willing to accept Ludwell either. A local man, Captain John Gibbs, gathered an armed force and claimed to have been elected by the Assembly to succeed Sothel. Gibbs failed when his claim was rejected in London, but the Proprietors decided to appoint Ludwell as the single governor of the whole province of Carolina and have him rule from Charles Town, present Charleston in South Carolina. This new arrangement, which called for the northern region to be ruled by a deputy governor, was something of an improvement, and most of the deputies appointed were longtime Albemarle residents who governed with a light hand from their plantations. One of these deputy governors, Thomas Harvey, owned the lands of the peninsula between the Yeopim and Perquimans rivers, an area still known as Harveys Neck.

In the early eighteenth century the population of the colony grew and spread beyond the confines of the Albemarle region, a fact recognized in 1710 when the Proprietors appointed Edward Hyde as governor of "North Carolina." Hyde soon had to deal with the uprising known as "Cary's Rebellion," led by Quaker supporters of the former deputy governor, Thomas Cary. Hyde was succeeded by Thomas Pollock, who was acting governor from 1714 to 1722. All three of these men owned plantations on the shore of the lower Chowan River.

No town existed in the Albemarle region until 1712, when the Assembly voted to establish a courthouse and lay off lots for sale on Queen Anne's Creek where it flowed into Albemarle Sound. In 1722, this town was named Edenton after Governor Charles Eden. The new town grew slowly, plagued by trouble with the Indians and the pirates that operated on the sound. William Byrd gives us an unflattering portrait of Edenton in 1728: "There may be 40 or 50 Houses, most of them Small and built without Expense. A Citizen here is counted Extravagant, if he has ambition enough to aspire to a Brick-chimney. Justice herself is but

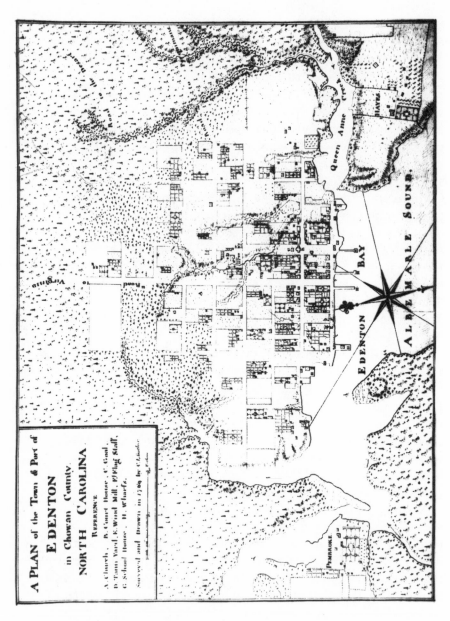

The Town Plan of Edenton, 1769, by C. J. Sauthier. (*Courtesy of Division of Archives and History, Raleigh, N.C.*)

indifferently Lodged, the Court-House having much the Air of a Common Tobacco-House. I believe this is the only Metropolis in the Christian or Mahometan World, where there is neither Church, Chapel, Mosque, Synagogue, or any other Publick Worship of any Sect or Religion whatsoever."

John Brickell, an Irish doctor who visited Edenton about 1730, provides us with a rather different description of the town. In his *Natural History of North Carolina*, published in 1737, he mentions Edenton's beautiful location and the fact that about sixty houses had been constructed. He is also enthusiastic about the inhabitants of the Albemarle region: "Most of the Plantations have a very noble and beautiful Prospect of large and spacious Rivers or Creeks, abounding with variety of Fish and Wild-fowl. . . . The Lands being thus richly adorn'd, and the Planters enjoying all these Blessings, are as hospitable People as any in the world, to all that come to visit them, there being few House-keepers, but what live decently, and give away more provisions to Coasters and Guests, that come to see them, than they expend among their own families."

A political change occurred that affected Edenton and the Albemarle. The English Crown and the Board of Trade had long felt that unrest in the North Carolina colony called for direct rule from London and that the Proprietors, who were looking primarily for profits, could never give it a stable government. In 1729, seven of the eight Proprietors, under pressure from the king, sold their shares to the Crown, and North Carolina became a royal colony. George Burrington, the first royal governor, was appointed by the king.

Up to this time the unofficial capital of the colony was Edenton, the chief meeting place of the Assembly. The second royal governor, Gabriel Johnston, sided with the settlers south of the Albemarle, and in 1746 a law was passed to establish the capital at New Bern. The Albemarle protested this move to the Crown but ultimately had to accept the fact that political power was shifting to the now more-populous areas of the south and west. The colonial capital of North Carolina was definitively established at New Bern in 1766.

Nevertheless, Edenton remained the most important town in

North Carolina. During the latter half of the eighteenth century, the town grew rapidly as a center of communications, shipping, and commerce. The post road, one of the best colonial roads, led north past the wilds of the Dismal Swamp to Williamsburg, Philadelphia, and New York. The mails and some travelers were transported along this track, which continued south to New Bern, Charleston, and Savannah. The fields and forests of the Albemarle produced naval stores, shingles, staves, tobacco, and corn, while shad and herring were seined from the rivers and sound. These products were exported from Edenton to New England, the West Indies, and across the seas. Roanoke Inlet, just south of present Nags Head across from Roanoke Island, was open during the eighteenth century, and Edenton was the chief landing of the port of Roanoke. (The term "port" was a regional designation in the eighteenth century.) The ships that called at Edenton carried cargoes of rum, spices, silk, linen, and sugar. They were shallow-draft vessels adapted to the coastwise trade. Larger ocean-going vessels could not navigate through the narrow inlets and the shallow sounds.

There was a grim side to the picture also. The large-scale production of the abundant raw materials of the Albemarle was possible only because of the application of slave labor. A plantation system developed built on human bondage. Slaves constituted more than a third of the population of the area. They contributed mightily to the prosperity of a colonial society in which they had little participation.

Edenton grew in population and stature. Tradesmen, cobblers, tailors, and blacksmiths opened shops. Lord Granville, the only one of the Lords Proprietors that had not sold his land to the king in 1729, established an office for the sale of land in Edenton, and Granville's unpopular agent, Francis Corbin, built the famous Cupola House on Broad Street near the waterfront. From this office he administered the sales, surveying, and money collection for the settlement of the vast Granville district. His questionable collection practices led the people to throw him into jail after a riot in 1759. St. Paul's Church, a handsome brick structure, was completed in 1766, and a beautiful Georgian-style pedimented courthouse surmounted by a cupola was built on a

St. Paul's Church, Edenton. (*Courtesy of N.C. Travel and Tourism Division*)

The Cupola House, Edenton. (*Courtesy of Division of Archives and History, Raleigh, N.C.*)

Chowan County Courthouse, Edenton. (*Courtesy of Division of Archives and History, Raleigh, N.C.*)

square facing Albemarle Sound in 1767. Taverns and public houses provided amusement for visiting sailors, travelers, and adventurers.

Other small ports and landings in the Albemarle region were developing into small villages as well. These grew into today's cities and towns, which owe their location to the eighteenth-century patterns of commerce and communication on Albemarle Sound. Each of the many rivers flowing into the sound had to have a landing for the on- and off-loading of goods for the surrounding area, since Edenton could not serve as a port for the many small necks of land and peninsulas of the region. The town of Hertford grew up at a landing called Phelps Point on the Perquimans River to serve the area of Harveys Neck. Nixonton, originally called Old Town, was a small port on the Little River. Windsor developed from a farmer's dock called Grays Landing on the Cashie River. Murfreesboro, on the Meherrin River, developed from Murfree's Landing, an eighteenth-century planter's wharf. Winton was an eighteenth-century port of entry on the upper Chowan River. Gatesville owes its origin to its location on Bennetts Creek.

Edenton almost tripled in size between 1728, when William Byrd saw it, and the end of the colonial period. By the eve of the Revolution, it was one of the leading towns in the colonies, and a remarkable group of leaders left their imprint during the early years of the new republic. Joseph Hewes came to Edenton from New Jersey to open a store and a shipyard. He also ran the post office and was a member of the colonial assembly. In 1773, Hewes and another Edenton citizen, Samuel Johnston, a leading member of the assembly and the owner of the nearby plantation called Hayes, helped organize a Committee of Correspondence, whose aim it was to communicate with other, similar committees throughout the colonies to present a united front against the taxation and trade policies of the British Crown. Hewes was one of the three North Carolina delegates to the Continental Congress in Philadelphia in 1774, and he signed the Declaration of Independence in 1776. During the Revolution, he led the Committee of Marine and helped organize the American Navy before he died in 1779.

Another early leader from Edenton was James Iredell, a lawyer instrumental in obtaining North Carolina's ratification of the Federal Constitution in 1789. Iredell was appointed to the United States Supreme Court in 1790. Although he had championed federal union, on the Supreme Court he became a defender of states' rights. His dissenting opinion in the case of *Chisholm* v. *Georgia* became the basis for the Eleventh Amendment to the United States Constitution, which prohibits suits against the states by citizens of other states or by subjects of foreign governments. Iredell's graceful white frame residence on East Church Street in Edenton is today operated as a state historic site.

Hugh Williamson, another Edenton resident, was a doctor educated in Scotland and Philadelphia. He originally came to Edenton to open up a trading business but was pressed into service treating the wounded during the Revolution. In 1787 he was the spokesman for the North Carolina delegation to the National Constitutional Convention and later was instrumental in persuading the North Carolina Assembly to vote to ratify the Constitution.

Although Edenton and the Albemarle supplied men to Washington's army, they were not major scenes of action during the Revolution. On October 25, 1774, fifty-one of the leading women of the Albemarle signed a document pledging to discontinue the use of East India tea as a gesture of protest. This action was ridiculed in Britain as the "Edenton Tea Party," but it helped show that mercantile interests in the southern colonies stood with the merchants of Boston in opposing British taxes. This was confirmed when, on April 12, 1776, in nearby Halifax on the Roanoke River, the Provincial Congress passed a resolution, now known as the Halifax Resolves, instructing the delegates to the Continental Congress to agree with any action leading to independence. After war broke out, Cornwallis's army marched through Halifax to the west, and the enemy occupied the Hampton Roads area to the north, but the Chowan River region was never invaded. Edenton became a supply depot for Washington's army since British vessels seldom dared to enter the North Carolina sounds. In May, 1781, the British galley *General Arnold*

The James Iredell House, Edenton. (*Courtesy of Division of Archives and History, Raleigh, N.C.*)

crept into Edenton harbor and captured an American schooner that was off-loading supplies. Men from Edenton pursued the vessel, recaptured it, and threw the English crew into Edenton's jail.

After the war years, Edenton no longer played a leading role in state and national affairs. The port declined as ships became larger and could not hazard the long voyage through shallow Albemarle Sound. The cypress and longleaf pine forests had been decimated, making the production of wood products no longer an important industry. The colonial post road through Edenton was avoided because of the long delays in catching a ferry across the sound. A steamboat service from Edenton to Plymouth, using a twenty-horsepower side-wheel craft called the *Albemarle*, was inaugurated in 1819 by a group of businessmen trying to revive trade, but this project failed in 1821. The principal overland routes shifted to growing population centers to the west.

The overwater trade of the Albemarle region shifted from Edenton to Elizabeth City in the early nineteenth century. The major cause of this change was the completion of the Dismal Swamp Canal in 1805, which connected Norfolk and the Chesapeake Bay with the Pasquotank River. Elizabeth City, which had been incorporated as Reading in 1793, was ideally located at the narrows of the Pasquotank River and soon became the focal point for the West Indies trade in the area. Elizabeth City is still the economic and commercial hub of northeastern North Carolina.

In the antebellum era of the nineteenth century, the plantation system held full sway in the Albemarle and the area was dominated by large "aristocratic" landowners and the institution of black slavery. Elaborate manor residences in the countryside and beautiful town houses that today grace the towns of the region were constructed by the wealthy few. The majority of the population lived a difficult life of subsistence farming and hard manual labor. The lands were productive and the sound and rivers were full of fish, so a period of stability and isolation resulted.

This society was shattered by the events of the Civil War. By dint of circumstance, the Albemarle was one of the earliest areas of the South to come under Union occupation. On February 8, 1862, as we have seen, a force under General Ambrose E. Burnside had captured Roanoke Island, which opened the way to operations against the principal North Carolina towns on the coastal rivers and sounds. Burnside did not waste any time. On February 9, he sent federal warships under Commander Stephen Rowan against Elizabeth City, which was defended by the "mosquito fleet" under Commodore W. F. Lynch. The Confederate schooner *Black Warrior* was moored across the Pasquotank River from Cobb Point, the site of a fort downriver. The federal boats "ran the river" and disabled the *Black Warrior*, and the Confederate militiamen deserted the fort. The other Confederate vessels of the mosquito fleet were either rammed or boarded. The people of Elizabeth City fled in terror, setting fire to several buildings as they ran. A crowd of jubilant blacks greeted the disembarking bluejackets as they took possession of the city.

Edenton was next. Commander Rowan sent Lieutenant Alexander Murray with several gunboats to Edenton harbor. The Edentonians offered no resistance to federal occupation, and the city was spared destruction. The town of Winton on the upper Chowan River was not so fortunate. Confederate authorities attempted to defend Winton because they regarded it as a key point in the line of defense for Norfolk and Weldon, the latter a crucial rail junction. Colonel William T. Williams placed his troops of the First Battalion of North Carolina Volunteers on top of a bluff overlooking the river. When Commander Rowan's flagship, the *Delaware*, came up the river, a mulatto named Martha Keen set a trap by waving to the vessel that it was safe to dock. Colonel Rush Hawkins, up in the crosstrees of the mast, saw the Confederate guns on the bluff and shouted, "Ring on, sheer off, rebels on shore." He descended to the deck so fast the Confederates reported that the lookout fell to his death. The Confederates opened fire and the ship was riddled, but it managed to get back into the main channel of the river and proceed upstream. The *Delaware*'s guns were then trained on the bluff, scattering the Confederates. The next day Winton suffered a terrible bombardment from Union guns, which was heard as far away as Gatesville. The bluejackets landed only to find Winton deserted. Colonel Hawkins then put the town to the torch, burning churches and the courthouse as well as homes and storage buildings. The effects of this destruction are evident today, and Winton is noticeably lacking in the handsome antebellum homes, churches, and buildings evident in many other cities and towns of the Albemarle region.

Federal occupation of the Albemarle region was peaceful except for isolated incidents. An armed band of blacks along with white Union sympathizers, known locally as "Buffaloes," established themselves at a plantation called Wingfield, seventeen miles above Edenton on the Chowan River. They mounted hit-and-run attacks until their power was destroyed by local authorities. In another incident, in 1864, Union Brigadier General Edward A. Wild led two regiments of Negro troops down the

Dismal Swamp Canal to Elizabeth City and across Camden and Currituck counties with the purpose of freeing Negro slaves. General Wild's troops freed about 2500 slaves but also took several ships and many horses and burned more than a dozen homesteads in the area before returning to Norfolk. On May 5, 1864, the Confederate ironclad *Albemarle* fought a three-hour battle with seven Union gunboats off Sandy Point in Albemarle Sound. The battle ended in a draw, but the *Albemarle* was later blown up at the wharf at Plymouth.

The Albemarle area was slow to recover from the Civil War. The landed estates were broken up, but blacks were still kept down, and the area remained poor and very isolated. The region lost population as increasing numbers of people, both black and white, left the land for higher-paying jobs in large cities.

In the present century, efforts began to be made to bring the Albemarle into closer contact with the state and the nation. Bridges constructed across the Chowan River and Albemarle Sound eliminated dependence on ferries. New industries were sought to broaden employment opportunities. People in Edenton awakened to the area's rich history and traditions, and the Historic Edenton Foundation was established to preserve the architectural heritage of the town on Queen Anne's Creek.

But ironically, the Albemarle region, the cradle of North Carolina colonial society, is today one of the least-known areas of the state. The counties above Albemarle Sound, some of whose names recall their seventeenth-century origins—Chowan, Perquimans, and Pasquotank—are sparsely populated areas far away from North Carolina's major cities. Under the influence of the Norfolk urban centers, they have, in a psychological sense, returned to Virginia. Yet the region still has remnants of its more than three-hundred-year history. And the major sources of income and employment today are those associated with the land and waters—agriculture, forestry, and fishing—just as they were in the eighteenth century.

The towns that were founded as river ports in the eighteenth century now straddle U.S. 17, the "Ocean Highway," which traverses the heart of the region. At the gateway to the ancient Albemarle, where the old plank road between Edenton and Halifax crosses the Cashie River, is the pleasant town of Windsor, the seat of Bertie County. Although it has a population of only 2300, Windsor is the commercial and industrial center for the county, which produces peanuts, tobacco, and other agricultural goods as well as lumber and wood products.

Across the mile-and-a-half-wide Chowan River is the town of Edenton, still the jewel of the Albemarle region. The eighteenth-century town plan has survived intact, as have many of the colonial-era houses and buildings. A wide range of building styles is to be seen here—Federal period, Greek Revival, coastal cottage, and the later Gothic Revival and elaborate Victorian types. Beautiful shade trees and the mirrorlike waters of Edenton Bay enhance the colonial-era charm of the town.

The countryside surrounding Edenton is rich with antebellum plantation homes. Bandon, the home of novelist Inglis Fletcher, who wrote historical novels about the Albemarle area, burned in 1963, but many others are in excellent condition. Hayes Plantation, constructed in 1817, still stands across Queen Anne's Creek on the bay. Its mansion has a magnificent columned double-porch facade, a common theme in the grander homes of the time. Farther east on Albemarle Sound are Sycamore, Athol, Mulberry Hill, and Sandy Point plantations.

Hertford, the seat of Perquimans County, is a beautiful old town built on the shores of the Perquimans River. The court-house was built about 1825, and many nineteenth-century homes remain along Front Street. George Fox, the founder of the Society of Friends, preached in this vicinity in 1672, and small communities nearby, such as Belvidere, were originally settled by Quakers from Pennsylvania in the early eighteenth century. South of Hertford in the Harveys Neck peninsula is the Newbold-White house, possibly the oldest structure in the state, and several other early plantation homes and sites.

Across the river in the Durants Neck area is the huge, brick plantation house called Leigh's Farm. Constructed by slaves, it has a gambrel roof enclosing a third-story ballroom and a double porch framed with six Doric columns. It is perhaps the largest of the old manor houses of the Albemarle. Governor Seth Sothel is said to be buried on its grounds.

Elizabeth City, with 14,000 people the largest city of the region, is the seat of Pasquotank County. Its antebellum buildings have suffered from twentieth-century demolition, but several dozen nevertheless remain. The waterfront, the site of a busy port in the nineteenth century, has been allowed to deteriorate, and access to the river is blocked by decaying buildings. Attractive neighborhoods of Victorian-era houses are found in the residential sections of the city.

The neck of land south of Elizabeth City is historically interesting. Nixonton, the county seat and chief port until the rise of Elizabeth City, is now an area of ramshackle homes and trailers, and the old customs house is a decaying reminder of busier times. At Halls Creek is the site of the first assembly of Carolina settlers in 1665, convened by William Drummond, the first governor of the province. Cobb Point is the site of the naval battle that resulted in the capture of Elizabeth City by Union forces in 1862. Nearby is Enfield Farm, where Culpeper's Rebellion began in 1677.

Across the Pasquotank River lies the peninsula of Camden County. This predominantly rural area produces mainly agricultural and forest products. A large second-home development is under way in the southern half of the county. Much of the population now commutes to either Elizabeth City or Norfolk to work.

The outstanding natural feature of the Albemarle is the Great Dismal Swamp in the northern part of the region and in southern Virginia. The early colonists called all coastal swamps "dismals," and this one merited the title of "great." Dense forests of cypress and gum grew in a permanently wet soil and in blackwater ponds. Originally, there were extensive stands of white cedar, called "juniper" by the locals. There are some unforested, open bogs covered with evergreen shrubs such as myrtle, swamp bay, and magnolia, and known as "lights."

Today the Great Dismal is a wet wilderness of about 210,000 acres, although it was originally twice as large. William Byrd tells us in his *Histories* that a party of surveyors under his direction ran the North Carolina–Virginia line through the Dismal in 1728. He tells of great forests of cypress and cedar and standing water "from which foul Damps ascend without ceasing, corrupt the Air, and render it unfit for Respiration." Even in the drier parts, his men found that their footprints through the mire immediately filled with water. They saw an area of the swamp that was barren of trees "but contains a large Tract of Reeds, which being perpetually green and waving in the Wind, it is call'd the green Sea." Byrd did not appreciate the beauty of the area, declaring, "Never was Rum, that cordial of Life, found more necessary than it was in this Dirty Place." He wanted to drain the whole swamp and suggested the possibility of building a canal to transport goods.

For the most part, Byrd stayed out of the Dismal, leaving the hard trek to his men, while he visited the inhabitants of the surrounding area. Calling at "John Ive's for a taste of good Water," he saw "several pretty Girls . . . wild as Colts, tho' not so ragged." Stopping for the night, he met his landlord's daughter, Rachel. "She was a smart Lass, and when I desired the Parson to make a Memorandum of his Christenings, that we might keep an account of the Good we did, she ask't me very pertly, who was to keep an Account of Evil? I told her she shou'd be my Secretary for that, if she wou'd go along with me."

After Byrd's time, the Dismal was indeed ditched and drained, much land was used for agriculture, and virtually the entire area was cut over at least once. Lumber companies used narrow-gauge railroads to cart out the huge logs. Relatively little of the original white cedar and cypress-gum forests remain; much of the regeneration growth has been loblolly and pond pine as well as mixed hardwood forest trees.

In this century, most of the remaining Dismal Swamp has been acquired by the U.S. Department of the Interior and the states of North Carolina and Virginia. A 14,000-acre tract in Camden County has been designated as a state park by North Carolina authorities, although there is no public access yet. With the forest lands now in public hands, there is a chance to manage this vast area so that the great cedar and cypress forests may return to some degree.

For the most part, the Albemarle is facing a quiet future. It is expected to remain a somewhat isolated, rural place, keeping to itself as it has always done. The old colonial cradle of North Carolina seems destined to continue to be unappreciated, even by North Carolinians. There is a treasure trove of architectural gems in the Albemarle, and it is available for all to see, if the effort is made. If not, the people will not be overly concerned. Edenton doesn't want to become another Williamsburg.

The biggest change taking place in the settlement and land-use patterns of the Albemarle is the increasing development of the shoreline of Albemarle Sound. Summer homes, retirement communities, and some industrial plants have located along the beautiful and extensive estuarine shoreline. The chief resource problem facing the region is how to reconcile this new development with the preservation of the sound.

Albemarle Sound is about fifty-five miles long and an average of seven miles wide. It is very shallow, little more than 18 feet deep anywhere. Much of the estuarine shoreline is covered by cypress, gum, and maple swamp forests. In some areas the shore is a bank of clay and sand five to twenty feet high. The wind tides and rising sea level are causing the shoreline to recede generally at a rate of two to three feet per year. In an effort to prevent this erosion in some places, the shoreline has been bulkheaded, but this is an expensive and at best a temporary solution. A much better way to handle erosion is to enforce setback and land-use requirements designed to leave the shoreline in its natural state. The fringing vegetation acts as a natural buffer that slows the erosion rate.

Since 1972, pollution of Albemarle Sound has been a major concern. That was the year of a big algae bloom on the Chowan River that was described as looking like a "pea soup." The lower half of the river was green from bank to bank. In some places, the tufts of algae appeared sturdy enough to walk on. This caused an outcry in the region as fishing was ruined, the shore was fouled, and recreational use of the river was rendered impossible. Particularly hard hit was the multi-million-dollar commercial catfish and herring fishery. The bloom died down during the winter months but has returned every year since.

People from Gatesville to Edenton have been frustrated and outraged by the pollution and the effect on their lives. At first they looked to the state water pollution control authorities to help them. But the state could not prevent the algae bloom. In their anger, residents started sending bottles of polluted water to their representatives in the General Assembly. I received a letter from a group in Gatesville who wanted me to file suit against the state. They said that they intended to ask Pete Seeger to give a benefit concert to raise the money for legal action. But by this time, in 1978, the situation had been allowed to deteriorate so much that even the courts could not enforce the law.

The Chowan River situation was the first large-scale algae bloom in coastal North Carolina. It has proved difficult to solve. Algae blooms are caused by the presence of too many nutrients—nitrogen and phosphorus mainly—in slow-moving water. The nutrients are produced by a variety of sources that are hard to control, such as seepage from septic tanks, runoff from agricultural lands, and forest and swamp drainage. Point sources of pollution from towns and industries contribute, too. No one discharger is to blame. In the case of the Chowan, the situation is complicated by the fact that the upper basin of the river is in Virginia, so that two separate sets of state authorities are involved. Neither North Carolina nor Virginia paid much attention to protecting the water quality of the river until the situation got out of hand.

The 1972 bloom was triggered by pollution from a fertilizer plant near Tunis, North Carolina, owned by the Farmers Chemical Company. Although not totally to blame, this company's discharges were enough to tip the critical ecological balance. When, in 1967, the company first announced it planned to build the plant, it assured the state that its operation would not pollute the Chowan. It planned to construct a nitrogen waste recovery system by 1972. In the meantime, the state allowed the plant to operate, and by 1972, two thousand pounds of nitrogen-rich wastewater per day were being discharged into the Chowan at a point where the river begins to widen and slow down. In that year, the state shut the plant down until the waste treatment facility could be built. But in 1976, after the plant had resumed operation, it was discovered that the grounds surrounding it had become contaminated with nitrogen-rich wastewater, which continued to seep into the Chowan. And the algae blooms have returned each year. State officials can do little but announce their "deep concern."

This sad episode could have been avoided had authorities been more diligent in enforcing the law. The time for action to stop pollution is before the trouble begins, not after fish start dying and the damage is felt. Albemarle Sound is, on the whole, a healthy estuarine system, relatively unpolluted, with abundant levels of oxygen. In addition to its beauty, it is an excellent habitat for anadromous fish such as striped bass and herring, as well as a nursery area for a wide variety of shellfish and finfish. Waste discharges into the rivers feeding this system and changes in flow from possible upstream diversions of water should be carefully evaluated before they are allowed to occur.

Now, as in the past, despite new industry and population growth, the prosperity of the Albemarle still depends in large measure on farming, forestry, and fishing. Future industrial and residential development should not be allowed to disrupt the essential resources—the rivers and sounds, farmlands and forests—that have been the strength of the region throughout its long history; they can provide the basis for future progress as well.

5

Currituck

BETWEEN THE HEAVILY POPULATED NORFOLK, VIRGINIA, region and the Dare County beach resorts, in the northeast corner of North Carolina, is the place called Currituck, as lovely and exotic as its Indian name. It consists of two peninsulas, one part of the mainland, the other a section of the Outer Banks, separated from each other by a coastal sound. To really get to know Currituck, an exploration by boat is essential. I made such a trip on a November day in 1978.

Our skiff glided through the still waters of Currituck Sound. We were searching for a small island, but our vision was obscured by a dense early morning fog that melted into the blue-gray of the waters of the sound. We could hear the call of the wild geese above the rumble of our motor.

Suddenly, we heard a dog bark in the distance. Diane called out, "Mushroom!" The dog barked again, and we navigated by the sound of the dog's barking until the dark outline of Monkey Island came into view. I saw the wooden dock and two buildings beyond it: a large hunting lodge said to be more than a hundred years old and a smaller caretaker's house. The rest of the island, only seven acres in extent, was thickly wooded with oak, pine, and gum trees. Along the shore, which was bordered by a wooden dike to retard erosion, was a fringe of freshwater marsh, cattails, giant cordgrass, and bayberry.

My companions, John and Diane Larocque, were home. They are employed by The Nature Conservancy, the national conser-

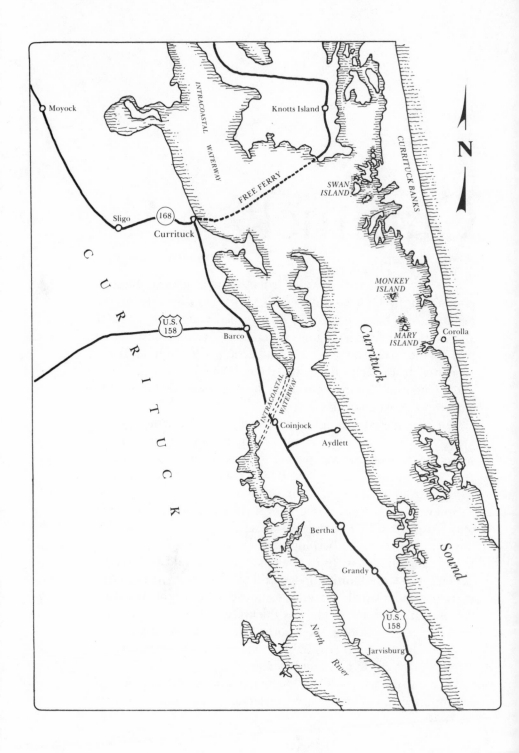

vation group that owns the island, to watch over it and an area of the Currituck Outer Banks. They live in the caretaker's house year-round except for a short time each winter when the waters of the sound freeze, making it impossible to ferry in supplies. Their busy time is through the hunting season, which begins during the week of Thanksgiving and continues until early January. The Nature Conservancy, which purchased the property in 1977, continues to lease the lodge and waterfowl blinds to the hunters that come to Currituck from all over the country.

The island has a long and interesting history. The name Monkey Island is said to come from the Pumonkey Indians, who venerated and buried their dead here. In the nineteenth century it began to be used as a private hunting club. In 1919 some executives of the American Tobacco Company purchased it and formed the Monkey Island Club, which was limited to nine members. One of these, Ashby Penn of Reidsville, North Carolina, bought out the others in 1931. Marcus Griggs, Mr. Penn's caretaker for thirty years, remembers that his employer was particularly fond of Monkey Island. When Penn died in 1975, Mr. Griggs scattered his ashes over the island. The Nature Conservancy acquired the property from the Penn heirs with the intention of preserving it and an adjoining area of the Outer Banks.

I asked Diane if she ever got bored living on the island. "Oh no," she said. "I watch the wildlife, do some painting, and explore the sound. There's always something new happening." In the summer, she explained, the island has a large population of nesting herons and egrets. There are all kinds: American, cattle, and snowy egrets; Louisiana, little blue, and green herons. Osprey nest on the channel markers in the sound. In the fall, the ducks, geese, and swans arrive. The sound is famous for concentrations of Canada and snow geese, whistling swans, and many kinds of ducks. "I saw some coots, too, the other day," she said. "The people around here call them bluepeters." With a smile she added, "I don't know why, but I asked one fellow and he said, 'If you spent as much time sitting in that cold water, yours would be blue too!'"

By this time the sun was well over the horizon, and the fog was burning off, revealing a clear, blue sky. A beautiful November day was in the offing. As the fog lifted, the contours of Currituck Sound became visible with the Outer Banks on one side and the mainland shore on the other side of the island.

The sound is the glory and the essence of Currituck. There is no other place like it in coastal North Carolina. About thirty miles long and three miles wide, it extends from Virginia on the north to the end of the Currituck peninsula across from Kitty Hawk on the south. Fresh water is fed into the sound from rivers to the north and west draining Virginia and North Carolina. There has been no direct link between sea and sound since New Currituck Inlet shoaled up in 1828. As a result, no lunar tides affect the sound, although a strong blow from the north or south can produce a wind tide of two to three feet. The waters of Currituck Sound have almost no salt content; it is like a big, freshwater lake.

There is something incongruous about such a large body of fresh water within a few hundred yards of the sea. The shining blue of the limpid water contrasts markedly with the darker appearance of the brackish water in the sounds to the south. It is so shallow that you can "pole" a boat across it by pushing an eight-foot oar off against the bottom. Freshwater grasses—wild celery, widgeon (or eel) grass, pondweed, and muskgrass—grow abundantly in the shallow water, providing a rich food source for wildfowl.

Currituck Sound has always been of crucial importance to the people of the area. For most of its history, Currituck has been a region of small farms and farming communities located along the axis of the north-south road—modern highways 158, 34, and 168—which runs down the spine of the mainland peninsula from Virginia to Point Harbor. People grew what they needed to survive, kept a cow for milk, and, in good years, shipped surplus corn and vegetables north for sale in the Norfolk market. Although they were only fifty miles from the Virginia population centers at the mouth of Chesapeake Bay, bad roads and the intervening swamps to the north protected their isolation. Large families were raised in small log and weatherboard farmhouses. The abundant wild ducks, geese, and fish of Currituck Sound provided an important supplementary source of income and food. Out of necessity, almost every man in the county was a hunter and fisherman as well as a farmer.

In the nineteenth century, wealthy northern businessmen discovered the wild ducks and geese of Currituck. They bought up vast tracts on the Outer Banks and the marshy islands of the sound. Sumptuous clubhouses and lodges were built on these tracts. In addition to Monkey Island, some of the most famous of these were the Narrows Island, Swan Island, Dews Island, and Currituck shooting clubs. Each fall and winter, members of these clubs and their guests would travel down to Currituck from New York, Philadelphia, and Baltimore, coming by train to Munden Point, Virginia, and proceeding by boats into the sound. The local people worked as hunting guides, caretakers, and laborers, and the clubs provided many of them with their principal source of cash income. In this heyday of market hunting, "battery-boxes" equipped with huge "punt guns" blanketed the air with shot and brought down a whole flock of birds with a single burst, until the practice was outlawed in 1918.

All was not harmony between the wealthy "Yankees" and the Currituck people. The hunting clubs took the attitude that the lands they bought in the sound were their property and tried to exclude the natives from hunting and fishing—what they called "poaching"—there. In 1887, the Narrows Island Club, which was organized in 1881 by a group of twenty-four New Yorkers, tried to block public access through Big Narrows, a vast area of Currituck Sound between two groups of marsh islands. The State of North Carolina took the club to court, and in 1888 the Supreme Court of North Carolina decided that since the waters of the sound were navigable, they could not be blocked off to the public.

This court decision did not end the argument, however. In 1953, the Swan Island Club sued three local men for trespass because they were operating duck blinds anchored in three feet of water on Currituck Sound. Once again, the court upheld the right of the public to use the waters and shoal lands of the sound.

During the past fifteen or twenty years, times have changed for the people of Currituck. Today, larger farms have to a great extent replaced the small, family farms, and since there is no industry in the county, more than half the work force commutes a half hour to Elizabeth City or makes the hour-and-a-quarter trip up a narrow two-lane highway to Norfolk. The old-timers insist that the hunting and fishing on the sound can't compare with what they were years ago. Tillman Merrell of Aydlett, who worked as a hunting guide for fifty years on Currituck Sound, remembers "clouds" of ducks and geese in the sound. "I've seen 'em come between you and the sun and just shadow it," he says. Today there are ten times as many hunters and less than half the game, he estimates.

Yet the links with the past are still strong. People who work in Norfolk shake their heads firmly when asked if they've considered moving there. They say they like the hunting, the fishing, and the outdoors in general, as well as a chance to have a big backyard garden. Fast-food places, shopping centers, and strip development are largely absent from the county. Much of the mainland is still forest land and swampland. The principal communities—Jarvisburg, Grandy, Bertha, Aydlett, Coinjock, Barco, Sligo, Shawboro, and Moyock—are small commercial centers consisting of a post office, a few gas stations and stores, and several houses.

Most of these places were named for the settlers who first had the presence of mind to apply to the U.S. Postal Service for a post office. A few, more modest, early postmasters adopted the name of a favorite child: the village of Bertha, for instance, was named for a daughter of Appolas Owens. A few towns, such as Moyock and Coinjock, have Indian names. Sligo was named by a homesick Irish preacher in 1783. The town called Currituck on maps, which is no larger than the other communities, is known simply as "the Courthouse" to most people. It appears to have changed little since the nineteenth century. A weathered red brick courthouse and jail dominate the community; both are more than a hundred years old, and the jail is said to be the oldest in the state. The rest of the town consists of a red brick church with a white steeple, a general store, and frame, weatherboard residences.

A ferry from the town of Currituck, which is located on the sound, provides the only North Carolina connection to Knotts

Currituck County Courthouse. (*Courtesy of Division of Archives and History, Raleigh, N.C.*)

Island, a peninsula physically connected to Virginia, on which there is a small farming and fishing community. Most of the peninsula is marshland administered by the Mackay Island National Wildlife Refuge. William Byrd's statement in 1728 that the people of Knotts Island lose "as much Blood in the Summer Season by the infinite number of Mosquetas, as all their Beef and Port can recruit in the Winter" seems apt today.

Although most of the old, exclusive hunting clubs have been sold, hunting is still very important today on Currituck Sound. Local people apply for permits to maintain hunting blinds in the sound, and during the short winter season, hunters who come from all over the country are lodged in private homes or in lodges on the mainland and then transported out to the blinds for the day by local guides. The going rate for a package deal including guide service, room, and board is $90 per day.

Sport fishing is also important on the sound, and the primary catch is largemouth bass. Crab pots and eel pots are much in evidence as well. Commercial fishing, once important, has declined in recent years. But the sound is an important nursery area for the young of many commercially important fish species. Small spot and croaker are present in large numbers during the winter and spring. Menhaden and trout appear during the spring and summer. Adult shad, alewives, and striped bass migrate through the sound to river spawning areas in the spring, and after hatching, the juveniles of these species move through the sound to the ocean.

John and Diane were ready to leave on the mile crossing from Monkey Island to Currituck Banks. We had to use an even smaller skiff than the one we had come in, they explained, because of the shallow water. We couldn't just head for a random landing on the banks, either. The sound side was fringed with dense marshes of giant cordgrass up to twelve feet high, cattail, marsh mallow, and black needlerush. We would have to head for one of the small creeks that drained from the banks into the sound.

"She's breezin' up," said Diane as we started the journey. "Sharp wind," John concurred.

I was excited to be under way. Traveling by boat across the sound was the only way a person could get to Currituck Banks without special permission. The public road from the south ends at the Dare County line. In the distance, I could see the Currituck Beach Light, erected in 1873. Surrounding the lighthouse, among the pines and live oaks is the little village of Corolla, with a population of only twenty-two, the only inhabited community on the banks. To the north a huge sand hill rose seventy-five feet or more above the tree line. This is Lewark's Hill, one of several huge, moving dunes that are found on this stretch of the Outer Banks. Another of these huge dunes, called Whale Head Hill, lies just south of the village of Corolla. Old-timers claim to remember that Whale Head Hill was once north of Corolla, and in the last fifty years gradually bypassed the small settlement. In the 1950s a dune called Pennys Hill moved completely over a small village called Seagull. The inhabitants were forced to leave as their homes gradually disappeared under the moving sands.

While we made the crossing, several V-shaped rafts of Canada

The Currituck Beach Light. (*Courtesy of Division of Archives and History, Raleigh, N.C.*)

geese graced the blue sky. Smaller flocks of ducks flew overhead, moving more swiftly, with less organization than the geese.

We were headed for Jenkins Cove, a small bay on the interior of the banks. Resting on the shoals at the entrance was a large flock of great black-backed gulls, herring gulls, and common terns. They rose at our approach. A pair of beautiful, white whistling swans moved in the distance. A great blue heron lifted slowly out of the marsh on its seventy-inch wings and lumbered off.

Soon the water became too shallow to use the motor, and we had to shove-paddle the skiff into the cove. We dropped the anchor and waded the last fifth of a mile to shore. "Keep an eye out for mocasins," John warned. "They're very aggressive and they can swim." The local people tell stories of water mocasins chasing people for miles. I had never seen one, but I cautiously looked around with every step.

On shore, we were in a wetland clearing in the midst of the marine forest at the back of the banks. The low forest canopy was mainly pine and live oak. These evergreen trees and the lushness of the marshland vegetation were reminders of summer on this warm, beautiful November day. But my eye wandered over a pastel of fall colors that would do credit to the mountains of Vermont. The rich red of the shining sumac and red maples and the yellow of the willow and black cherry trees stood out against the green of oak and pine. Along the edge of the forest were yaupon holly bushes with their scarlet berries. Wax myrtle and bayberry shrubs with dark green foliage were heavy with bluish-purple berries. I counted more than twenty different kinds of flowers and bushes still in bloom, silvery-white baccharis shrubs, yellow wild daisies, marsh pinks, goldenrod, reddish-brown plume grass, sedge, and blue asters. The sands were marked with the tracks of deer, raccoons, and a feral hog which had come down to the sound for water.

As we walked toward the ocean, the forest canopy disappeared and we were in an area of small dunes vegetated with grasses, *Spartina patens*, sand burr, spurge, and marsh elder, as well as low shrubs, wax myrtle and bayberry. We startled three wild horses grazing on the *Spartina*. They quickly disappeared into a stand of shrubs.

The roar of the ocean grew louder as we neared the beach. A marsh hawk rose out of a depression between the dunes and flew off. The dominant vegetation was now American beach grass and sea oats. A flock of sanderlings and knots flew up as we crossed the frontal dune to the beach. There in the surf were the stumps of large trees, some two feet in diameter and three to five feet high. It was an eerie sight to behold; I was looking at the remains of a forest that grew here perhaps in the sixteenth century. At that time I would have been standing on the sound side of the island. Now the weathered wood was slowly succumbing to the sea.

A wild beach is rare on the east coast of the United States. The lack of development of Currituck Banks is all the more unusual because more than a million people live in the cities a few miles to the north. A further irony is that Currituck was one of the earliest places explored and settled by the Europeans.

The first explorers of the area, the Spanish expedition of 1566, named the region San Bartolomé. The Indian name for the Currituck Sound was Titepano. The first settlers who came down the North and North Landing rivers from Virginia in the 1660s called the area "Coratank," which was the Indian word for wild goose. The first recorded grant of land was for 600 acres on Indian Creek, a tributary of the North River, made by Lord Berkeley, the Governor of Virginia, to John Harvey in 1663. At this time, Algonkian Indian tribes, especially the Poteskeet, lived on the mainland shore, but not on the Outer Banks. Additional settlers from Virginia paid the Indians for permission to settle on their lands.

By 1665, when King Charles II extended the grant under the Carolina Charter of 1663 to the eight Lords Proprietors to include the lands between Albemarle Sound and the present North Carolina–Virginia line, several families were probably already living in Currituck. Confusion grew about where the boundary line was located. In 1680 people living near the border, who claimed to live in Carolina, refused to pay taxes to Virginia, even though they held grants from the Virginia land office. In response, Virginia authorities began collecting the taxes by force. They also denied the Carolinians the use of Virginia ports to ship tobacco grown in the Albemarle region. The Lords Proprietors pressured the English Crown to survey and mark the boundary between the two colonies to clear up the dispute.

Only in 1728 did the two colonial governments agree to run the line. Virginia's boundary commission was led by the aristocratic planter, William Byrd II, and Carolina's commission was headed by Chief Justice Christopher Gale. William Byrd has given us an account of the settlement of the boundary dispute in his *History of the Dividing Line betwixt Virginia and North Carolina*. He also wrote another version called *The Secret History of the Line*, which was an inside account of some of the dissensions that arose during the expedition.

The major problem at the outset was that the 1665 grant described the boundary between Virginia and Carolina as "To run from the North End of Corotuck Inlet, due West to Weyanoke Creek . . . and from thence West, in a direct Line, as far as the South Sea." By this time, no one knew what "Weyanoke Creek" referred to; the name had been lost. So it was decided to begin at Currituck Inlet and survey the line due west.

There was no love lost between the snooty Virginia planters and the rustic settlers of North Carolina. Byrd frequently referred to North Carolina as "Lubberland." The two boundary commissions exchanged sarcastic letters at the outset. The Virginians wrote, "We shall be provided with as much Wine and Rum as will enable us and our men to drink every Night to the Success of the following Day, and because we understand there are many Gentiles on your frontier who have never had an opportunity of being Baptised, we shall have a chaplain to make them Christians." To which the North Carolinians replied, "Now you force us to expose the nakedness of our Country and to tell you we can't possibly meet you in the manner our great respect to you would make us glad to do. . . . So all we can answer . . . is that we will endeavor to provide as well as Circumstances of things will permit. What we may want in necessaries we hope will be made up in Spiritual Comfort we expect from Your Chaplain of whom we shall give notice as you desire to all lovers of novelty and doubt not of a great many of Boundary Christians."

On March 5, 1728, the two groups met on the desolate north shore of Currituck Inlet. On sixteenth-century maps, two inlets are shown breaching Currituck Banks, and the sound was a saltwater lagoon. Currituck Inlet was just south of the present state line, and Musketo Inlet was several miles further south. Musketo Inlet shoaled up and disappeared in the 1670s. Byrd's account tells us that in 1728, Currituck Inlet was "an Opening of not quite a Mile, which at this day is not practicable for any Vessel whatsoever. And shallow as it now is, it continues to fill up more and more, both the Wind and the Waves rolling in the sands from the Eastern Shoals." He describes the power of the sea. "The Breakers fly over . . . with a horrible Sound and at the same time afford a very wild Prospect." He tells us that a "new inlet" had opened up in 1713, about five miles south of the old one. This was New Currituck Inlet, which remained navigable until 1828. Currituck Sound was used by ocean-going ships during this time. Near the present village of Currituck was a customs house and a dock. Byrd says that a New England sloop was riding in the sound when he passed through on his way to the banks. But Currituck Inlet silted up entirely in the 1730s, shortly after Byrd was there, and in 1828 New Currituck Inlet closed, transforming Currituck Sound into the freshwater body it is today.

The Carolina commissioners treated the Virginians to breakfast out on the banks. Byrd remarks disparagingly that the Carolinians were "much better provided for the Belly than for the Business." After that, there was a "sharp dispute" over where to begin the line. The Virginians wanted to run it from the end of a spit of sand that marked the north side of the inlet. The Carolinians argued in favor of the first high land to the north. The Virginians finally gave in "for Peace-sake." Byrd tells us that two "Credible Witnesses" (undoubtedly in cahoots with the North Carolinians) swore that the spit of sand had advanced two hundred feet to the south since the boundary dispute had begun. So even in the eighteenth century, inlet migration was causing problems for human notions of fixed and settled property lines. The North Carolinians understood how inlets work better than the Virginians did, and they used this knowledge to win the argument and gain the advantage in the boundary dispute.

Byrd also remarks about some of the people then living nearby. On the "South Shore" or North Carolina side of the banks, he writes, "dwelt a Marooner, that Modestly called himself a Hermit, tho' he forfeited that Name by Suffering a wanton Female to cohabit with him. His habitation was a Bower, cover'd with Bark after the Indian Fashion, which in that mild Situation protected him pretty well from the Weather. Like the Ravens, he neither plow'd nor sow'd, but Subsisted chiefly upon Oysters, which his Handmaid made a Shift to gather from the Adjacent Rocks. Sometimes, too, for a change of Dyet, he sent her to drive up the Neighbor's Cows, to moisten their Mouths with a little Milk. But as for raiment, he depended mostly upon his Length of Beard, and She upon her Length of Hair, part of which she brought decently forward, and the rest dangled behind quite down to her Rump."

William Byrd's observations on the early settlers of Currituck are not very complimentary. "The Truth of it is, these People live so much upon Swine's flesh, that it don't only encline them to the Yaws, and consequently to the downfall of their Noses, but makes them likewise extremely hoggish in their Temper, and many of them seem to Grunt rather than Speak in their ordinary conversation." Yet he tells us that he "called at a Cottage where a Dark Angel surprised us with her Charms. Her Complexion was a deep Copper, so that her fine Shape and regular Features made her appear like a Statue in Bronze done by a masterly hand."

Except for the disappearance of the inlets, the Currituck Outer Banks remained essentially as William Byrd saw them until well into the twentieth century. The frequent northeaster storms and hurricanes often pushed the ocean waters over the flat barrier beaches into the sound. Some people tried to farm the banks and graze cattle on them, but no one stayed very long.

In the nineteenth century, when the U.S. Lifesaving Service established lifesaving stations every six to eight miles along the banks, weatherboard buildings were put up at places called Wash Woods, Pennys Hill, Whale Head, Poyner Hill, and Seagull. The lighthouse was erected at Currituck Beach. Small settlements for the lifesaving crews and their families grew up around these stations.

Of these small settlements, only Corolla has survived. According to one account, this village received its name when someone noticed many wild violets growing there and remarked that the outside of the flower is called the corolla. This seems doubtful, but it is as good an explanation as any. The town consists of a post office, store, church, school, and several private residences.

The Whaleshead Club. (*Courtesy of Division of Archives and History, Raleigh, N.C.*)

Nearby is the Corolla Lighthouse, one of the six historic light-houses of the Outer Banks, a brown brick tower one hundred and sixty-three feet high.

Corolla is the site of the largest and most elaborate of the old hunting lodges of Currituck, the Whaleshead Club. This huge, gabled structure built in the Italian style has a green, copper-tile roof. Edward C. Knight, a railroad magnate from Philadelphia, spent $383,000 on its construction from 1922 to 1925. Incredibly ornate, it has brass plumbing and corduroy walls, thirty-six rooms and twelve baths. After Knight's death in 1936, the lodge was sold at a tremendous loss to Ray Adams of Washington, D.C., for $25,000. It was too expensive to maintain, and during World War II the building was leased to the Coast Guard. Then it became a school and a rocket fuel test station. It is now a vacant shell, slowly decaying in the salt air.

In the 1930s, an extensive dune-stabilization program was carried out on the Outer Banks. Workers of the Civilian Conservation Corps erected sand fences and bulldozed up a continuous frontal dune to prevent overwash of the banks. Yet the banks were not developed because no road was constructed behind the stabilized dunes. The Back Bay National Wildlife Refuge, which included several miles of beach between Sandbridge, Virginia, and the North Carolina–Virginia line blocked the way south from the Norfolk area, and population concentrations were not sufficient for the State of North Carolina to construct a road from the south. The number of people living on the banks actually declined as the lifesaving stations were abandoned.

In the 1970s, after a long period of stable population, Currituck County began to grow. The 1970 census showed the population to be 6,900. By 1980, this had grown to 10,600, with several thousand additional summer residents. By the year 2000 the permanent population is predicted to be 30,000, with 21,000 seasonal residents. This increase is the result of an influx of people working in the Norfolk metropolitan area, new retirement settlements, and vacation home development. Many trailer parks have been set up, areas such as Bell's Island and Church's Island have been subdivided for expensive homes built on finger canals cut into the marshes bordering the sound, and beach cottages are going up on the Currituck Banks.

A land boom is in full swing in Currituck County. The state Department of Transportation is widening highways 168, 34, and 158, the north-south corridor to the Norfolk area. When this is complete, most of the county will be less than an hour from the city over a good road. The mainland peninsula will come firmly within the orbit of this metropolitan area. As the region becomes a surburban and resort community, can the beauty of Currituck Sound be preserved? Will it retain its links with the pastoral, rural, and agricultural past?

Most of the Currituck Outer Banks was purchased by land development companies. There is a potential for subdividing this area into more than 8,000 individual lots. The roads of the county are studded with beguiling signs: "Sanderling. Life as it used to be"; "Southern Shores. More than just real estate. It's a state of mind." These two developments are to the south, in Dare County, but some people would like to duplicate them on the Currituck Banks. Beach cottages, mobile homes, and a grid pattern of roads have already appeared in many sections of the banks. Hundreds of four-wheel-drive vehicles run over the beaches and dunes. Finger canals have been dredged through the marshes on the sound side of parts of the banks. Many people question the wisdom of this scale of development. The sandy soil is not suitable for individual septic tanks, yet only one developer has put in a sewage treatment plant—and it has not functioned adequately. The widespread use of septic tanks could endanger the purity of the water of the sound and pollute the small supply of groundwater under the banks. Other forces have to be reckoned with as well. The huge moving sand dunes can completely bury houses in their paths. Storm surges from hurricanes are capable of inundating the entire banks or cutting new inlets. The Ash Wednesday Storm of March, 1962, wiped out what remained of the little Coast Guard station village of Pennys Hill. A major hurricane has not hit since the 1930s, but this has been very unusual. The big storms will surely return.

Certain groups tried to stem the tide of development. In 1977, The Nature Conservancy quietly purchased two of the old hunting lodge properties, Monkey Island and Swan Island, including more than 6,000 acres of land on the Outer Banks. The National Audubon Society acquired Pine Island, including almost two miles of oceanfront property just north of the Dare County line. The active hunting organizations, such as the Currituck Shooting Club, own several thousand acres of marsh and banks property. These groups wanted to preserve at least part of the Currituck Banks in a natural state.

By the late 1970s, the issue was clearly joined between the environmentalists and the developers over the future of Currituck Banks. Both sides were keeping their powder dry, and the least spark would set it off. That spark came in 1978, in the form of a proposal to build a public road north from the Dare County line.

Why a simple road would cause so much commotion takes a little explaining. The main reason that this twenty-three-mile stretch of Outer Banks had never been developed was a lack of what bureaucrats call "access." The public road from the south ended near Duck, at the county line. On the north, just across the Virginia line, the Back Bay refuge blocked the way. For years there were attempts to break this impasse.

In 1949, development interests had gotten a law passed by the North Carolina General Assembly which created a special "municipal corporation," called the Carolina-Virginia Coastal Highway, for the purpose of building a toll road north to the Virginia line. This attempt failed when in 1953 the North Carolina Supreme Court decided that the law under which this body had been created was unconstitutional.*

In 1963, a similar effort was made when a law was passed creating the North Carolina Turnpike Authority to build a road. This prompted litigation with the hunting club. This time, in 1965, the North Carolina Supreme Court upheld the law and the legality of the Turnpike Authority.† Despite this, the road was never built because the Authority couldn't come up with the financing.

In the early 1970s, the road issue again got hot. With the dramatic rise in the value of beach property, the developers brought political pressure to bear on the state. By this time, the environmental movement was strong enough to have a significant effect. A compromise was reached in an effort to satisfy both groups. In 1974, with great fanfare, the state and county governments adopted the so-called "Currituck Plan," which was hailed as a model solution. The bargain struck was that development was to be allowed to proceed on Currituck Banks in clusters, called Planned Unit Developments, each with a relatively high population density. Each developer was to provide open space and water and sewer utilities. The state agreed to purchase part of the land on the banks for a state park. The key element of the plan was that the state would also provide bridge and ferry service across the sound. The idea was to create lateral access instead of the north-south beach road. Currituck Banks was to be a "destination" beach instead of a strip beach development. A

*The major reason for this decision was that the court found a violation of the legal principle that the legislative power cannot be delegated. See *Carolina-Virginia Coastal Highway* v. *Coastal Turnpike Authority*, 74 S.E.2d 310 (N.C. 1953).

†*North Carolina Turnpike Authority* v. *Pine Island, Inc.*, 143 S.E.2d 319 (N.C. 1965).

moratorium was declared on development until the bridges and ferries could be put into service.

The deal started coming apart within a year. The state announced it did not have the money to buy the parkland and also dragged its heels on providing bridge and ferry service. The county quietly shelved the Currituck Plan and went back to a business-as-usual approach to development on the banks.

So thousands of lots were plotted on the banks, and it looked like the beginning of the end for the wildness of Currituck Banks. But although a few thousand lots were sold, actual development languished. The squeeze was being put on at each end of the banks. On the north, the Back Bay refuge cut off access down the beach. The refuge officials felt this had to be done to protect the refuge from what would surely become a steady stream of traffic to and from Virginia Beach. The Fish and Wildlife Service issued regulations requiring special permits to travel to Currituck Banks. These permits were granted sparingly even to property owners (less than fifty are now in effect). A howl of rage went up and litigation ensued, but the restrictive regulations held up in court.

Coming up the banks from the south was no easier. Just north of Duck, at the county line, a big steel gate and an armed guard blocked the road. Casual visitors were told that the road was private and closed to public access. Only permanent residents of the banks and visitors with special permission were allowed to pass. This arrangement was set up and maintained by a private developer and the Pine Island Hunting Club to keep out the tourist hordes. The town of Corolla was cut off, as well as other areas of the banks up to the Virginia line.

In late 1977, the Currituck county commissioners decided to do something about this situation. They proposed that a north-south beach road be built as soon as possible. The financial stakes by this time were tremendous. One of the commissioners, the most vocal in pushing for the road, predicted that the value of the lots on Currituck Banks would triple if a public road were built. He freely admitted that he had a personal stake in one of the land development companies.

It happened that one of the county commissioners was an old

college friend of Governor James Hunt. In February, 1978, the commissioners met with the governor. After this meeting, the word was passed that the governor had agreed to have the state build the road. In March, the commissioners sought help in Washington as well. Two members met with Congressman Walter Jones and the two North Carolina senators at that time, Jesse Helms and Robert Morgan. After lining up their political support, the county commissioners held several meetings with officials of the North Carolina Department of Transportation to make sure the road would get a priority approval. All this was done very quietly; it looked as if the road would be approved before any effective opposition could be mounted.

Potential opponents of the road included more than just environmentalists. The Fish and Wildlife Service of the Department of the Interior was watching the situation closely. As early as 1964, Interior officials had considered the idea of buying and preserving Currituck Banks. Secretary Stewart Udall flew over the area and floated a trial balloon of a Currituck Banks National Seashore. Nothing happened. Then, after the wreckage of the Currituck Plan became apparent, the Fish and Wildlife Service studied the area. In a confidential memorandum, written in 1977, acquisition was recommended. The Nature Conservancy, having purchased the Swan and Monkey island tracts, was prepared to use them to block development and to transfer them to Interior as the nucleus of a wildlife refuge at the appropriate time.

Another opponent was Earl Slick, the owner of the Pine Island property protected by the guardhouse. He was concerned about what a public road would do to the privacy of his property and horrified that it might become a throughway to serve developments to the north. In order to protect the attractiveness of the area to waterfowl and wildlife, he donated a tract along the oceanfront to the National Audubon Society, which adamantly opposed development and the road. Taking into account the reality of the developments to the north, Slick granted an easement to the Coastland Corporation, which was developing the tract just north of Pine Island, but he required it to maintain the guardhouse to prevent general access to the area. Coastland also opposed the state road, partly because it already had access by private road.

Coastland had other reasons for opposing the other developers on the road issue. Its property was laid out at the time when cluster development and water and sewer systems were required by the county under the old Currituck Plan. But now those requirements had been rescinded by the county. The other developers, Kabler and Riggs and Whalehead Properties, were going ahead without putting in those costly facilities. Coastland was afraid of losing its competitive advantage. It had given an easement to Whalehead across its property in return for Whalehead's promise to abide by the Currituck Plan. When Whalehead reneged, Coastland cut off the easement. Coastland and Whalehead were fighting it out in the courts. Whalehead was owned by Kabler and Riggs, the biggest developer to the north. One of the county commissioners was a minority owner of Whalehead. In short, the tangle of interests and counter-interests was bizarre. It was harder than reading a Russian novel to determine who was doing what to whom and why.

I became involved in this situation in the summer of 1978 through my research for this book. It was hard to determine the facts, since all the parties were playing it very close to the vest. I finally put the pieces of the puzzle together. I talked the situation over with some people in Currituck County, but they were not aware of the situation and took the attitude that politics of this sort is a game played by the "big boys" and that there was little that could be done.

I decided to try to get some help from John Curry, an attorney, an old friend, and at that time the representative for the Natural Resources Defense Council in North Carolina. He was also on the board of the local Audubon Society. I explained the situation and told him that I thought this was the most important issue we faced on the coast. It was not just a question of a road. I felt that the whole future of the Currituck Banks hung in the balance. We agreed that the road should not be built without a full review of what was going to happen to the region.

John got in touch with all the conservation groups and alerted them to the situation. He also contacted officials of the Coastland

Corporation at their Virginia Beach headquarters. Our strategy gave first priority to short-circuiting the quick approval of the road. The conservation groups alone were not enough to prevail. John thus very effectively began to put together a coalition of the environmental groups and the Coastland Corporation. The old saw "politics makes strange bedfellows" never rang more true. The militant Natural Resources Defense Council was acting hand-in-glove with one of the large Outer Banks developers.

On October 4, 1978, Curry, together with Jim Johnson and Jack Sherrill of Coastland and Ben Taylor of Envirotek, Inc., the architectural firm that had drafted the old Currituck Plan, met with Tom Bradshaw, the secretary of the North Carolina Department of Transportation. Bradshaw told them that the road was a "legitimate request" and that his department could acquire the necessary right of way to construct it. The money for construction could come from the county's share of the secondary road maintenance funds. He said that he would go ahead with the project if the county commissioners continued to support it and if the reaction of the public was favorable. Johnson, Sherrill, and Taylor explained that the road would have disastrous consequences for the Outer Banks, and that its true purpose was to facilitate the developments to the north. They called for a revival of the old Currituck Plan. Curry had reservations about the Currituck Plan, but he agreed that it was better than the north-south road. Bradshaw was not moved by the arguments, and the meeting broke up. Curry and the others felt that the meeting had been useful; at least Bradshaw would know that there were going to be some important voices raised against the road.

Later that day, the group also met with Anne Taylor in the North Carolina Office of Policy Development. Anne had been an extremely effective lobbyist for the Sierra Club before joining state government. She listened sympathetically and agreed to try to get the state to look into developing a policy for the future of Currituck Banks.

Meanwhile I resolved to bring the problem to the attention of some other groups in state government. As a member of the North Carolina Marine Science Council, a body appointed by the governor to study and advise him on coastal and marine policy, I brought up the subject of Currituck Banks at the council's November, 1978, meeting. My ten-minute speech, explaining the issue and recommending that the council get involved in the brewing controversy, was met by studied silence from the group. There was little sentiment for taking on the governor, the Department of Transportation, and the Currituck county commissioners. The best I could do was to get a resolution that Currituck be put on the agenda for the next meeting.

In December, the Department of Transportation held a public hearing on the road in Currituck County. All the players in the game were there, and they reiterated their positions. The Fish and Wildlife Service said they were studying acquisition of a part of the banks. Curry made a particularly effective presentation, calling on the Department of Transportation to do an environmental impact statement, which would study all the consequences of building the road and the alternatives for the future of the area.

I felt we were making progress. We had perceptibly slowed down the blitz aimed at quick approval, and we were raising the important questions involved. I knew that if the road were left to the Department of Transportation (DOT), we wouldn't have a chance. If that happened, the best we could hope for would be for the situation to degenerate into an adversary process, with ensuing litigation. That would be a last resort, but now there was still hope to work things out in a reasonable fashion.

My main strategy at this point was to get groups in state government involved that would force DOT to face the larger issues. On January 11, 1979, the Marine Science Council met at Pine Knoll Shores, and the Currituck question was on the agenda. Fortunately, on that day we were having a joint meeting with the Coastal Resources Commission and the Coastal Resources Advisory Council. So the principal state bodies concerned with the coast would be together under one roof. In my speech I argued that the Currituck issue was too important to be left to DOT, and I asked that a committee of these groups be formed to consider the matter together with DOT. When I finished speaking, Anne Taylor got up and agreed that it was time to make a comprehensive review of state policy for the area. John Curry then reiterated the importance of an environmental study. We won our point, and the three bodies resolved to form a joint committee on Currituck Banks. I left the meeting elated; we now had a vehicle and an official mandate to look into the issue. I was one of nine people appointed to the joint committee.

Now the problem for the joint committee was to get involved in the actual decision-making process at DOT. On February 9, 1979, the committee held a hearing in the county to start the fact-finding process and to establish its own credentials. Then in a meeting with key DOT officials on April 12, the committee obtained DOT's promise of full cooperation in addressing the access issue.

At this point, high officials in the North Carolina Department of Natural Resources and Community Development were becoming interested in what all the excitement was about. Secretary Howard Lee and his deputy, Walton Jones, felt that events were overtaking their department. If the fate of Currituck Banks was to be determined, they wanted some control. Jones decided to appoint yet another official committee, which was named the North Carolina–Virginia Currituck Committee. I regarded this as a positive development despite the obvious duplication of effort involved. It gave hope that the larger issues would be addressed. Governor Hunt himself moved in this direction when, on May 8, he sent a letter to the U.S. Fish and Wildlife Service warning them that they should not consider federal acquisition without "assuring a full perspective of the interrelationships of many issues . . . in order to avoid isolated decisionmaking."

Now that the decision-making process had been effectively opened up, it was time to see if people could be induced to cooperate in putting together a deal that would hold up for Currituck Banks. That would take some doing, because so many different groups were involved, and each tended to suspect the others' motives.

The person who saw this most clearly was Dave Owens, an attorney and staff member for the Coastal Resources Commission. He decided to use the land-use planning process of the Coastal Area Management Act to start things off. He approached the county commissioners about the idea of updating their land-use plan by doing a thorough fiscal analysis of development on the Currituck Banks. Baxter Williams, the chairman, was receptive to the idea since one of the main reasons for developing the banks in his mind was to improve the tax base of the county. The commissioners passed a resolution authorizing the fiscal analysis on June 13.

Owens quickly arranged for a $6,000 grant for this purpose and hired as consultants the firm of Roberts and Eichler of Atlanta to do the work. Throughout the summer he worked closely with the consultants on the preparation of the report. He also made a point of going to the meetings of all the other groups involved and keeping everyone informed of the developing situation. In August the Coastal Resources Commission endorsed the Currituck Plan update and recommended that the issues of water quality, water supply, density of development, beach access, and emergency evacuation from the beach be considered.

Meanwhile, DOT was moving toward completion of its feasibility study of the north-south road. This was a critical decision point, since if the Board of Transportation approved the road, the opportunity for achieving a consensus on how to proceed would be lost. Through informal channels, it was learned that DOT planned to come out in favor of the road without waiting for the other groups to act. Fortunately this did not happen. The two Currituck Committees and the Coastal Resources Commission all endorsed the preparation of an environmental impact statement before a final decision was made on the road. DOT received pressure from outside the state government as well. John Curry had organized a group called Friends of Currituck, which was headed by John Caldwell, the former chancellor of North Carolina State University, and Jerry Wright, a Currituck native. This group lobbied for the environmental impact statement, as did most of the members of the academic community involved with marine resources. Secretary Lee also played a key role by personally calling Secretary Bradshaw of DOT to argue in favor of the impact statement. Faced with this united front, the Department of Transportation voted on September 14 to do an impact statement and delayed their decision on the road.

Two weeks later, the results of the fiscal impact study were presented. These showed that while tax revenues from a developed Currituck Banks would exceed costs, the net gain would be very small and there would be a financial drain on the county during some periods. It also concluded that the purchase of the area north of Corolla by the U.S. Fish and Wildlife Service would be the best alternative financially for the county and would alleviate environmental problems associated with water quality and erosion control. On October 1, the county commissioners endorsed the report by a 3-to-1 vote; Ernie Bowden was the lone dissenter.

These key developments finally made it possible for county and state officials to work together with federal officials at Interior to provide a comprehensive solution for Currituck Banks. And Owens became the key figure, holding the trust of all three and acting as an intermediary between them. In December, the U.S. Fish and Wildlife Service released its draft environmental statement recommending the purchase of all the lands north of Corolla and the marshlands to the south to create a wildlife refuge. Instead of taking a hard-line position with the state, as before, it worked with Owens to allow permanent residents of the banks access through the Back Bay refuge for an additional year. (Access had been scheduled to end completely on December 31, 1979.) This, in turn, helped persuade state and county officials to work with Interior. The state began a serious review of Interior's proposal for a refuge on Currituck Banks. Owens continued to play the most important role, participating in hearings on the impact statement and negotiating with Interior to get assurances that state and county interests would be addressed.

All this hard work paid off. On March 5, 1980, Assistant Secretary Herbst of the Department of the Interior gave the state the assurances it had been seeking. Interior promised that full refuge revenue-sharing payments would be paid to the county and that the refuge would provide recreation facilities and not interfere with traditional hunting and fishing activities. A compromise was also reached on the road issue, providing that if the DOT impact statement recommended that a public road be maintained up to Corolla with adequate environmental safeguards, Interior would not oppose it. But no road would be built north of Corolla.

Now all the pieces of a comprehensive plan for the future of Currituck Banks seemed to be falling into place. On March 17, the county commissioners endorsed this solution in another 3-to-1 vote. On March 19, the two advisory committees approved it. The final step was to get Governor Hunt to agree, and a draft letter for his signature was prepared. Hunt took the material home for the weekend, and on March 31 signed a letter to Interior stating that "we consider establishment of the refuge to be in the best long term public interest and acceptable to North Carolina." On November 12, 1980, after the final environmental impact statement on the establishment of the refuge was published, Governor Hunt reaffirmed his support of federal acquisition, calling Currituck Banks "one of North Carolina's most precious resources."

Regretfully, the purchase of Currituck Banks was vetoed by James Watt, the Secretary of the Interior in the Reagan administration. After so much work to find a solution, there was bitter disappointment at Watt's decision. Thus the conflict with the real estate developers on Currituck Banks is unresolved. In 1983, Congress authorized a half measure: the purchase of the Nature Conservancy land north of Corolla. The Currituck National Wildlife Refuge officially came into being, but at a fraction of the size of what was envisioned a few years before. The state also established the Currituck Banks Estuarine Reserve in the marshlands. The state has completed a road up the banks as far as Corolla, but public access stops there. The area of the banks still in private ownership—from Corolla near the Virginia line south to Currituck refuge—is cut off, including about fifty families who try to live year-round on Currituck Banks.

Nevertheless, the Currituck Banks wildlife refuge proposal— if it can be fully implemented—seems the best solution to the Currituck controversy and will allow this area to retain its cultural and historical traditions. It would be disastrous to allow Currituck to become an intensely developed, highly populated area. Not only would the esthetic and tranquil setting be lost, but the productive and fragile sound—long a paradise for hunters and fishermen—would be irretrievably damaged. Development would result in pollution and in depletion of the limited fresh water on the banks. It would also be economically unsound since studies have shown that the government services that would have to be provided would at times exceed the tax revenues produced. Development would also increase the danger of a hurricane disaster and would produce pressures for the expenditure of many additional millions in public money for hurricane and erosion protection measures.

Creating a national wildlife refuge on Currituck Banks would preserve the sound as well as the barrier island habitat and something of the cultural and historic life-styles of earlier residents on the banks. The public could be allowed to visit the banks by ferry and on foot for recreational purposes. Historic sites such as the old hunt club lodges and Coast Guard stations would be preserved. The extraordinary hunting and fishing resources of the area that have always sustained visitors and the local population would remain intact. The county would gain economically, from increased tourist business, and could develop more slowly in a smaller area. Currituck would remain a unique and magical place.

6

South Albemarle

THE SOUTHERN SHORE OF ALBEMARLE SOUND IS MARKED by rivers and creeks that lazily drain the swampy flatlands of the interior. At the western end, the Cashie and Roanoke rivers enter the sound, forming Batchelor Bay. To the east is Bull Bay, the drowned mouth of the Scuppernong River. Still farther east, the estuary of the Alligator River, more than two miles wide at the point it enters the sound, cuts a deep gash into the low-lying land.

Early settlers from the Albemarle to the north explored this area, hunted, trapped, and traded with the Indians in the late seventeenth century. Soon trading posts and farms were established. In 1702 Thomas Blount built a sawmill on Kendricks Creek on the site of the present town of Roper. After Blount's death, Thomas Lee married his widow and continued the business. The settlement came to be known as Lees Mills. After Edenton was founded, Thomas Bell operated a ferry across the sound to serve the growing population, and a post road was constructed from the mouth of Kendricks Creek south to Pamlico Sound. The ferry was later known as Mackeys Ferry, after its subsequent owner, William Mackey, and it gave the name Mackeys to the present town at its former southern terminus.

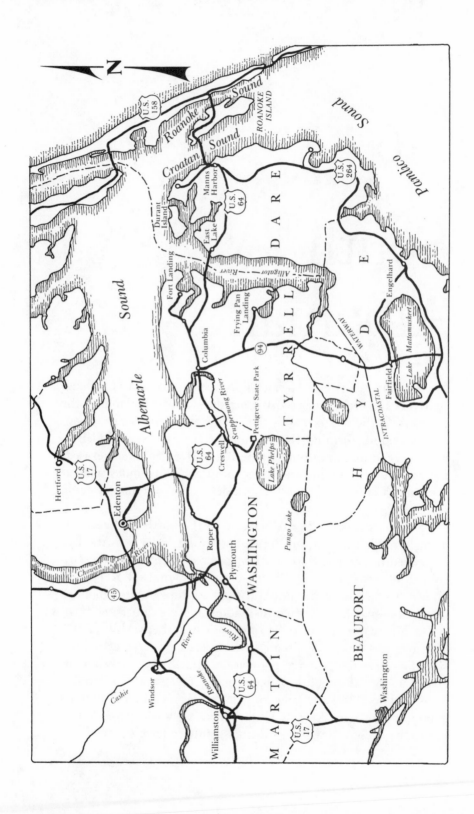

Additional settlements were established on the sites of present-day towns. Columbia, on the east bank of the Scuppernong River, was a trading post known as Shallop's Landing in the eighteenth century. The site of the town of Plymouth on the Roanoke (in colonial times the Moratucke) River, was settled in 1723 by William Rhodes, who built a "Brick House" that is a landmark on early maps. In 1729 Tyrrell County was established, and a courthouse was built in 1748 on Kendricks Creek near the present town of Roper.

The first towns in the area were founded in the last years of the eighteenth century. Plymouth began in 1787 when Arthur Rhodes sectioned off a hundred acres of land from his plantation on the Roanoke River and subdivided it into 172 lots. After ten years, all the lots had been sold, and the town was named after Plymouth, Massachusetts. The eighteenth-century plan of the town has survived intact. Plymouth soon became a center of trade and travel for the Roanoke River valley and in the nineteenth century was one of the principal ports of North Carolina. A lumber mill and shipyard were established on the waterfront. In 1799 Washington County was created, and Plymouth was designated the county seat in 1823.

The settlement at Lees Mills (Roper) on Kendricks Creek served as the first county seat of Washington County from 1799 to 1823. Although surpassed by the growing importance of Plymouth, the town was an agricultural and lumbering center throughout the nineteenth century. In 1889 the sawmill was taken over by J. L. Roper, who gave his name to the modern town. The cypress forests of the region were exploited unmercifully. By 1921, when milling operations ended because readily accessible trees were no longer available, more than 990,000 acres of virgin timber had been logged off.

These early towns served the large plantations that were established in Washington County beginning in the eighteenth century. These large farms began the process of cutting the magnificent forests and draining the huge swamps for agriculture, using the technology of the day—slave labor. The first plantations were on the higher lands near Plymouth and Lees Mills. The best known of the early planters was Joseph Buncombe, who had come from St. Kitts in the West Indies. He purchased 1,025 acres of land and built a house on Kendricks Creek south of Lees Mills. His son Edward Buncombe constructed an elaborate fifty-five-room house known as Buncombe Hall, which became a center of social and economic life for the area. During the Revolution, the younger Buncombe trained and equipped a regiment of troops at the plantation and took them to fight in Washington's army. He died of wounds received at Germantown, Pennsylvania, in 1777. Nothing now remains of the former Buncombe estate.

Later, more plantations were established in the low swamplands to the east. Some of the most famous of these were located on the shore of Lake Phelps, a 16,600-acre natural, freshwater lake. This shallow, round body of water went undiscovered for more than fifty years after the first settlements of the area, although it is only twelve miles from Albemarle Sound. The reason for this was that most of the interior of the South Albemarle peninsula was a dense, forbidding swamp forest, known as the East Dismal. In 1755, the story goes, a group of hunters were making their way through the soft, mucky swamplands. One of them, Benjamin Tarkington, climbed a tree and sighted the lake. Josiah Phelps, a companion, ran to the lake and was the first to reach it, thus gaining a share of immortality when the lake eventually acquired his name. This was not immediate, however, for in the eighteenth century the lake was known as Scuppernong, from an Algonkian word meaning "at the place of the sweet bay tree." It acquired the name Lake Phelps in the nineteenth century.

In the 1780s a group of Edenton men formed a company to drain Lake Phelps and to farm its fertile soil. This plan was abandoned, but a second company was formed in 1784 by Samuel Dickinson, Nathaniel Allen, and Josiah Collins of Edenton to drain and farm the surrounding swamplands. In 1787 slaves were put to work digging a six-mile-long drainage canal, which still exists, between Lake Phelps and the Scuppernong River. The project was a success, and the plantation was soon producing rice and wood products.

By 1816 Josiah Collins had become the sole owner of the plantation, and upon his death in 1819 it passed to his descendants. One of these, Josiah Collins III, took over the property with his wife Mary after his graduation from Harvard. In 1830 he built a fine home of heart cypress on the banks of Lake Phelps and called it Somerset Place. He accumulated fine furniture, a library, and art treasures in the spacious three-story home, and his lands were maintained by more than three hundred slaves. He extended the lands under cultivation by the construction of additional drainage canals and established another plantation known as Western Farm near the present community of Cherry. Somerset Place was famous as the center of an elegant social life for the wealthy planters' families. By contrast, the slaves who sustained these people lived in crowded slave cabins nearby.

Other large plantations in the vicinity were owned by the Pettigrew family. Charles Pettigrew, who was the rector of St. Paul's Church in Edenton, built a mansion called Belgrade, completed in 1814, near the present town of Creswell on the Pettigrew Canal. Another Pettigrew plantation, Bonarva, was built on the shores of Lake Phelps near Somerset. This was the birthplace of the Confederate general James Johnston Pettigrew, who led a charge at the Battle of Gettysburg and was killed during the retreat of Lee's army following the battle.

The Civil War caused the breakup of the plantation society of the South Albemarle. James Johnston Pettigrew and Collins financed a company of men for the Confederate cause, and as we have seen, Pettigrew went to war himself. The Union army came up Albemarle Sound and occupied Plymouth in 1862, and the Federals were able to control traffic on the Roanoke River, cutting the South Albemarle region off from the rest of the South. Collins fled inland to Hillsborough, where he died in 1863.

The Confederates staged a hit-and-run raid on Plymouth on December 10–11, 1862. Colonel John C. Lamb led a cavalry charge on Union troops who had formed a line across Main Street. His artillery disabled the Union gunboat *Southfield*, which was forced to fall back. The Federal forces broke and ran, and Lamb's men set fire to the Union headquarters and other buildings before leaving the town.

After this episode, the Federals decided to fortify Plymouth. A 2,800-man garrison under the command of Brigadier General W. H. Wessells constructed forts and breastworks that ringed the town. The anchor of the fortifications was Fort Williams at the south center of the defensive line. Fort Gray was built two miles up the Roanoke River, across from Tabor Island. Several gunboats were attached to this force. Plymouth became one of the major supply depots of Federal troops in North Carolina.

The Confederates decided to mount a major attack to drive the Federal forces out of Plymouth. To be successful, the Union gunboats had to be cleared from the Roanoke River. For this purpose, Gilbert Elliott, a nineteen-year-old inventor from Elizabeth City, designed an ironclad, 152-foot Confederate gunboat christened the *Albemarle*. It was built of yellow pine with a ram of oak and was covered with iron plates.

Assured of the assistance of the *Albemarle*, which was slowly making her way downriver, Brigadier General R. F. Hoke marched on Plymouth on April 17, 1864. He captured a Union outpost, Fort Wessells, and dug in to await the *Albemarle*'s arrival. The ironclad had problems getting under way, but on April 19 she steamed past Fort Gray without difficulty, the bombardment barely denting her strong hull. Two Union gunboats, the *Southfield* and the *Miami*, prepared to engage her. The *Albemarle* rammed the *Southfield*, which sank immediately. When the *Miami* fled downstream out of range, the *Albemarle* had command of the river. The next morning Hoke's men advanced upon the town from all sides, and the Federals were left holding only Fort Williams, which was soon surrounded by Confederates. General Wessells' position was untenable, and he surrendered his force of about twenty-five hundred men, twenty-eight pieces of artillery, horses, and supplies. The victory was complete, and there was great rejoicing among partisans of the Southern cause. The Confederates now had a base on Albemarle Sound to launch further attacks to drive the Federals out of coastal North Carolina.

The victory was short-lived, however. Lieutenant William B. Cushing devised a plan to destroy the *Albemarle* at her moorings at the Plymouth dock. He outfitted a small launch with a torpedo device and proceeded up Albemarle Sound the night of

Somerset Place plantation house and outbuildings. (*Courtesy of Division of Archives and History, Raleigh, N.C.*)

October 27, 1864. Under a hail of Confederate bullets, Cushing guided the launch into a boom of cypress logs which protected the *Albemarle*. Standing in the prow of the launch, he lowered the torpedo device and exploded it under the *Albemarle*, which sank with a hole as big as a wagon in her bottom. The force of the explosion blew Cushing's launch apart, and he escaped by swimming downriver. With the *Albemarle* gone, the Federals easily retook Plymouth on October 31 and once again dominated Albemarle Sound.

At the end of the Civil War, Plymouth was a battle-torn village of eleven buildings that had somehow survived the destruction. The great plantations of the area were abandoned or sold. Without slave labor, the great mansions could no longer be maintained and fell into ruin. Many of the old drainage canals were neglected, and the swamp forests returned to some degree, although the second-growth trees were primarily pines. The region became an area of small towns and farms. Paper and wood product companies eventually bought large tracts of forest land to operate as tree farms.

Today, Plymouth, a town of about five thousand people, reposes quietly on the shore of the Roanoke River. Except for a few markers erected by the state, there are not many reminders of its long and interesting history. Instead, the town is dominated by the huge smokestack of the Weyerhaeuser paper mill, belching sulfur-laden smoke into the air. "We get very few complaints about our smoke," said a Weyerhaeuser official. "The prevailing winds around here are from the south, so it almost always gets blown out into the sound." "Nonsense," one town resident replied when he heard this. "The reason no one complains is that over half the county depends on the plant to make a living. Without the paper mill, this county would dry up and blow away. The state doesn't dare make them clean up their emissions. And if you think the air pollution is bad, you should go take a look at the water downstream from the plant. It is black with pollution, and all that stuff goes into Albemarle Sound."

One senses in Plymouth a certain feeling of inferiority when it compares itself with Edenton, the stately, beautiful old village across Albemarle Sound. "Plymouth thinks of itself as just a stinky old mill town," one resident told me. "People always say we can't compare with Edenton. But they forget that during the Civil War, Edenton wasn't worth fighting over; Plymouth was!"

In spite of this, the distinctive character of Plymouth will be revealed to the person who looks closely enough. The old city retains the street plan laid out by Arthur Rhodes in 1787. Several antebellum structures have survived the changing times. The Latham House at 233 Main Street is one of the most interesting of these. Built in 1850 by Charles Latham, a lawyer and political figure, it is a two-story, frame, Greek Revival structure with a central-hall floor plan. During the Battle of Plymouth in 1864, many citizens took refuge in its basement. Musket-ball holes from the battle can still be seen. Today, this elegant house is empty and badly in need of repair. It has fortunately been acquired by a foundation, but funds are needed to restore its former beauty.

Most of the black population remaining in the area live in Plymouth. Years ago many blacks left to work in northern cities. Now some of them are coming back. I talked to one old black man who had left Plymouth in the 1930s to get a job with the railroad in Baltimore. He told me he couldn't get a job in Plymouth and hated the bigotry of the town. In 1976 he returned to live in Plymouth with his wife. I asked him what he thinks of Plymouth now. "People have changed," he said to me with tears in his eyes.

East of Plymouth, astride Highway 64, is the old town of Roper, formerly Lees Mills, now a sleepy farm village. Its past is reflected in the commercial district, a unified set of brick and frame buildings dating from the late nineteenth and early twentieth centuries. The former plantation lands to the north of Roper are now farm and commercial forest lands, and the southern shore of Albemarle Sound is dotted with recreational homes and developments. Some reminders of the antebellum past are Blount House on Albemarle Sound near the mouth of the Roanoke; Westover Plantation, a Greek Revival frame house on State Road 1300; and Rehobeth Church, constructed by slaves in 1853 on the south side of Highway 64 near the community of Skinnersville.

The Blount House on Albemarle Sound. (*Courtesy of Division of Archives and History, Raleigh, N.C.*)

South of Roper, the vast area of the East Dismal Swamp was transformed in the 1970s into agricultural lands on a scale undreamed of even by the nineteenth-century planters. Corn and soybeans are being raised on the once impenetrable swamp forest lands by huge corporate farms owned by trucking companies and French and Japanese investors, among others. Modern land-clearing technology has been used by these farms to prepare the land. First, drainage canals are cut to collect the excess water, which is then pumped or allowed to flow into the rivers and creeks and eventually into Albemarle Sound. Then the area is clear-cut, and the trees and vegetation are bulldozed into piles and burned. The earth is then worked by huge rollers and tractors that break up roots and till the soil. Thousands of acres have been transformed in this manner. The harvest crop acreage of Washington County has doubled in the last ten years. The result is a landscape that resembles the plains of Kansas and Nebraska. Near the center of the former swamp, the huge grain storage elevator of First Colony Farms now dominates the area. In addition to cropland, large numbers of hogs and cattle are being raised.

These corporate farms were allowed to transform the landscape of a significant area of coastal North Carolina with almost no consideration of what the effect would be on the people and the resources of the region. The legal tools that could have been used to control the situation were not applied. In 1974 and 1975, when the decisions were made *not* to require the farms to obtain permits for their ditching and draining activities, federal and state water pollution laws were ambiguous as to whether such activities were covered. The state Environmental Management Commission and the U.S. Army Corps of Engineers took a conservative position—to let the farms alone. Subsequent court decisions have since proved them wrong in this judgment; by their decision to play it safe they lost an opportunity to prevent some of the problems caused by the farms' operations.

By 1976 some of the impacts of corporate farm development were becoming clear. Not only was there a direct loss of thousands of acres of wetland, forest land, and prime wildlife habitat, but there were adverse impacts on the waters of the coastal sounds. The artificial drainage canals that were being built were designed to drain water very quickly from the new farmland. As a result, the increased volume of freshwater runoff lowered the salinity of Albemarle Sound below levels necessary to sustain shrimp, crabs, and other shellfish, as well as finfish. The water flow also brought increased quantities of pesticides, sediment, bacteria, and nutrients into the sound.

When I looked at the state's file on First Colony Farms recently, I saw that as far back as 1973, there had been warnings about pollution of the sound by field personnel of the Environmental Management Commission. I found a monitoring report flatly stating that violations of water quality parameters had been found and recommending enforcement action. The report concluded that the state might have to choose between farming and the fishing industry in this area. It appeared the two were incompatible. But I found no record of any action taken as a result of this report; rumor has it that it was simply ignored.

The file also contained a letter, dated May 7, 1975, from the assistant secretary of the North Carolina Department of Natural and Economic Resources, Arthur Cooper, to Colonel Homer Johnstone of the Army Corps of Engineers. The letter lists six

First Colony Farms after reclamation of the swamp forest. (*Courtesy of Winston-Salem Journal-Sentinel*)

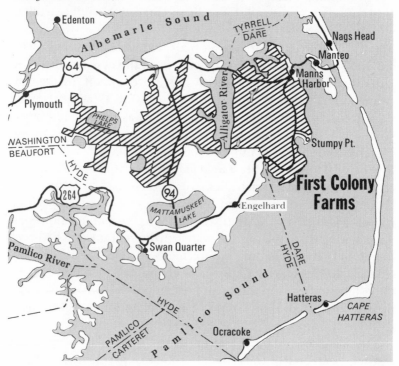

First Colony Farms now dominates a large area of coastal North Carolina. (*Courtesy of Winston-Salem Journal-Sentinel*)

pages of questions that Johnstone was asked to address in preparing an environmental impact statement for First Colony Farms. The questions go into the economic, social, and environmental impact of the corporate farm operations. Had this request been carried out, the federal government would have been in a position to stop some of the adverse effects of the farms. But the Corps of Engineers took no action. It was not until 1979, after the problems with the large land-clearing operations had become apparent, that the state decided to begin a study of the impact of corporate farming in eastern North Carolina. This effort is laudable, but it came several years too late.

Now only remnants of the old East Dismal Swamp—Lake Phelps and Pungo Lake, a national wildlife refuge—survive in the midst of the new farmlands. These are two of the curious Carolina bay lakes that are common in the tidewater peninsulas of North and South Carolina. They usually occur in the middle of swamp-peat bogs in flatland areas just a few feet above sea level. Shallow and elliptical in shape, they maintain their water level by collecting rain and groundwater. They are surrounded by a rim of higher ground, tapering off into lowlands that are often lower in elevation than the lakes themselves.

No one knows exactly how these lakes were formed. Some of the local people maintain that a huge prehistoric meteor shower impacted the land, slanting in from the northeast. Indian legend has it that they were created by peat fires that burned down to the water level. Modern-day geologists theorize that they are either remnants of ancient lagoons formed as the sea retreated from the land, or sinkholes created by the subsidence of lower, soluble rock strata.

Lake Phelps is in the center of a bowl-like basin surrounded by a ridge twelve to fourteen feet above sea level. It is seven feet deep in the center. No creeks or rivers feed into the lake because it is actually higher than the surrouding land, but drainage canals have been constructed around its perimeter so that its level is now artificially maintained by man. Many ducks and geese winter in the area, including several thousand Canada geese, pintail, and ring-necked ducks. Wood ducks nest on the shore, and ospreys, kingfishers, and herons are permanent residents. The lake itself provides habitat for largemouth bass, catfish, and white perch. Black bears, white-tailed deer, and bobcats are found on the shore, as well as many kinds of smaller fur-bearing animals. People in the area have also reported sighting cougars in the wilds of the south shore. Bald eagles are occasionally seen as well.

The northern shore of Lake Phelps is fringed with a beautiful bald cypress forest, with individual trees up to three hundred years old. The western and southern shore is an open canopy of pond and loblolly pine with an evergreen understory of bay and other shrubs. On one stretch of shore, there are mobile homes and vacation cottages. Sailing, fishing, and recreational boating are increasing on the lake.

Pettigrew State Park is being developed on the north shore of Lake Phelps. Visitors can picnic or camp among the huge cypress trees, and there are boat-launching facilities. Nature trails and a swimming beach are planned. Somerset Place, the old mansion of Josiah Collins, is the major attraction of the park. A splendid line of century-old cypress trees conducts the visitor up the old carriage road to the house on the shore of Lake Phelps. Distinctive for its three sets of double-gallery porches and constructed of heart cypress, it is one of the most magnificent coastal plantation houses still surviving in North Carolina. In front of the house, the old 1787 canal still drains the lake, and beyond is a lawn with centuries-old trees. Brick walls enclose the outbuildings of the old plantation, while nearby a path passes through the remains of the old slave residences, chapel, and hospital. In the same vicinity are the sites of the old Pettigrew plantation and family cemetery.

The nearest town to Pettigrew State Park is the small but fascinating community of Creswell, located just off Highway 64. The commercial district is a unique grouping of late nineteenth- and early twentieth-century frame stores and shops with large gable fronts. Although some of these buildings have unfortunately been abandoned, many are still in use, giving the tiny village an atmosphere of small-scale autonomy. Lucy's Department Store, Bill's Soda Shop, and Davenport's Market are vestiges of a time before Sears, Kroger, and Tastee-Freeze spread throughout the land. Creswell is a vivid, living example of early twentieth-century America.

The residences of Creswell are neat frame dwellings from the same period. Their decorative features are drawn from the Greek-Revival and Victorian periods as interpreted by local carpenters. Belgrade, Charles Pettigrew's Federal-style house, still stands, as does St. David's Chapel, a frame church nearby constructed in 1803 by Pettigrew and remodeled in 1857.

Tyrrell County to the east has the smallest population of any in the state. Most of the county is still swampland, excellent wildlife habitat as well as commercial forest land. Large corporations such as Weyerhaeuser and First Colony Farms own large portions of the area. And most of the 4,000 people of the county live near the mouth of the Scuppernong River, on the shores of Albemarle Sound, or to the south, along the upper Alligator River in the residential area of Gum Neck. Tyrrell County has been declining in population, and there is little industry apart from that associated with agriculture, forestry, fishing, and recreation. Columbia, the county seat, is an interesting, compact little village of nine hundred people on the Scuppernong River. It was laid out in 1791 and in the nineteenth century was an important fishing center. During the Civil War, in March, 1862, it was captured and ransacked by New Hampshire troops. The commercial district today is a series of two-story brick buildings with an early-twentieth-century flavor. The abandoned Columbia Hotel near the waterfront is a reminder of more prosperous times.

Across the two-mile-wide mouth of the Alligator River, the southern shore of Albemarle Sound is still largely undeveloped. Highway 64 winds through pinelands and pocosin, broken only by small cleared fields and the communities of East Lake, famous during Prohibition for "East Lake Rye" and now distinguished by its fine frame church, and Manns Harbor, a fishing village on Croatan Sound. The shore of the sound is an extensive freshwater marsh and cypress swamp. Durant Island, at the mouth of the Alligator River, is a beautiful, isolated natural area thirty-five hundred acres in extent. The small community of Mashoes is the only populated area on the eastern end of the sound. West of Highway 264 lies the peat-rich Dare County pocosin, still a wilderness with a forty-five-thousand-acre bombing range leased to the U.S. Air Force.

The South Albemarle region today is a relatively poor area of declining or stable population. There is little prospect or desire for new industry, so its future prosperity will continue to depend upon agriculture, forestry, fishing, recreation, and tourism.

The corporate farm operations are expected to expand, but at a somewhat slower pace than before. The large corporations have gone into the business of preparing the land for farming and selling out or leasing to individuals and smaller corporate farmers. If economic conditions are favorable, large areas of Tyrrell and Dare counties will also be converted from swamp-forest to agriculture.

First Colony Farms also plans to exploit the huge quantities of peat that underlie the bogs and pocosins of the area. More than 146,000 acres of peat could be mined to supply fuel for a series of peat-fired electric power plants that may be constructed to generate electricity. This would transform the land more dramatically than large-scale farming, since strip mining four to six feet of surface peat from an area only a few feet above sea level would present difficult problems of land maintenance and rehabilitation. This time the state, to its credit, is proceeding under the Coastal Area Management Act to do an environmental assessment of the proposed peat mining before it is allowed to go forward.

Great attention must be given to the management of the further expansion of recreational development, large-scale agriculture, forestry, and mining to ensure the survival of the traditional resource base of the region—the air, waters, and extensive wildlife habitat. Several major problems must be solved. Emissions into the air from pulp and paper mills, grain-drying operations, and possible peat-fired electric power plants must be controlled. The water level of Lake Phelps, a major source of the recharge of groundwater resources of the area, must be maintained, and development must be controlled to prevent pollution and destruction of wildlife habitat. The waters of Albemarle Sound should be protected from fertilizer and pesticide runoff, increased freshwater flows from farm drainage canals, and paper mill and septic tank discharge. Significant preserves of wildlife habitat need to be maintained especially along the rivers and creeks flowing into the estuarine system. In the future, farm-clearing and peat-mining operations should be carried out according to performance standards that guarantee the survival of the ecological baseline of the area. It will take a great deal of effort and planning to accommodate these new activities and the traditional pursuits of the people of this region.

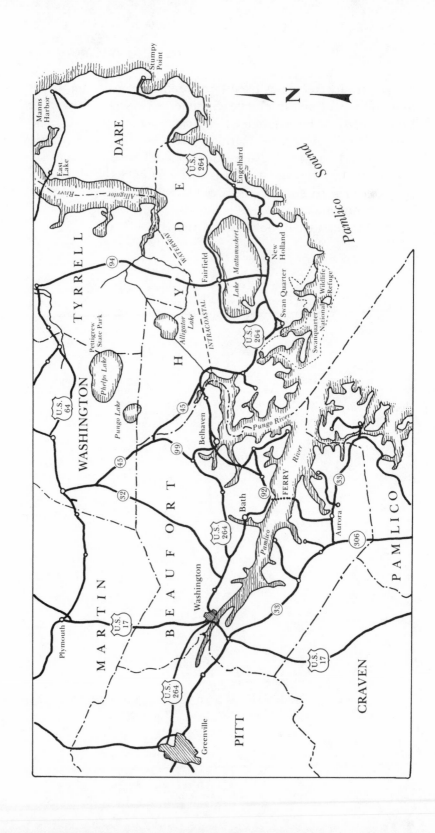

7

Bath Town and the Pamlico Shore

ON JULY 11, 1585, SIR RICHARD GRENVILLE, THE ENGLISH adventurer, left his temporary encampment on present Ocracoke Island, sailed north across Pamlico Sound, and explored the Pamlico shore. His party included Ralph Lane, John White, and Thomas Hariot. The notes of the voyage are regrettably sketchy, but he must have struck the mainland at Wyesocking Bay, where he encountered the Indian town of Pomeioc. The Indians apparently took him to see the great inland lake Paquipe, now Lake Mattamuskeet. Following the shore westward, he discovered another village, Aquascogoc, on the Pungo River estuary, perhaps at the site of the modern Belhaven. Still farther west, he came to the town of Secotan, where the group was "well intertayned" by the Indians. John White probably made his famous painting of this village at that time.

These were the lands of the Algonkian tribe known to the English as the Secotan, after their principal village. At that time they occupied the area north and south of the Pamlico River estuary, one of the principal arms of Pamlico Sound. In later times the tribe was known as the Machapunga, which was probably what they called themselves.

A nasty incident marred this first exploration of the Pamlico estuary. Grenville's group discovered that a silver cup had been stolen by one of the Indians of Aquascogoc. Returning to this village, they demanded it back. When the Indians refused, Grenville's men burned the village and the nearby cornfield, driving the Indians away.

Despite this early reconnaissance of the Pamlico, it was not until about 1690 that the first Europeans, French Huguenots from Virginia, settled the lands along the river. The Indians had been decimated by a smallpox epidemic, and the new settlements grew rapidly. In 1696 Governor Archdale formally proclaimed this region a new county, which he named Bath, in honor of one of the Lords Proprietors.

The growth of the new county was aided by the fact that by the beginning of the eighteenth century the inlets of the Outer Banks north of Cape Hatteras were shoaling up, but Ocracoke Inlet was still passable. A town on the Pamlico shore could become a major port because of proximity to the inlet.

This consideration probably provided the impetus for the founding, in 1705, of Bath Town, which has the distinction of being the first incorporated town in North Carolina, although permanent settlements already existed in the Albemarle region to the north.

The co-founders of Bath Town were John Lawson, Joel Martin, Sr., and Simon Alderson, who bought the town site and laid off and sold lots. Lawson was a recent arrival in the English settlements. He had come from Yorkshire by way of Charles Town in present South Carolina. In 1700 he set out from Charles Town on a fantastic thousand-mile journey by boat and on foot through the Carolina wilderness, ending at the Pamlico settlements. Staying on for several years, Lawson was appointed surveyor-general of the colony, participated in the founding of Bath Town, and wrote a book, *A New Voyage to Carolina*, containing an account of the wilderness trek and a wealth of information about the natural history and the Indians of the region. This was published in London in 1709 and is still a classic of American colonial literature.

The heart of the new town was Front Street and the area along Old Town (Bath) Creek. The plan made provision for a town common, a marketplace, and a glebe, a three hundred-acre farm set aside to attract a minister so that a church would be provided for the colony. By 1708 twelve houses had been built, and the town had a library donated by the Anglican Church, which sent a missionary to preach in the new parish.

This small town was the center of what was called the Pamptecough Precinct, after the Pamptecough (or Pamlico) Indians, and small farms and plantations had been established on both sides of the present Pamlico River estuary. The northern shore of Pamlico Sound, modern Hyde County, had also been settled by 1708 and was known as the Wickham Precinct. Bath Town and the Pamlico settlements were soon enveloped by fighting and discord.

To begin with, the conflict known as Cary's Rebellion caused destruction of homes and crops and brought about civil strife in the region. When Governor Edward Hyde attempted to take office in 1711, he was contested by a Quaker faction led by former Governor Thomas Cary, who owned a plantation near Bath Town. In May, 1711, Hyde brought an armed force to the Pamlico in an unsuccessful attempt to defeat Cary. In June, Cary and his men went north to the Albemarle and attacked Hyde at the home of Colonel Thomas Pollock on the Chowan River. Cary was eventually forced to flee and later captured by marines sent by Governor Alexander Spotswood of Virginia, but the events left the Pamlico region weak and unprotected.

On the heels of Cary's Rebellion came the Tuscarora uprising of the autumn of 1711. The Tuscarora under King Hancock, whose chief town was Catechna on the Neuse River, conspired with the Machapunga and Pamlico Indians to attack the white towns and settlements simultaneously in order to drive the whites out of the region for good. On September 22, 1711, about five hundred Indian warriors attacked and killed the settlers on the Neuse and Pamlico rivers. Bath Town became a refugee center and a garrison for those who were able to flee the slaughter. Another fortification was hastily thrown up at the Lionel Reading plantation on the south side of the Pamlico shore across from Chocowinity Bay.

The Albemarle region to the north was quiet, since Chief Tom Blount, leader of the Tuscaroras in that area, had remained neutral (for which his people later received a large grant of land in eastern Bertie County still known as "Indian Woods"), but Governor Hyde could not send sufficient aid. An appeal was sent to South Carolina for help, and Colonel John Barnwell was dispatched in command of a force of 30 whites and 500 friendly Indians to quell the uprising. Barnwell, who acquired the name "Tuscarora Jack," reached Bath Town on February 10, 1712, and was joyously welcomed by the weary settlers. Gathering additional men, Barnwell proceeded to King Hancock's fort on the Neuse and obtained his surrender on April 17. The North Carolina government was furious that Barnwell had not destroyed the Indians, however, and Barnwell led his men back to South Carolina. On the way, some of his men seized some Indian slaves. This opened the way for new Indian uprisings, which continued throughout the summer of 1712.

In December, Colonel James Moore, with a force of nine hundred friendly Indians, arrived from South Carolina to take another crack at breaking the Indians' power. The Tuscaroras were holed up in Fort Neoheroka, a log and earthen fortification on the Neuse. This time victory was complete, and 950 Indians were killed or captured, the remainder fleeing into the wilderness. A remnant of the Tuscaroras remained in North Carolina until 1765, when they went to New York to join the Five Nation Iroquois confederation.

The Machapungas were still operating in the swampy wilderness of the interior of the peninsula between Albemarle and Pamlico sounds, however, and Moore skirmished with them during the summer of 1713, before he gave up and returned to South Carolina. The war continued sporadically throughout 1714 and until February 11, 1715, when the hostile Machapungas signed a treaty agreeing to accept a reservation at the eastern end of Lake Mattamuskeet between present Engelhard and the south side of Wyesocking Bay. By the nineteenth century these Indians had sold their lands and become assimilated into the general population.

Bath Town grew and prospered despite this time of troubles. A growing number of ships called at the town, and the General Assembly of the colony designated the region Port Bath in 1715. Another factor that made Bath a colonial center was the post road that led north to Edenton and the Albemarle settlements through a vast lowland wilderness (which the colonists called a "desert"). This road was eventually extended to the south as well when ferry service was established across the Pamlico River.

Bath was resurveyed in 1715 to accommodate the increase in population. As the seat of the county court and the commercial center of the Pamlico region, it fostered a lively social life in its inns, taverns, and homes. A number of important people lived in the area. Christopher Gale, chief justice of the colony, had a plantation called Kirby Grange on the Pamlico River and a town house on Bay Street. Governor Charles Eden, who had succeeded Edward Hyde in 1714, owned a home in town.

One of Bath's most famous—or infamous—citizens was the pirate Edward Teach, who was known as "Blackbeard" because of his jet-black beard, which he often braided and festooned with small bits of rope. He came to Bath in 1717 after a career of piracy during which he had used a forty-gun ship called the *Queen Anne's Revenge* and a fleet of several smaller vessels to terrorize shipping in the West Indies for several years. Blackbeard was received in Bath by Governor Eden and exonerated under the recently passed Act of Mercy, which prescribed a pardon for pirates who surrendered to authorities. He married a girl of sixteen and pretended to settle down in a home at Plum Point on Bath Bay.

This home was well situated to keep track of the ships entering and leaving the harbor, and Blackbeard continued to slip out of Ocracoke Inlet and fly the pirate flag over his new ship, the *Adventure*. Governor Eden looked the other way, and Tobias Knight, the secretary of the colony, who lived at Bath, gave Blackbeard protection in exchange for a share of the loot.

During the middle years of the eighteenth century, Bath Town

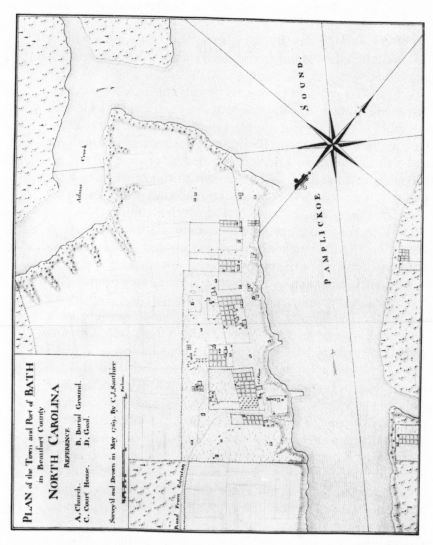

Sauthier's plan of Bath, 1769. (*Courtesy of N.C. Division of Archives and History, Raleigh, N.C.*)

reached the height of its development as a colonial center. Although it never contained more than about thirty houses, it was the second-largest town in the colony, surpassed only by Edenton. Several colonial governors resided in Bath, and the Colonial Assembly met there in 1744 and 1752. Ships from the West Indies and New England called at its port, bringing goods from England and carrying away lumber, naval stores, and foodstuffs. Traders, adventurers, and other travelers journeyed along the post road through Bath and the other Carolina settlements. One of these was the famous religious reformer and preacher George Whitefield, who passed through the town in 1747 and again in 1764 and 1765, "hunting in the woods, these ungospelized wilds, for sinners," he wrote. Apparently Whitefield's sermons did not have a big impact on the rough frontier town; it was known for the gaiety of its tavern life. Legend has it that "Whitefield's curse" is what caused the decline of Bath, condemning it to become a cultural and commercial backwater.

The real reason why Bath slipped quietly into obscurity after the colonial era was that the center of population was shifting toward the west as more settlers came into the region from the northern colonies. The post road also was moved west to avoid the long and inconvenient ferry crossings over the coastal rivers and sounds.

Political power, too, slipped away. In 1738 Hyde County was created out of the eastern part of the Pamlico region, and Bath became the county seat of Beaufort County. In 1746 Bath was considered and rejected as a suitable place to locate the capital of the North Carolina Colony; adding insult to injury, the General Assembly in 1755 voted to remove the county seat of Beaufort from Bath to satisfy landowners to the west. This was prevented only by a compromise measure creating Pitt County, which severed Beaufort County's western territory. This move was ultimately unsuccessful, however, since in 1785 the county government was permanently shifted to the newly incorporated city of Washington, several miles upstream from Bath on the Pamlico River. Washington soon eclipsed Bath as a port since it was farther upriver as well as on the axis of the new north-south road.

St. Thomas Episcopal Church in Bath is the oldest existing church building in North Carolina. (*Courtesy of N.C. Travel and Tourism Division*)

Today Bath is an isolated place that one must make a special effort to see. A modern building, the visitors' center operated by the Historic Bath Commission, is the first stop for most people. Most of the town still has the feel of a nineteenth-century village. The eighteenth-century street plan has survived largely intact, and the visitor can walk over the same streets and fields that the surveyor Claude Joseph Sauthier saw when he drew the earliest surviving map of Bath in 1769.

From the time of the Revolution, the city of Washington overtook Bath as the principal town of Beaufort County. Today it is a pleasant city of about nine thousand that has successfully preserved its waterfront on the Pamlico River. The center of town has also retained its eighteenth-century plan, and several nineteenth-century buildings remain. North Carolinians usually refer to the town as "Little Washington" to differentiate it from the nation's capital, but the local chamber of commerce calls it the "original Washington" because its founding preceded the establishment of Washington, D.C. The Beaufort County courthouse, begun in 1786, still stands at the corner of Second and

Market streets. It is a brick structure topped with a clock tower. During the nineteenth century, Washington was a port and a center for the shipment of naval stores to the West Indies.

As the principal town of the region and one of the largest cities of the North Carolina coastal area, Washington received major attention from both sides during the Civil War. Things started out quietly when a Federal expeditionary force from General Ambrose Burnside's army captured the town without a fight on March 21, 1862. Confederate troops had pulled back to Greenville, leaving the town undefended, and two-thirds of the twenty-five hundred inhabitants had fled, burning stores of corn and cotton on their way out.

The Confederates began to harass and test the Federals in the fall of 1862. On September 6, a raiding party of North Carolinians under Colonel S. D. Pool launched a surprise attack on the town. Colonel Edward Potter, in command of Washington, was on his way to aid Plymouth with men and artillery. Hearing the firing back in Washington, he returned to oust the North Carolina troops after two hours of heavy fighting.

Next, the Confederates tried a siege in order to recapture the town. General D. H. Hill erected batteries on the north bank of the Pamlico River both above and below Washington. On the south bank, at Rodman's Point, artillery was set up also. Beginning March 30, 1863, both sides settled down to a daily artillery duel. Two Federal squadrons sent up the Pamlico River to break the siege were repulsed. The commanding officer at Washington, General John Foster, decided to try to break the blockade by running down the river himself. On April 15, he outfitted the steamer *Escort* with baled hay to protect her and successfully got through a hail of Confederate shells. He loaded up with supplies and returned to Washington, again running the blockade. General Hill, feeling that his plan to take Washington by siege had failed, withdrew in bitter disappointment.

The Confederates finally did retake Washington in the spring of 1864. After the Confederate victory at Plymouth, Union general Edward Harland, then in command at Washington, received orders to evacuate the city. For three days, from April 27 to 30, the departing Federal troops sacked and pillaged the city, setting

The Palmer-Marsh House in Bath was built about 1744; note the chimney windows. (*Courtesy of N.C. Division of Archives and History, Raleigh, N.C.*)

fire to buildings and whatever stores they could not carry with them. By the time Confederate troops entered the deserted town, more than half of it was in ashes.

The victory and all the destruction went for nought. After the Confederates were driven out of Plymouth on October 31, Washington once again fell under Federal domination until the end of the war.

The aftermath of the Civil War also changed the Pamlico River hinterland. Prior to that time, the region had a relatively prosperous small-plantation economy. Afterward, small farms were the rule, and the area experienced a steady decline in population. In the present century, wage and salary jobs became available as lumber companies, small manufacturing plants, and recreation-related industries were established.

The southern shore of the Pamlico estuary contained only small, isolated farming villages until one of the world's largest deposits of phosphate was discovered there. In 1964, Texas Gulf Sulfur, a multinational company, began open-pit phosphate mining in the area of Lees Creek north of Aurora. The town of Cho-

cowinity has grown also, as a result of its proximity to the Washington area and the influx of several small industries.

The north Pamlico shore, Beaufort and Hyde counties, is a
region of small towns and crossroad agricultural communities
clustered on or close to the main highway, U.S. 264. The population density diminishes as one proceeds east on this road. A
number of antebellum homes may be seen as lingering reminders
of the plantation economy that once dominated the region. Especially remarkable is Belfont Plantation near State Road 1411
about ten miles east of Washington near Latham. This Georgian,
gable-roofed structure has massive end chimneys that are similar
to those of the Palmer-Marsh House at Bath.

At the eastern end of Beaufort County is the quaint town of
Belhaven. A walk down Main Street is a journey back to the
early years of the century. On Front Street, stately old homes
face the estuary of the Pungo River. The principal industry of
the town is fish and crab-meat processing, and Belhaven is a
boating center on the route of the Intracoastal Waterway between New York and Florida.

On a quiet, tree-lined street in Belhaven stands the River Forest Manor, a turn-of-the-century mansion that is now a gracefully decadent resort hotel. The house, surrounded by beautifully
landscaped grounds and tennis courts close by the Pungo River,
was built in 1899 as the private residence of a railroad magnate,
John Aaron Wilkinson. After Wilkinson's death in 1947, Axson
Smith of Belhaven turned it into a country inn. The visitor today
enters through a porch surmounted by huge, double-story, white
Ionic columns, and emerges into a large lobby with elegant oak
paneling outdone only by the hand-carved Italian ceiling sup-
porting crystal chandeliers. A poster on the wall says: "Coil up
Your Ropes/And Anchor Here/Till Better Weather/Doth Appear." The guest rooms feature antique beds, fireplaces with
carved oak mantels, and huge bathrooms with double tubs. The
evening buffet at the River Forest includes seventy-five separate
dishes. The "small" noon buffet offers fish and meat, ten different vegetable dishes, several varieties of salad, and dessert.

The visitor to Belhaven also should not miss the Belhaven
Memorial Museum. This unforgettable institution takes up the

entire second floor of the City Hall, a red brick building surmounted by a droll, blue-roofed bell tower that tilts forward on its axis like a misplaced Leaning Tower of Pisa. Ascending the rickety wooden stairs, the visitor emerges into a huge room bursting at the seams with an unbelievable collection of all manner of objects, the *chef d'oeuvre* of which is an exhibit of clothed fleas on pins. After examining this unique spectacle, the guest can pass on to the thirty-thousand-piece collection of buttons and several decades of North Carolina automobile license plates. The voyeur is sure to notice the exhibit of women's "divided unmentionables" and the grass skirt from the South Pacific. Animal lovers will be horrified to see a man's tie made out of the skin of a rattlesnake, an armadillo-shell basket, and a collection of birds' wings. Those who fancy medical curiosities will want to see the gallstones of various sizes and the aborted fetuses. The albino snake and the eight-legged pig will delight all who enjoy the unusual and bizarre. More conventional persons may enjoy the collection of old books, turn-of-the-century farm implements, old coins, and shells.

All this was accumulated by the late Mrs. Eva Blount Way, a Belhaven resident who seems to have kept everything she ever owned. On top of that, people for miles around gave her whatever they could no longer use, so that her house became a repository for just about everything. She stored things in all the rooms of her house, and her penchant for collecting was tolerated by her husband and five children, who courageously lived amid the growing mountain of objects. After the First World War, Mrs. Way began guiding visitors through her house and giving their donations to the Red Cross. Her hobby became an all-absorbing passion. Her daughter, Catherine Wilkerson, says, "Mama taught us [children] how to cook and do the chores and turned everything over to us." Mrs. Way's poetry expressed her liberated attitude: "I like to be happy/I like to be gay/But how can I be that/In the kitchen all day?"

By the time she died in 1962 at the age of ninety-three, Mrs. Way was known far and wide for her unusual collections. The Belhaven Memorial Museum was established in 1965 to keep the bulk of what was in her house when she died. The visitor today

The River Forest Manor, Belhaven. (*Courtesy of N.C. Travel and Tourism Division*)

can confirm the truth of her daughter's observation: "She simply couldn't throw anything away."

East of Belhaven, across the wide estuary of the Pungo River, the deeply-indented, low-lying shore looks out on the broad expanse of Pamlico Sound. The road (U.S. 264) skirts richly beautiful and productive estuaries, such as the nine-thousand-acre Rose Bay, near Sladesville. Three fishing villages, each with a population of a few hundred people, are the principal settlements of this region. Their appearance reflects their relative isolation; travel to or from these towns was primarily by water until the 1920s. Swan Quarter, the seat of Hyde County, is a cluster of homes and stores with three turn-of-the-century churches. Engelhard is at the head of a small stream, and Stumpy Point, in Dare County, overlooks the beautiful Stumpy Point Bay. In these small villages, life has for generations centered around the waters of the sound and the religious and social life of the churches. North and west of Stumpy Point there is still a vast wilderness, the realm of the black bear and bobcat. Beautiful, cypress-fringed small lakes and creeks exist east of the Alligator River.

Between Engelhard and Swan Quarter, on the Pamlico shore, are farmlands and rural communities that have been settled since the early years of the eighteenth century. The weathered houses, dark pine forests, and fields of soybeans and corn give the countryside an air of great peace and antiquity. Especially notable are the churches of the region. The Amity Methodist Church (built in 1854) is a jewel-like structure, with the pure classical lines of Greek Revival architecture. Just west of Engelhard, along Route 264, is a treasure trove of nineteenth- and early-twentieth-century frame dwelling houses and churches, reflecting the richness of this small-farm culture. A rare octagonal house dating from 1840 and covered with cypress shingles is in this vicinity; a campaign is under way by Engelhard residents to raise money to restore this unusual building.

Also worth exploring are the rural farming communities between the main road and the sound. The country roads were clearly laid off to go around—not through—the farm fields. The motorist today driving south from Engelhard to Middletown comes to a dead end against a crossing perpendicular road. A sign pointing to the right reads "Middletown 2 miles." Immediately next to it is a sign pointing to the left—in exactly the opposite direction—reading "Middletown 2 miles." Both signs are correct.

Just north of this historic agricultural district is the major physical feature of Hyde County, Lake Mattamuskeet. The largest of the Carolina bay lakes, more than eighteen miles long and six miles wide and fringed with cypress trees and freshwater wetlands, it has been the focal point of the area since Indian times. The name Mattamuskeet is an Algonkian phrase meaning, "It is a moving swamp," which describes it well. The surface of the lake is three feet below sea level, and it is one and one-half to five feet deep. According to Indian legend, the lake was formed by an ancient drought which allowed peat fires to burn unchecked for thirteen moons. Modern science has been unable to fully explain its origin.

The Pumping Plant at Lake Mattamuskeet was constructed to drain the lake and maintain the lake bed as cropland. (*Courtesy of Division of Archives and History, Raleigh, N.C.*)

The shallow waters of Lake Mattamuskeet and the surrounding farms produce an abundance of food for wildfowl, so that the lake has one of the largest concentrations of wintering ducks and geese anywhere in the eastern United States. Well over a hundred thousand birds are on the lake at the height of the winter season. Particularly beautiful are the thousands of whistling swans, about one-fifth of the entire North American population, that come to the lake each fall. It's a never-to-be-forgotten sight to look out upon scores of these birds in pearly white plumage, gliding gracefully and haughtily through its still waters. Unfortunately, an average of seventy-five of these beautiful birds die of lead poisoning each *week*, the legacy of the lead pellets lying on the lake bottom from past hunting activities.* Besides swans, Lake Mattamuskeet is famous for its bald eagles. A few of these rare birds are usually around the lake. At one time, more than one hundred thousand Canada geese arrived on the lake each fall, but this has dropped to about twenty-five thousand as a result either of hunting pressure or the greater availability of food elsewhere.

*The use of lead pellets has now been prohibited by the federal government.

Historically, the people of Hyde County hunted and fished the lake and derived a cash income by guiding hunters and fishermen from outside the area. Today Mattamuskeet is managed by the U.S. Fish and Wildlife Service as a national wildlife refuge. Hunting swans is now against federal law, although fishing and duck hunting are still permitted on a limited basis.

Another important function of the lake since the nineteenth century has been to serve as the receptacle for the drainage of the productive agricultural lands that surround its perimeter. A series of canals, many of which were dug by slaves before the Civil War, are essential in removing water from these low-lying lands to make them arable. Permission to drain into the lake is restricted to those lands that were part of the drainage district prior to 1974, the year the lake was acquired by the Fish and Wildlife Service. The lands in this category are for the most part small farms that have been under cultivation for generations.

For many years men dreamed of bringing the bed of Lake Mattamuskeet itself under cultivation. As early as 1835, the North Carolina General Assembly authorized the draining of the lake, but no money was appropriated for the task. In 1915 a group of investors purchased the lake from the state and laid off the town of New Holland with the idea of applying Dutch reclamation techniques to Lake Mattamuskeet. In the succeeding years a series of canals, which still exist, were constructed from the lake to Pamlico Sound, and a three-story pumping station was constructed. The pumps handled a million gallons of water per minute, and the lake bed was dried and planted with corn and vegetables. A commemorative sign erected to celebrate the success of the project reads:

> This plant is dedicated to the spirit of cooperation
> Which has here transformed a great lake into dry land
> And so created a new and fertile principality
> For the use and possession of man.

For two years the pumping continued and the crops were harvested. It was soon apparent, however, that to combat the constant heavy rains and the high water table the pumps had to be operated almost continuously. In the end the lake won the battle for survival. It was just too expensive to keep up the constant pumping of water through the canal into the sound. After the expenditure of more than a million dollars, August Hecksher of New York, the principal owner of the company, ordered the project suspended. The lake waters returned, and the farm disappeared. The investors sold the lake to the government, which established the wildlife refuge in 1934. Today, the abandoned pump house and the sign are ironic reminders of the attempt to farm the lake. The smokestack of the pump house is now used as an observation tower from which to view wildlife.

A causeway and road have been constructed across the center of Lake Mattamuskeet, and on the northern shore is the agricultural village of Fairfield. This little community reached the height of its prosperity in the nineteenth century, when a canal dug by slaves in 1840 forged a connection with the Alligator River to the north. Small steamers such as the *Lizzie Burrus* plied this waterway to Elizabeth City until the early years of the twentieth century, when the construction of the Intracoastal Waterway bypassed the village and made this route obsolete.

Fairfield today retains an ensemble of interesting buildings that give an idea of its nineteenth-century prosperity. The United Methodist Church, constructed in 1877, is a fine Gothic Revival building with Italianate flourishes and an exquisite three-tiered belfry. The Fairfield commercial district retains two fine nineteenth-century frame structures, and several elegant homes from the same period are in the vicinity. The town appears little changed from the last century.

The northern half of Hyde County above Lake Mattamuskeet was a wilderness until the late 1960s, when the large corporate farms began to buy the land and prepare it for cultivation. The longtime residents of the county welcomed the employment opportunities offered by the new farming operations but mourned the passing of the wilderness of the countryside. Approximately one hundred thousand acres have been cleared and drained in the last ten years. What once was pocosin and swampland is now cornfields and rangeland. "There has been a total change in the ecosystem of plant and animal species," says Steve Frick, the manager of the Lake Mattamuskeet National Wildlife Refuge.

"The black bear is gone; there is no bear season in Hyde County anymore. Deer have begun to graze on crops because their natural food is gone. On one corporate farm they shot two hundred deer out of one soybean field last summer."

Others question the motives of the corporate farms. "They didn't come down here to make money on farming," one resident told me. "They haven't made a penny on that new land. Tax write-offs and land speculation is what they're interested in. That raises the price of land for the local people."

The commercial fishermen of Hyde County have also been affected by the rise of the large corporate farms. Since new drainage into Lake Mattamuskeet is prohibited, the new lands cleared by the farming companies are drained into canals that lead directly into Pamlico Sound. As discussed in Chapter 6, the fishermen feel that their livelihood is being sacrificed in favor of large farming operations because the massive amounts of drainage water have altered the salinity levels and degraded the water quality of the sound.

Another resource-management problem in the region is raised by the proposed expansion of phosphate mining. Underlying the entire eastern half of Beaufort County and extending into Hyde County is one of the largest deposits of phosphate-bearing sediments in the world. The beds of the lower Pamlico and Pungo rivers are also rich in this mineral. World demand for phosphate for use in agricultural fertilizer is expected to increase. Texasgulf, Inc., already has a large open-pit phosphate-mining operation at Lees Creek on the southern shore, and several other companies such as Weyerhaeuser and North Carolina Phosphate Company are poised to increase dramatically the mining of these sediments on both shores as well as in the rivers.

These mining activities have the potential to upset the resource base of the estuary and the adjacent shorelands. Not only will their operations encroach on the small villages, agricultural lands, and forests of the region; they could cause the further degradation of the water quality of the rivers and sound. In addition, mining processes require the extraction of large amounts of water, which could both deplete the resource and allow the intrusion of salt water into the aquifer. Governmental authorities must establish adequate standards for phosphate mining that ensure the survival of the productivity of the estuary and shore-lands and maintain the existing groundwater resources.

Another increasing problem is the impact of waterfront development in the region upon the plant and animal ecosystems of the sound and shore. The natural shoreline contains a variety of plant communities of value to man as well as to wildlife. Fringing much of the Pamlico shore are brackish marshlands containing wild rice, saw grass, seashore mallow, and black needlerush, as well as woody plants such as wax myrtle, red bay, red cedar, and bald cypress. On higher ground there is an association of evergreen shrub thicket with larger trees and shrubs such as the loblolly bay, black and tupelo gums, and bald cypress. The presence of this shore vegetation is a buffer against erosion, a habitat for wildlife, a source of productive nutrients for fish, and a guaranty of the water quality of the rivers and sounds.

Some of the Pamlico shore is protected against development that would destroy these values. Goose Creek State Park east of Washington and Swanquarter National Wildlife Refuge preserve these habitats and offer interesting opportunities for studying them. Excessive shoreland development has been a problem, however, particularly in Beaufort County. Subdivisions have been built near Washington and near Bath that have caused excessive pollution of the river from septic tanks and unnecessarily severe alteration of the natural landscape. In the future we should take better care of this beautiful area.

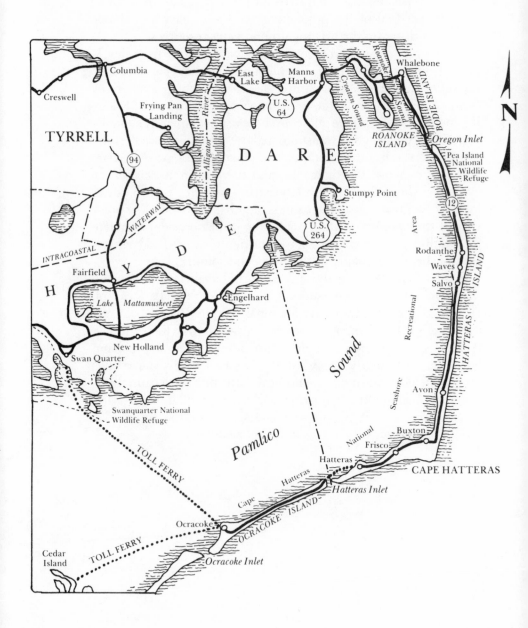

8

Cape Hatteras Seashore and Ocracoke

IN 1953, A SEVENTY-TWO-MILE STRETCH OF THE OUTER Banks, from the southern limit of Nags Head to Ocracoke Inlet, was designated the Cape Hatteras National Seashore. The creation of this seashore park "for the benefit and enjoyment of the people," according to its charter, was not easy. Congress first authorized its establishment in 1937 but refused to spend money for its acquisition. Both land developers and oil companies hoping to strike oil fought the proposal. Finally, in 1952, Paul Mellon and his sister donated $800,000 to buy the area, and when the State of North Carolina matched this gift, the park became a reality.

The major entrance to the seashore is through a place called Whalebone Junction, a picturesque name for the unattractive intersection of the main north-south road down the banks and the highway west to Roanoke Island. Not far from there the Nags Head development abruptly ends, and the road traverses a landscape of low trees and shrubs growing precariously in the sandy soil.

Bodie Island Lighthouse. (*Courtesy of N.C. Travel and Tourism Division*)

This is Bodie (pronounced *body*) Island, still called by this name even though Roanoke Inlet, which separated this section of the Outer Banks from the banks to the north, has long since disappeared. The most prominent feature on Bodie Island is the brick lighthouse with its distinctive horizontal stripes, built in 1872. This is the third lighthouse at the site; earlier buildings were erected in 1848 and 1859. The two-story, brick building nearby that housed the keeper's quarters is now a National Park Service visitors' center and museum. Another structure, the Bodie Island Lifesaving Station, was built about 1890. A day-use swimming beach and recreational center has been developed at Coquina Beach. The remains of the *Laura A. Barnes*, a four-masted schooner wrecked off Bodie Island in 1921, are exhibited; this is one of the hundreds of vessels wrecked on the dangerous shoals of the Outer Banks through the years.

At the south end of Bodie Island is Oregon Inlet, today the principal passage into or out of Pamlico Sound. Fishing vessels from Wanchese on Roanoke Island as well as the mainland communities of Stumpy Point, Manns Harbor, Engelhard, and Swan Quarter utilize this inlet. Although the channel is constantly dredged, it is also constantly shifting with the winds, waves, and tides. Even experienced captains sometimes run aground on the shallows and must be rescued by the Coast Guard.

Oregon Inlet did not exist in colonial times; it was opened during a hurricane in 1846. In 1963 the Herbert C. Bonner Bridge was built across it to Pea Island, and the isolation of the Outer Banks was ended. The existence of bridges from the mainland across Currituck and Croatan sounds and from Roanoke Island to the banks meant that millions of tourists and vacationers can ride down State Highway 12 as far as Hatteras by private car.

Another bow to mass recreation in the national seashore is the concession for the operation of the Oregon Inlet Fishing Center Marina. The main attraction is offshore sport fishing in the Gulf Stream from chartered vessels. Trophy fish such as white marlin, blue marlin, and sailfish—some weighing more than five hundred pounds—are caught by the hundreds every year. Other charters take fishermen out into the inlet or Pamlico Sound for a day of angling for flounder, bluefish, spot, croaker, and trout.

Stretching for thirteen miles south of the Bonner Bridge is the Pea Island National Wildlife Refuge, managed by the U.S. Fish and Wildlife Service as a resting and wintering ground for ducks, geese, swans, and other birds. A significant percentage of the total North American population of snow geese congregate here each winter, as do twenty-five species of duck and numbers of shorebirds, gulls, and terns. For those interested in viewing the wildlife, there are raised observation platforms and a four-mile nature trail around North Pond. The visitor here may catch

The Bonner Bridge over Oregon Inlet. (*Courtesy of N.C. Travel and Tourism Division*)

sight of rare or endangered species such as the peregrine falcon or the brown pelican. In order to provide as much food and habitat as possible for the ducks and geese on the refuge, dikes have been erected on the sound side of the island, making freshwater ponds and marsh in which food plants such as sago pondweed, widgeon grass, bulrush, and spike rush grow. The wax myrtle and other shrubs are regularly burned on the refuge to permit the growth of rye grass, a food for wildfowl.

Across the road from the wildlife refuge headquarters are the ruins of the Pea Island Lifesaving Station, the only one to have had an all-black crew. A portion of the ruins is on the beach in front of the dune, an indication of the erosion that has taken place here. Just to the south, in the ocean surf, a shipwreck is visible—gaunt, black, and battered by the crashing waves.

Immediately south of the Pea Island refuge is the settlement of Rodanthe, an enclave of privately-held lands allowed to remain within the national seashore. On early maps of this area beginning with John White's sketch in 1585, a prominent headland known as Cape Kenrick is shown. Apparently this feature was eroded in the seventeenth century and reduced to shoals charted by James Wimble in 1738 and afterwards known as

Wimble Shoals. By 1730, an inlet was opened just to the north of this former cape and was given the name New Inlet. It divided what became known as Pea Island on the north from Hatteras Island to the south. New Inlet shoaled up with the opening of Oregon Inlet in 1846, although it periodically reopened after this time. The last time New Inlet was open, from 1933 to 1945, wooden bridges were built across it; these may still be seen west of the road at the southern end of the Pea Island refuge.

Rodanthe is the modern name for the ancient Outer Banks settlement of Chicamacomico. In the seventeenth century this was apparently one of the widest areas of the banks, with extensive woods on the sound side. A few families settled in these protecting woods. They lived by grazing cattle, raising vegetables, and taking fish from the abundance of Pamlico Sound. The ocean provided additional sustenance. A beached whale was a bonanza supplying oil and meat. When a passing ship foundered in the shallows or in a storm, the contents of her hold were fair game for the bankers. By 1850, thirty-seven families were living here. In 1874, when postal service was established, the U.S. Post Office Department, in a bureaucratic pique, insisted that the name of the town be changed to something easier to spell and pronounce. The beautiful Indian name Chicamacomico, from which Cape Kenrick is also derived, was discarded in favor of Rodanthe. The adjoining settlements to the south acquired the names Waves and Salvo respectively.

Today the permanent population of these communities is about two hundred, and the focal point of development is now along Highway 12. Tourism is the main industry, and all available private land is being subdivided for vacation homes, campgrounds, and other visitor facilities. The summer population is about five hundred, and this is expected to double in the next ten years.

The most distinctive building in Rodanthe is the old Chicamacomico Lifesaving Station, which was closed in 1954. The main building, with its hip-roof gables covered with shingles, is, together with the lookout tower, stables, and outbuildings, the most complete surviving lifesaving station on the North Carolina coast. Through the efforts of Carolista Baum and the Chicamacomico Historical Society, the station has been acquired and re-opened as a historic site.

This building is a testimonial to the great era of ship disasters and lifesaving efforts on the Outer Banks. With the growth of the coastwise trade and passenger service in the nineteenth century, craft of every kind plied the sea lanes a few miles off the shores of the banks. Storms, northeasters, and hurricanes often came up without warning, catching vessels far from the protection of the few harbors of the North Carolina coast. Errors in navigation also caused ships to run aground on the many offshore shoals. Hundreds of ships were lost, and hardly a mile of the Outer Banks has not been the scene of a terrible disaster.

In 1874 the U.S. Lifesaving Service opened seven stations on the North Carolina coast, including Chicamacomico. Eventually, additional lifesaving stations were added so that at seven-mile intervals down the banks a station and lookout tower with a permanent crew were in operation. A constant watch was maintained by the men who patrolled the beach on foot or kept watch from the lookout towers for vessels that were too close to the shore. Through the use of lanterns and flares, ships were warned away from the dangerous shallows. Even so, disaster often struck and a ship would be driven or would run aground near the shore. It is easy to imagine the terror of such a situation, with passengers or crew clinging desperately to the rigging or helplessly trying to swim for the shore, while the waves crashed and battered the beached vessel as it broke apart. The crew of a lifesaving station would attempt a rescue of the survivors, often at great risk to themselves. If the ship was close enough to shore, a line would be fired over the wreck and a basket called a "breeches buoy" sent out to haul the survivors one-by-one to safety. If the ship was too far out to make this feasible, the lifesaving crew would launch a surfboat and go out to the wreck to pick up the terrified occupants. At the Chicamacomico station, the most famous rescue effort occurred in 1918 when Captain John Allen Midgett, Jr., and his crew saved forty-two British seamen from the burning wreck of the tanker *Mirlo* after it had been torpedoed by a German submarine. Five of the six surfmen

The Pea Island National Wildlife Refuge is a haven for wintering wildfowl.
(*Courtesy of N.C. Travel and Tourism Division*)

Chicamacomico Lifesaving Station. (*Courtesy of Division of Archives and History,
Raleigh, N.C.*)

helping with the rescue were also named Midgett, the main clan of Chicamacomico and a legendary family on the Outer Banks.

During the Civil War, Chicamacomico was the scene of one of the most bizarre battles in military history. A Union force, six hundred troopers from Indiana under Colonel W. L. Brown, established a base at Chicamacomico in 1861 to keep an eye on the Confederate fortifications on Roanoke Island. The Union tug *Fanny* was sent up Pamlico Sound from Hatteras with a load of supplies. While anchored off Chicamacomico, on October 1, 1861, the *Fanny* was attacked and captured by those small Confederate sound steamers we have already discussed known as the "mosquito fleet." The seized provisions were taken to Roanoke Island, where it was reported that a large Federal army was poised to strike the Confederate garrison.

The Confederate commanding officer at Roanoke Island, Colonel A. R. Wright, decided to strike the first blow. His plan was to use the mosquito fleet to mount an amphibious operation against the Federals. A regiment of Georgians would land above Chicamacomico, and North Carolina troops would be landed below the village, closing a trap upon the Federal force.

Colonel Brown watched the Confederate fleet loaded with troops coming down Pamlico Sound the morning of October 5 and guessed what was happening. He gave the order to beat a hasty retreat south to Hatteras. The Indiana regiment, leaving everything behind, began to run down the beach to avoid the trap, with the Georgia troops in hot pursuit. Even though it was October, there was a hot sun, and the march without food or water was painful.

The North Carolinians meanwhile were having trouble making a landing on the banks. Their transport vessels grounded in the shallow waters of Pamlico Sound. At first they started to wade ashore but encountered deep water and returned to their ships. The Union troops slipped the trap, moving down the banks on the ocean side and reaching Hatteras Lighthouse, where they spent the night.

The Georgia troops encamped just north of the lighthouse. The next morning they learned that the North Carolinians had failed to land, so the Georgians retreated north up the banks.

Now it was their turn to run for safety. A New York regiment was on its way up from Hatteras, and the Union steamer *Monticello* shelled the Confederates from Pamlico Sound. Eventually, the Georgians returned to the safety of Roanoke Island, and the Federals abandoned their Chicamacomico base.

In the annals of Civil War history, this battle is referred to as the "Chicamacomico Races." Each side claimed to have defeated a major enemy offensive movement. In reality, no advantage was gained by either side.

Several miles south of Chicamacomico (or Rodanthe) is another enclave within the national seashore, the town of Avon. In colonial times, this area of the Outer Banks was forested, and a shipbuilding industry flourished. The settlement was known by the Indian name of Kinnakeet before the Post Office Department adopted the modern name of Avon in 1883. In 1874 one of the original lifesaving stations was established about two miles north of here—the Little Kinnakeet Lifesaving Station, a structure that still stands. It was moved to its present site, west of the road, because of erosion on the oceanfront. Next to the 1874 building is a larger structure and a lookout tower built in 1904. Decommissioned in 1953, it is now owned by the National Park Service.

Avon was a center for hunting and fishing but is now primarily a summer vacation home development. The population of about eight hundred swells to around fifteen hundred in the summer months. The old town, located on the back side of the island, is dominated by oceanfront development.

South of Avon the island narrows, and we know from ancient maps that an inlet called Chacandepeco existed here until the middle of the seventeenth century. Because it was convenient to transport goods from ocean to sound over the narrow sand barrier, the area was known as "the Haulover" in later times. During the Ash Wednesday Storm in 1962, the sea broke through once again, cutting the road and forming a new inlet. This was filled in and the road rebuilt at a cost of 1.5 million dollars.

At Cape Hatteras itself, the sand ribbon reaches the limit of its thrust into the Atlantic and changes its mind, bending sharply to the west. A large, barren sand flat signals land's end, and the very point, which confronts an almost encircling sea, is constantly being shaped and changed by the winds and waves. The breaking waves beyond signal the shallows known as Diamond Shoals, the feared, submerged tail of the cape, which stretch seaward for several miles.

It is not hard to imagine the significance of Cape Hatteras to early mariners. A short distance shoreward is the beached wreck of the *Altoona*, a sailing ship from Maine lost in a storm while rounding the cape in 1878. She was buried by sand and lost for nearly seventy-five years. The shifting sands exhumed her in 1963, and only the skeletal spars remain.

The most famous shipwreck off Cape Hatteras is the Civil War ironclad, *Monitor*, which lies 16 miles out to sea in 220 feet of water. After her celebrated battle with the Confederate warship, the *Virginia* (formerly the *Merrimac*), which saved the North's blockade of Confederate ports, this "cheese-box-on-a-raft," as the *Monitor* was called, was swamped by gale-driven seas while on her way to Charleston on December 31, 1862. Sixteen members of her crew perished.

The location of the *Monitor* was lost for more than a hundred years. Then, in 1973, the Duke University research vessel *Eastward* discovered the wreck. She lies upside down resting on her turret. A systematic study of the wreck is under way, and artifacts from the ship are slowly being recovered and preserved. The wreck itself is deteriorating rapidly in the turbulent waters where the warm Gulf Stream meets the cold Atlantic currents.

The Cape Hatteras Lighthouse, a massive brick structure built in 1873, towers 208 feet above the low dunes. Painted with black-and-white spiral stripes, it is one of the most famous landmarks of the North Carolina coast. Until the advent of modern communication systems, the beacon of this lighthouse was, together with the Diamond Shoals Lightship anchored several miles off the cape, the major navigational aid for coastwise traffic. Recent erosion has cut into the beach, and, unless it is protected or moved, the celebrated Cape Hatteras light will soon fall into the sea. Nearby are the ruins of the first lighthouse, constructed here in 1803. The two-story, frame structure that

An old photo of the Cape Hatteras Lighthouse in its original glory. (*Courtesy of N. C. Travel and Tourism Division*)

The Diamond Shoals Lightship, anchored several miles off Cape Hatteras, was formerly used to warn vessels of the existence of the treacherous shallows known as Diamond Shoals. (*Courtesy of Division of Archives and History, Raleigh, N.C.*)

Cape Hatteras from the air. (*Courtesy of N.C. Travel and Tourism Division*)

housed the keeper's quarters is now a National Park Service museum.

The presence of motels, stores, and residences in this area signals another enclave of private lands, the town of Buxton, called simply The Cape in the nineteenth century. This is one of the widest and most forested sections of the Outer Banks. In the sixteenth century, this part of Hatteras Island was called "Croatoan" by the Roanoke Island colonists. It was one of the few places on the banks inhabited by Indians, and Indian artifacts have been found near Buxton. According to Ralph Lane's accounts, the Indians here were friendly, and John White in 1590 expected to find the lost colonists on this island. The Croatoan Indians were known as the Hatteras tribe in later times, and the name of the cape is derived from the name of that tribe.

Behind the cape is Buxton Woods, one of the most beautiful maritime forests on the Outer Banks. Growing on a series of high dune ridges, called relict dunes because they are the remnants of the ancient shoreline, is a dense, low overstory of live oak, red cedar, hornbeam, and holly trees, festooned with Virginia creeper vines and Spanish moss. In their shelter grow dogwoods, myrtle, and yaupon holly. Trunkless sabal palmettos burst from the ground in a fan of green. Freshwater ponds and marshes lie back of the dunes. The Seashore preserves about nine square miles of this, and a nature trail conducts visitors over the area.

At the western edge of Buxton Woods is the community of Frisco, known as Trent in the nineteenth century. This was the site of Creeds Hill Lifesaving Station, built in 1918, a weatherboarded structure that is now a private residence.

West of Frisco, the banks narrow, and Sandy Bay cuts deeply into the sound side of the island. This is a very unstable section that is a prime candidate for the formation of a new inlet by some future storm. Below Sandy Bay the banks are once again wide and forested at the site of the village of Hatteras, a small tourist community and former lifesaving station. A ferry departs from here, providing transportation across Hatteras Inlet.

This inlet, opened by a storm in 1846, was one of the state's major shipping channels by the time of the Civil War. By 1861, the Outer Banks was the perimeter of a fortress designed to keep out of the state the Federal warships lurking offshore. Two forts, Hatteras and Clark, were constructed at Hatteras Inlet. Privateers operating out of the inlet waylaid Union merchant ships.

The Federal capture of the Hatteras Inlet forts occurred almost by accident. In August, 1861, General B. F. Butler and Commodore Silas H. Stringfellow took seven warships and some troopships to the inlet to carry out a hit-and-run raid on the Confederate forts. Butler landed 318 men on the beach. The Confederates in Fort Clark ran out of ammunition and retreated to Fort Hatteras. The Union fleet then simply lined up offshore, just beyond the range of the Confederate guns, and shelled the fort. After several hours the Confederates surrendered. To occupy the forts General Butler had to violate his orders, but new orders were soon sent from Washington. The Union had established a small but vital beachhead on the North Carolina coast. This was followed up when, in January, 1862, General Ambrose Burnside crossed the bar at Hatteras Inlet and carried out his successful attack of Roanoke Island, the key to the control of coastal North Carolina.

Across Hatteras Inlet lies the storied island of Ocracoke, now part of the Cape Hatteras National Seashore except for the 775 acres that comprise Ocracoke Village. This island was known to the earliest European visitors, and Sir Richard Grenville weighed anchor here in June, 1585, on his way to Roanoke Island. The earliest name was "Woccocon," an Indian word meaning *fort*, and this was corrupted by various stages to "Ocacock" and "Ocracoke." A more colorful, but spurious, explanation of the name is that one day the pirate Blackbeard, waiting for the dawn, shouted "Oh crow cock!"

The island has changed its shape since colonial times. John White's map of 1585 shows an island about eight miles long, since Old Hatteras Inlet went right through the middle of the present island, and what is now Hatteras Inlet did not exist. Old Hatteras Inlet closed in the 1750s, and Ocracoke was attached to Cape Hatteras until the new Hatteras Inlet opened in 1846. Ocracoke Inlet, on the south end of the island, has existed continuously at least since 1585.

Today Ocracoke is about sixteen miles long and for the most

The "Governor Edward Hyde" Ferry plies Pamlico Sound between Ocracoke and Swan Quarter. (*Courtesy of N.C. Travel and Tourism Division*)

Silver Lake and the village of Ocracoke. (*Courtesy of N.C. Travel and Tourism Division*)

part very narrow, covered with low shrubs of myrtle and yaupon growing under the protection of a frontal barrier dune. A small herd of wild ponies, some of which are said to be descended from stock brought by Grenville in 1585, still live on the island and are carefully maintained now by the National Park Service. The only way to get to Ocracoke is by ferry, from the mainland by way of either Swan Quarter or Cedar Island, or across Hatteras Inlet.

In the early eighteenth century, Ocracoke was used as a rendezvous point for pirates who slipped in and out of the inlet. It was here that the British lieutenant, Robert Maynard, charged by Governor Spotswood of Virginia with apprehending Blackbeard, caught up with the pirate on November 22, 1718. Maynard was getting the worst of the fight; his ship *Ranger* was no match for Blackbeard's cannon power and his ship *Adventure*. Maynard used a ruse to draw Blackbeard on board. He ordered his men below deck and convinced Blackbeard that only Maynard and the helmsman were left alive. When Blackbeard boarded the *Ranger*, Maynard's men poured out of the hold. Blackbeard fought to the death, falling only after his throat was slit and he had twenty-five wounds on his body. The place where this fight is said to have occurred is known today as "Teach's Hole." After the battle, Maynard triumphantly sailed to Bath exhibiting Blackbeard's severed head.

In 1719 Ocracoke was granted by the Lords Proprietors to John Lovick, who came from New Bern to establish a farm. He was the first of a line of settlers who lived by raising stock and growing vegetables on the island.

As a result of the increasing volume of traffic through Ocracoke Inlet, a village was established on the south end of the island, in Ocracoke's only area of maritime forest. Experienced pilots were needed to guide ships through the treacherous channel. The colonial assembly passed an act for the settling of pilots on Ocracoke in 1715. On early maps the settlement created was called "Pilot Town." In 1747 the Spanish, at war with the British, took possession of Ocracoke Inlet to block trade and travel, and plundered the island. During the Revolution, Ocracoke Inlet was largely ignored by the British, who concentrated their blockade on Beaufort Inlet and the Cape Fear River to the south.

Ocracoke became a link in an important supply route for provisions destined for Washington's army.

After the Revolution, trade through Ocracoke Inlet continued to grow, and piers and warehouses were established on Shell Castle Island, in the middle of the inlet, for the unloading and storage of goods. Because of the shallowness of the sound, ocean-going ships were unloaded on arrival and their cargo transferred to shallow-draft vessels for transport to New Bern, Bath, or Washington. This procedure was called "lightering." Shell Castle and the town of Portsmouth, across the inlet from Ocracoke, were the centers of the lightering trade because the channel was on the south side of the inlet. Nevertheless, the lighthouse was constructed on Ocracoke in 1824, after complaints that the one on Shell Castle Island was not sufficiently visible to ships at sea.

There was some attempt to fortify Ocracoke Inlet in the nineteenth century. A fort was constructed on Beacon Island during the War of 1812. This did not prevent a British raid on Ocracoke under Admiral Cockburn on July 11, 1813. During the Civil War, the fort was occupied by the Confederates. After the fall of Hatteras, however, it was abandoned without a fight.

In the post-Civil War period, commercial fishing and the lifesaving stations at each end of the island provided the mainstays of the economy. Traffic through the inlet waned, and the village grew more isolated. Tourism began about 1885, however, when a group of businessmen built the Ocracoke Hotel as a vacation resort for their families. During the summer, there was periodic ferry service to and from New Bern and Washington. The hotel burned in 1900.

Until the World War II period, Ocracoke remained isolated, without roads, electricity, or telephones, although the Coast Guard provided an emergency radiotelephone hookup when necessary. The narrow, sandy streets with weathered houses were shaded by live oak trees. The only regular service to the mainland was by mail boat.

Ocracokers felt the direct impact of the war more than most other Americans. German submarines lay in wait for Allied tankers and merchant vessels, which had to swing wide at Ocracoke to clear the Cape Hatteras shoals. Older residents claim that at least one ship a day was sunk at the height of the German siege, and that far more went on than was ever reported in the press. People started calling the seas off Ocracoke "Torpedo Junction," and the bodies of unfortunate seamen washed ashore on the beach. A small "British Graveyard" can be seen on the island.

The U.S. Navy built a base and training center on Ocracoke, and the first paved roads were constructed on the island. The Ocracokers were prohibited from being on the beach at night. There were rumors of Germans landing on shore. The story was told of the capture of a German submarine whose crew had ticket stubs from a movie theater in Norfolk.

The war and the increased tourism that followed it have modified the culture of Ocracoke. A paved road now runs the length of the island. Ferries run several times a day. A national seashore visitors' center has been built at the ferry slip. The island even has a pub and a liquor store: no longer does the thirsty tourist have to use the mail boat to smuggle ale disguised as cans of evaporated milk for the island's undernourished children—a scheme one longtime visitor relates having used in 1949. Today electricity, a new water system, private phones, modern restaurants, and motels have come to the island.

Yet a good bit of the old Ocracoke remains. In this age of the automobile, there are few places in the country that absolutely cannot be reached except by ferry. The center of the village is still Silver Lake, a snug harbor with fishing trawlers encircled by wheeling gulls. No fast-food or motel chains have supplanted the traditional frame and shingled houses. Many of the streets are sandy lanes, and the soft-white lighthouse is still the dominant landmark. "We don't have any movie theater, golf course, miniature golf course, bowling alley, nightclub, or drive-in," explains one resident. "We don't want to encourage that sort of thing." For this reason you don't come to Ocracoke with someone you don't like.

Man has lived on and with this part of the Outer Banks— Hatteras and Ocracoke—for hundreds of years. During almost all of that time he has been subject to the tremendous forces of winds, waves, and tides that are a part of these exposed and stressed sand reefs. The Indians hunted and fished on the banks

Ocracoke Lighthouse. (*Courtesy of N.C. Travel and Tourism Division*)

but did not live there, except in the most stable areas such as the wooded dune ridges of Hatteras Island. The European settlers and their descendants placed their farms and small villages on the sound side at the widest and most forested areas of the banks.

Beginning in the 1930s, however, an effort was begun to apply technology to make this region "stable and productive." The essence of this idea was to control the erosion of the banks, to "rebuild" the dune, and to build a coastal highway down the banks from Nags Head all the way to Beaufort. The proposal was made on the heels of two 1933 hurricanes, which had opened new inlets and devastated beach houses on the banks. Politicians and state officials knew that only the federal government in Washington had the money to carry out such an ambitious project. They proposed the creation of a national seashore park to "save" the Outer Banks, bring in large numbers of tourists, and contribute to the prosperity of the local economy.

The first step was to persuade the federal Public Works Administration to provide funds to employ workers to build a continuous line of frontal dunes along the ocean. The project was sold on the theory that the work could provide much-needed jobs during the Depression.

There were two assumptions underlying this dune-building and stabilization. One was the belief that high dunes were the natural condition of the banks, and that they had been destroyed by the impact of storms and man. The second was that in earlier times the banks were densely forested and that overgrazing and timber cutting had denuded the former lush forests.

In David Stick's book, *The Outer Banks of North Carolina*, he quotes State of North Carolina officials, dramatically illustrating the attitude of the time:

State Forester J. S. Holmes: "This beach section can be made one of the finest timber producing areas of the country."

State Geologist H. J. Bryson: "There is no question but that reforestation along this beach would stop the erosion to a large degree."

H. D. Panton of the North Carolina State Highway Department (on the Outer Banks Highway): "One of the easiest jobs of this whole program, because it will come after everything else has been planned."

Frank Page, former chairman of the North Carolina Highway Commission: "I consider that this general program of coast development means the preservation of Eastern North Carolina for the future."

The Civilian Conservation Corps went to work, putting up 557 miles of sand fences, planting 3,254 acres of beach grasses, and setting out 2.5 million trees and shrubs. By 1940, the frontal barrier dune system formed a vegetated wall against the ocean fifteen to twenty-five feet high. Erosion at the Cape Hatteras lighthouse had been arrested, and the building was usable again. The initial cost was more than three million dollars.

The coming of World War II caused a temporary hiatus in the stabilization program, but the project was resumed in the 1950s. The national seashore was established, and the all-weather highway was completed to Hatteras and on Ocracoke Island. In order to create opportunities for private enterprise, the enclave communities in the seashore were not incorporated into the park. These communities began to become intensively developed, with motels and subdivisions expanding toward the oceanfront to take advantage of the improved access and the protective dune line. Land values soared in these areas. The transition was made to a local economy based on tourism and recreation.

The problem with this project is that it was based upon a false conception of the natural forces acting upon the islands. They are not, as was supposed, stable geological structures where extensive forests grew under the protection of a frontal high dune ridge. Rather, they are in a state of perpetual shifting and migration that alone enables them to survive the tremendous energy of the winds, storms, waves, and tides that act upon them.

The forces causing this migration and shifting are among the most elemental in nature. The sands of the beach are reworked by the seasonal waves and tides; the gentle waves of summer build up the beach, and the harsh winter storms carry sand away to the offshore bars. The longshore drift shifts the sand of the beach laterally; transport occurs both north and south, but on the Outer Banks the net deposition is to the south.

The dunes of the natural system are active, shifting structures. They do not keep out the storm surges that accompany hurricanes and northeasters but instead permit overwash onto the island. Overwash allows new sediment to be deposited, building up the island's elevation and extending its width on the sound side. The system returns to equilibrium as marsh plants grow on the sound side, salt-resistant vegetation quickly colonizes the overwash "fan," and the dune re-forms in a new location. The maritime forest is not a universal feature of the Outer Banks ecosystem; trees can grow only in relatively high and protected areas that are virtually never subject to overwash.

The opening and closing of inlets is also a part of this natural system. Inlets are opened by storm surges that can occur from either the ocean or the sound side. They allow the vital mixing of salt water with fresh water in the estuary. The deposition of sediment in the inlet by the incoming tides forms what is called a "flood-tide delta" that provides a surface for the growth of marsh grasses, widening the sound side of the barrier island.

These mechanisms have allowed the Outer Banks to bend and migrate intact in a generally westward direction in response to rising sea level and the high energy winds and waves. It is thought that Cape Hatteras has shifted about 4,000 feet since it was first seen by European explorers in the sixteenth century. Scores of inlets have opened and closed in this relatively short period of time. The Outer Banks are retreating, not washing away as was supposed in the 1930s.

By the 1970s, the inevitable consequences of the management policies of prior years began to be felt. Where the high, stable dune held fast against the waves, beach sand was scoured out, and "beach nourishment" had to be undertaken to pump new sand onto the beach. The places where the sand was taken, called "borrow areas," were unsightly holes. Sometimes the protective high dune was breached by overwash or inlet formation. This necessitated repairs of the dune as well as of the highway and utility lines. Although few major storms have recently occurred on the Outer Banks, by 1973 the National Park Service had spent $20 million on beach nourishment and dune stabilization. Officials also realized that these expenses would be a recurring item indefinitely.

Other disturbing signs also appeared. Studies of erosion on

the National Seashore show that 63 percent of the shoreline is eroding, 31 percent is accreting, and only 6 percent is stable. Severe erosion is occurring at the south end of Bodie Island, on Pea Island, and on the shoreline fronting Rodanthe, Avon, and Buxton. Cape Hatteras point and the southern end of Ocracoke are accreting.

This erosion is not unexpected. What is unusual is that data compiled by the National Seashore indicate that erosion is also occurring on the *sound* side of the Outer Banks. It is thought that the prevention of overwash and of inlet formation has precluded deposition of the sediment that is necessary for the widening of the islands and their natural retreat. So we may have inadvertently found the formula for washing away the Outer Banks in our effort to preserve them.

Another impact of the artificial dune system has been to change the vegetation and so the ecology of the Outer Banks. Before dune stabilization, an extensive area of grassland occurred just behind the natural dunes. Plants such as salt-meadow cordgrass (*Spartina patens*), broom sedge, and rushes grew here, able to tolerate occasional saltwater flooding. Shoreward out of the salt spray are found shrubs such as myrtle and yaupon and, in a few areas, the mature maritime forest. With the managed dune system, however, there is less grassland, and the shrubs grow right up to the edge of the dune. If overwash should occur, these species would die, leaving the area barren, whereas sand and overwash would not harm the grasses, which are specially adapted to resist them.

The managed dune system of the Cape Hatteras seashore also affects the Pamlico Sound estuary, the large, shallow-water body behind the barrier islands. This sound is a very productive environment for fish and wildlife and is essential to the fishing industry of the state. The primary food producers are the eelgrass and phytoplankton as well as organic material from the saltwater marshes. Many species of finfish and shellfish that are important to man depend on the maintenance of a mid-range of salinity in the sound. Clams, oysters, and scallops live on the estuary bottom, filtering out nutrients and phytoplankton from the large volumes of water they pass through their bodies. Blue crabs, shrimp, and menhaden spawn in the ocean but migrate into the estuary to spend their critical juvenile stage. Anadromous fish such as shad, striped bass, sturgeon, herring, and alewives pass through the estuary to spawn in freshwater rivers and spend their juvenile stage in the estuary before they are mature enough to swim as schools through the inlets out into the ocean.

The managed dune system disrupts the estuary by preventing the normal flow of salt water into the system and by decreasing the productivity of the marshlands on the sound side of the barrier islands. This adds more stress on the estuarine system already threatened by excessive pollution and overfishing.

In 1973 the National Park Service, realizing these problems, announced a change of policy with respect to management of the seashore. The government would no longer attempt to stabilize the Outer Banks artifically but would let natural processes take their course. Lawrence C. Hadley, a Park Service official, summed the situation up this way: "We have reached the conclusion that what we have been doing is not the way to go at all. It is time to set out on a different course that would allow those coastal landscapes to shift with the natural forces. We will always have to do some manipulation and minimal development."

Some longtime residents agree with this new policy. Alonzo Burrus, who has lived in Ocracoke all his life except for a stint with the Coast Guard, remembers a hurricane that struck in 1944. The island was completely under water, and residents drilled or chopped holes in the floors of their houses and opened their doors to let the waters pass freely. "Otherwise the houses would have been swept away," he says. "You just can't do anything about the ocean—many have tried, but it always wins."

Burrus believes the stable dune line will last only until the next hurricane, and that ironically the destruction will be intensified because of it. "When the storm passes over, we won't get hit until it's on the back side of the island. A lot of water collects up in the rivers and creeks of the estuary. This will come back in a great wave on the sound side and crash over the island. If the dunes weren't there, the storm waves would flow over the island more gradually from the ocean side, and we could handle that better."

Other islanders are bitter against the Park Service. Bill Dillon of Buxton complains, "What the Park Service really means when they talk about ocean overwash and letting nature have her way is letting us who live here wash out to sea." He makes the point that when the national seashore was created, the Park Service promised to protect the coastal communities from the ocean. "First the government stole the land from us, broke every promise they ever made, and now they want to abandon us."

Up to now the Outer Banks have been eerily quiet; the expected storms have not occurred, and the new policy has not been put to the test. But what will happen when the inevitable hurricane strikes the Outer Banks? Will the dune line be repaired? Will new inlets be allowed to stay open? Will the coastal highway, the economic lifeline of the commercial developments, be abandoned? The Park Service will continue to be haunted by past policy mistakes. Their decision to let nature take its course is fundamentally correct and the only possible choice in the light of the tremendous forces operating on the Outer Banks. Yet the Park Service cannot afford to ignore the people of the banks and its past promises. There is no easy solution to this dilemma; hard decisions lie ahead.

Another federal agency with extensive management responsibilities affecting the Cape Hatteras National Seashore is the Army Corps of Engineers. Its mission is to dredge the ship channels in shallow Pamlico Sound and to maintain the inlets to keep them open for navigation. This is a never-ending job, since the shifting sand always fills in the dredged channels.

Dredging is carried out by using hydraulic systems to pump sand and bottom material to adjacent areas. This creates what are called "spoil islands" in the sound and around inlets. Although dredging destroys some marine life and bottom organisms, it has recently been found that spoil islands serve as important nesting sites for seashore birds that can no longer find suitable barrier island nesting grounds because of man's activities. Terns and oyster catchers nest on unvegetated new spoil areas. If the islands are allowed to grass over, pelicans, laughing gulls, black skimmers, and willets will use them. More densely vegetated islands will be colonized by egrets, herons, and ibises.

These birds add immensely to the coastal environment. Spoil deposition should be carried out with regard to the impact on these nesting birds wherever possible. The Corps should plan its dredging so that new spoil is not deposited on active nests and a diversity of vegetated spoil islands are maintained to accommodate different species of birds.

The most ambitious project planned by the Corps of Engineers is the stabilization of Oregon Inlet. This is being proposed for several reasons. The Herbert C. Bonner Bridge, constructed in 1963, has been structurally weakened because of the natural shifting of the inlet, which is migrating southward. (Since the inlet opened in 1846, it has shifted nearly two miles to the south, but this was ignored when the bridge was built.) The channel through Oregon Inlet is shallow and constantly shifting, despite periodic dredging. Stabilizing and deepening the channel would allow larger vessels to get through. This would tie in with another Corps project, the enlargement and deepening of Wanchese Harbor to create a seafood industrial park on Roanoke Island. It is thought that commercial fishermen in the sound-side communities such as Wanchese will be able to use larger trawlers if the inlet is stabilized, and this will be an economic boon to the seafood industry.

The Corps plans to construct a jetty out into the ocean on each side of the inlet. The north-side jetty would be 10,000 feet long with a 3,500-foot shore anchorage system. The south-side jetty would be 8,100 feet long. The project is costly, about $75 million initially with an additional $5.5 million each year for upkeep.

This project, to be carried out in the middle of the Cape Hatteras National Seashore, contrasts markedly with the Park Service's decision to "let nature take its course." The Department of the Interior opposes this project because of the impact on the natural system and on the national seashore. This would be the first attempt at inlet stabilization on the Outer Banks. A study has also recommended the stabilization of Ocracoke Inlet to the south.

In the operation of the natural inlet, sandy shoals called the ebb tide delta form on the ocean side. Sand is reworked by the longshore current and carried across the inlet. In the case of Oregon Inlet, the net transport of sand is to the south; thus the jetties will cause sand to build on the north and "starve" the beaches to the south. This will erode the National Seashore and Pea Island wildlife refuge lands. The Corps plans to compensate for this by a sand bypass system capable of moving 450,000 cubic yards annually across the inlet. It is not known whether this will be sufficient because, unlike the natural system, the Corps will only bypass sand during times when wave action is low, chiefly the warm weather months. It is doubtful whether the amount and timing of sand deposition by the natural system can be duplicated.

The inlet stabilization would have other unknown impacts as well. The flood-tide delta on the sound side of the inlet would not receive sufficient sand. This would prevent the deposit of sediment on the sound side of the Outer Banks that is necessary for their widening and retreat from rising sea levels. Oregon Inlet is the only one in the northern portion of the Outer Banks. Will it be able to continue to function as a passage for marine organisms once it is stabilized? Will the stabilized system create new pressures for the opening of a new inlet through the banks?

No one can answer these questions because geologists tell us that we simply do not know enough about inlet mechanics and migration to predict what will occur in the future. There are too many variable factors at work; the attempts of the Corps of Engineers to build models of how inlets work are simplistic failures. Like other events in nature—volcanic eruptions and earthquakes, for instance—inlet mechanics are responses to powerful forces that we do not fully understand and cannot control. We should plan our activities to stay out of their way.

It is sheer folly to try to stabilize these inlets of the Outer Banks. The millions of dollars spent on these projects will only necessitate the spending of many millions more when the projects go awry and people discover they have been falsely assured of a stable, deep-water passage. The experience of the Bonner Bridge is an excellent illustration of the problem. It was built at a cost of $2.8 million in order to provide easy access to Cape Hatteras. By 1978, erosion had caused subsidence of the south end, requiring a repair job costing $1.8 million. Now further maintenance is scheduled, costing more than $5 million. Once the process of engineering is begun, there is no end to the money that must be spent to try to salvage the job. And we know that in the end the ocean will win. It would be best to abandon attempts to stabilize inlets on the Outer Banks and to let the Bonner Bridge fall into the sea.

Yet another problem faced by the National Park Service on the Cape Hatteras Seashore is the growth in the number of people using off-road recreational vehicles (ORV's) on the Outer Banks. More than 2 million people come to the seashore each year, and more than 100,000 of them bring four-wheel-drive vehicles, jeeps, and beach buggies. Some of these are commercial fishermen who set their haul nets in the surf, anchored at one end on the beach. After circling their prey, they bring the other end of the net to shore, and the net is pulled in. This manner of fishing is one of the oldest uses of the Outer Banks, except that in earlier days a pony was used instead of a truck. The legislation creating the seashore preserves the commercial fisherman's right to use the beaches. But most of the traffic nowadays is due either to the sport fishermen who cast into the surf for bluefish, spotted sea trout, and red drum schooling just offshore or to people who just like to drive over the beach.

ORV use can kill vegetation and disturb nesting birds. The Park Service has accordingly restricted vehicles to marked trails and access points, except on the beach face, which is most resistant to adverse impacts. Under current regulations, ORV's are permitted within 150 feet shoreward of the tide line, but no closer to the vegetation line than 20 feet. Portions of the beaches are closed during the summer to protect nesting birds and sea turtles. Beaches less than 100 feet wide are closed as well.

These regulations have been controversial. Many fishermen object to having to get a permit to use the beach or think the 100-foot criterion is too strict and that too many beaches will be unnecessarily closed. The Park Service's restrictions appear to be a reasonable compromise, however, between those that want unrestricted access and those that wish to bar all vehicles from the beach.

There will also be increasing conflicts between the Park Service and the enclave communities of the Outer Banks. Although their growth is restricted because they are surrounded by National Seashore land, the banks communities are destined to develop right to the edge of the parkland. The Park Service is constantly asked to provide utility services and to protect these enclaves against encroachment by the sea, although this will prove unreasonably expensive in the long run.

Unanswered questions and unsolved problems abound at the Cape Hatteras National Seashore. It will be impossible to satisfy and reconcile all the demands being made upon this resource. The day of reckoning must inevitably come.

9

New Bern and the Neuse Shore

THE BROAD ESTUARY OF THE NEUSE RIVER TRACES A GIANT curve for almost fifty miles before passing between the last marshy headlands into the open vastness of Pamlico Sound. Along this course the river is fringed with wetlands and penetrated by numerous tributary streams and creeks.

On the northern shore, fields of corn and soybeans alternate with pinelands and pocosin. Small farming and fishing communities coexist with vacation home subdivisions advertising "wooded and waterfront lots." The largest town is Bayboro, the seat of Pamlico County, with a population of about 600. The most picturesque place is Oriental, a fishing village and retirement community on the shore of the Neuse. White-painted houses with tin roofs are clustered under oak and magnolia trees. In the little harbor, shrimp trawlers with names such as "Starduster" and "Grey Cloud" are tied up alongside expensive yachts that have put in from the nearby Intracoastal Waterway. Highway 306 bisects the county from north to south, following the ridge of a prehistoric beach. The northeastern neck of the county, Goose Creek Island, is a game management area too wet to farm.

This isolated region has been settled since the eighteenth century, but the first town was incorporated only in 1857. This was the little village of Jackson, whose name was defiantly changed to Stonewall after the Civil War. Other towns grew up in the late nineteenth century, and summer camps and a resort were established on the Neuse at Minnesott Beach after World War I.

The southern shore, deeply indented by rivers and creeks, is more heavily populated. A large U.S. Marine Air Base, Cherry Point Marine Air Station, is located near the Craven County town of Havelock, a tacky area of strip development. To the east is a peninsula of bogland, pocosin, and swamps known as Open Ground. Recently several thousand acres in this area were cleared and drained by a corporate farm owned by Italian investors.

The lands surrounding Cherry Point constitute the 155,000-acre Croatan National Forest. Away from the road corridors—U.S. 70 and N.C. 101—that pass through the area is one of the largest remaining pocosin lands in North Carolina. Interspersed with the extensive forests and swamplands are several shallow Carolina bays, home to wildfowl and the American alligator.

As we discussed in Chapter 1, the term *pocosin* (an Indian word meaning "raised bog") accurately describes these lands. They are thought to have been formed over a period of several thousand years by changes in the level of the sea. Originally covered by the sea, the area was transformed into freshwater marsh and then, as organic material accumulated, into a swamp forest of cypress and tupelo gum trees. The further deposit of organic materials and the receding sea allowed species to survive that were adapted to high-acid soils and nutrient deficiency and that were capable of growing in the organic muck. The dominant tree is the pond pine with a dense undergrowth of titi, zenobia, and greenbrier vines. In the high pocosin, where drainage develops, pond pines grow tall, and cypress and oak are also present. In the low pocosin, tree growth is stunted, and there are extensive open areas. Here the unique insect-eating plants, Venus fly trap, pitcher plant, and sundew thrive.

Docks at the town of Oriental on the Neuse River. (*Courtesy of N.C. Travel and Tourism Division*)

The Croatan National Forest is managed for timber production and wildlife. Commercially valuable hardwood trees such as cypress, oak, and gum are cut on an eighty-year cycle. The faster-growing pond, loblolly, shortleaf, and longleaf pine are managed on a cycle of shorter duration. Several stands of virgin pine have been left undisturbed, providing habitat for the rare red-cockaded woodpecker. Parcels of roadless and undeveloped areas in the forest are managed as wilderness areas.

On the Neuse shore are several recreation areas. At Flanner Beach, the Neuse River Recreation Area is a designated site for camping and swimming. This was a cotton and tobacco farm until the turn of the century, with a gristmill, cotton gin, and ship landing. Another recreation area, Pinecliff, near Cherry Point, is a place for swimming and picnicking. The Neusiok Trail, a hiking path, begins here and passes through thirteen miles of forest and swamp to the Newport River to the south.

Upstream, at the confluence of the Neuse with the Trent River, is the stately town of New Bern. This old colonial capital has aged gracefully, like a grandame in the midst of the golden years of her maturity. Church steeples and spires dominate her skyline, rising above quiet streets and tree-shaded brick and clapboard buildings. Because of its location, New Bern has been the natural crossroads and principal town of the region since the eighteenth century.

The Neuse River estuary was visited by the Englishman Sir
Richard Grenville on his exploration of Pamlico Sound in 1585.
At that time the shore was inhabited by the Neusiok Indians,
and the river retains the name of these people. In the upper
reaches of the river was the land of the Tuscarora.

In the early eighteenth century, settlers began to come to the
Neuse and its tributary creeks, seeking cheap and unoccupied
land. The Indians did not bother the handful of newcomers,
who purchased their land on an individual basis. Quakers and
French Huguenots, outsiders in the more settled lands to the
north, sought the isolation of the lower Neuse estuary. Adventurers, in search of mineral wealth or simply curious about the
country, also wandered into the Neuse wilderness.

One of the latter was John Lawson, the co-founder of Bath. In
1705 he visited the Neuse country, staying for a time among the
Indians of Chatooka, a Tuscarora Indian town of about twenty
families on the site of present New Bern. From this experience,
Lawson gave a glowing account of the fertility of the country,
the friendliness of the Indians, and the cheapness of the land,
one-fiftieth the price of the more settled lands of the Virginia
colony.

By 1709 Lawson was in London looking after the publication
of his book, *A New Voyage to Carolina*. While there, he was approached by several men from Bern, Switzerland, who wanted
information about the American colonies. One of these, Georg
Ritter, was in charge of a company that, with the blessing of the
Bern government, wanted to settle a group of paupers and religious dissenters, Anabaptists and Mennonites, in the New
World. Two others, Christophe de Graffenried and Franz Lud-
wig Michel, were interested in obtaining mining rights in the
colonies. Based largely upon Lawson's advice that the Neuse region offered both cheap land and possible silver mines, the Swiss
decided to negotiate jointly with the Lords Proprietors and the
English Crown to found a settlement in North Carolina.

A deal was struck which served the interests of all sides. The
Lords Proprietors wanted people to settle the Neuse to colonize
the empty lands between the Albemarle colony and Charles
Town. This would strengthen their hold against the Indians to

the west and the Spanish to the south. The English Crown was looking for a place to transport German refugees from the Palatinate, who had come to London in 1708 after their farms and towns had been destroyed by the French during the War of the Spanish Succession. The Swiss investors were granted mining rights, allowed to buy land, and given provisions to start the new colony in return for transporting the Swiss and Palatines to the shores of the Neuse. Graffenried, a Swiss nobleman who had been the governor of a small province, was placed in charge of the operation and given the title of Landgrave.

The new colonists sailed from England in 1710. The Palatines went first, in January, accompanied by John Lawson. Graffenried stayed behind to make final arrangements for the Swiss settlers. The winter voyage on the stormy Atlantic caused terrible hardship, and more than half the Germans died en route. When the survivors reached the lands on the Neuse, at the site of present New Bern, they found that the promised supplies had not been delivered, so they traded clothes to the Indians and existing settlers in exchange for food.

Graffenried and the Swiss arrived in September, 1710. He was distressed by the condition of the colony and disappointed by its location. He blamed Lawson for choosing the southern shore, which was regarded as hot and unhealthy compared with the northern bank of the river. An additional problem was that Lawson had chosen the site of the Indian village of Chatooka, inhabited by two hundred families led by King Taylor.

Graffenried brought supplies and persuaded King Taylor to leave by paying for the land. During the negotiations, Michel got drunk and picked a fight with one of the Indians. He also grabbed King Taylor's headdress and threw it as far as he could. Graffenried had Michel seized and taken away. He assured the Indians this conduct would not be repeated and, to make sure, sent the unhappy Michel away to do some surveying on the White Oak River. When Michel returned, Graffenried was afraid of more trouble, so he sent Michel to Pennsylvania to explore for silver mines.

Graffenried had John Lawson lay out a town on the point of land between the Trent and the Neuse rivers. Three acres were allotted for each family, and two streets were established, one from the shore of the Neuse into the forest, and the other extending from the Trent to the Neuse. A church was planned at the crossing of the two streets, but this was never built. Farms of 250 acres each were laid out on both sides of the Trent River. The little settlement was named "Neuse-Bern" or Bern-on-the-Neuse, but people soon started calling it "New Bern."

All at once, Graffenried, a Swiss who only wanted to turn a profit on a good business deal, found himself one of the most important men in the North Carolina colony. The New Bern settlement of about 400 was suddenly the rival of Bath and Edenton, and Graffenried as its leader was expected to wield political power. During Cary's Rebellion, the uprising of the Quaker minority, he was courted by both sides and wisely chose to support the Lords Proprietors, whom he looked to for help and supplies. Graffenried was offered the presidency of the colonial council, but he declined, deciding to keep out of politics.

The founding of New Bern was the last straw as far as the Indians were concerned. They had been paid for their lands but did not fully realize that this meant exclusive possession by the whites. The clash of cultures inevitably caused unfortunate incidents. Graffenried relates that one day a white woodchopper noticed an Indian statue painted red and black, representing evil. The woodchopper thought this an insult to his native city, whose official colors were red and black. He therefore took an axe and chopped the statue in two. Only with great difficulty was Graffenried able to calm the Indians afterward.

In September, 1711, John Lawson talked Graffenried into taking a canoe trip up the Neuse River. Lawson, ever the adventurer, at first said he wanted to look for wild grapes; then he suggested that they look for a passage to the mountains or to Virginia. Graffenried reluctantly agreed to go, and they took provisions for fourteen days on the river.

Lawson and Graffenried could not have picked a worse time for their trip. Unknown to them, the Tuscarora Indians upstream were preparing a coordinated assault on the white settlements along the Trent, Neuse, and Pamlico rivers. A few days after their departure, both men were seized by the Indians and taken to Catechna, the main Tuscarora village. The men were forced to listen to speeches about the grievances the Indians had against the settlers. King Hancock, their chief, wanted to know why Lawson and Graffenried had not stopped by on their way to pay him their respects.

When King Taylor of old Chatooka reproached the men, Lawson lost his temper and quarreled with him. Graffenried tried to restrain Lawson without success. The Indians reacted by holding a council of war and condemning Lawson and Graffenried to death. Graffenried bitterly scolded Lawson for getting them into this predicament.

The next day the prisoners were bound and forced to wait while the Indians, their faces daubed with war paint, danced and prepared for the executions. Graffenried tried everything to save himself. He took aside one Indian who spoke English and pleaded with him, saying that Lawson alone was to blame. Just before the execution was to be carried out, he gave a speech in English promising all kinds of services and favors to the Indians and warning that the queen would avenge his blood. At the last moment, Graffenried was spared when one of King Taylor's braves spoke for him. He was led away to a hut and given food to eat. The unfortunate Lawson was executed. Graffenried recounts, uncertainly, that he was either burned or hanged or that his throat was slit with his own razor.

The Indians kept Graffenried prisoner while they ravaged the white settlements, beginning at sunrise on September 22. The town of New Bern was spared at first, but the settlers, not knowing that the town would be a refuge, went to William Brice's fortified plantation across the Trent River. When Graffenried returned and urged peace with the Indians, the settlers were in no mood to follow his advice. They distrusted him and followed Brice's hard line against the Indians.

Graffenried left the colony, bitter at this turn of events. After staying with Governor Spotswood in Williamsburg for a time, he returned to his native Bern in 1714. There he entered business and wrote *An Account of the Founding of New Bern*, the story of his Carolina adventures and a justification of his role as head of the colony. He died in 1743 at the age of eighty-two.

Meanwhile, peace and new political status came to the ravaged New Bern colony. The Neuse River Tuscaroras were subdued with the help of John Barnwell and James Moore; the *coup de grace* occurred when the Indian fort Neoheroka, about thirty miles upriver from New Bern, was captured by South Carolina troops under Colonel Moore in March, 1713. The Neuse region, which had been part of Bath County until it was designated the Archdale Precinct in 1705, was renamed the Craven Precinct around 1712, after William, Lord Craven, one of the Lords Proprietors. It remains Craven County today.

New Bern and the Neuse settlements were slow in recovering after the political and Indian problems attending their early years. For several years after the Tuscarora War, New Bern was a ghost town; in 1741 there were only twenty-one families living there. Title to the lands of the town had passed from Graffenried to his major creditor, Thomas Pollock, a wealthy landowner of the Albemarle region. The original Swiss and German settlers had never owned the land, and now the Pollock family demanded payment. Only a few could afford to pay, and the rest of the original colonists were dispersed in 1749, when the English Crown, seeing their plight, gave them a grant of 250 acres each of new lands to the west. New English-speaking settlers arrived in the area, and New Bern soon lost its original German heritage and became a British-American town.

Yet New Bern had a bright future because of its central location in the colony. After North Carolina became a Crown colony in 1729, the royal governors began to hold some meetings of the colonial assembly in New Bern. Governor Gabriel Johnston, who owned land in the Cape Fear region, wanted to shift the center of government from Edenton, the unofficial capital, to a town farther south. He knew that the Cape Fear region would be unacceptable, but he succeeded in getting the assembly to pass a law in 1746 designating New Bern as the permanent capital and reducing the number of delegates of the Albemarle counties. This did not stand up, however; the Albemarle settlers protested the law and refused to pay their taxes until the British Privy Council disallowed the law in 1754.

In that same year, Arthur Dobbs was appointed royal governor. He, too, wanted a permanent colonial capital. Rejecting both Wilmington and New Bern because of their unhealthy climates, Dobbs wanted to locate the capital near present Kinston. Ill health and political squabbles caused by the French and Indian War prevented Dobbs from carrying out his plan.

When Lieutenant Governor William Tryon arrived to take over his duties in 1764, the people of New Bern, led by the newspaper editor James Davis, were ready to restore the capital to their city. When he visited New Bern, Tryon was given a warm reception, and a large house was made available as a center of government. Tryon accepted the offer and, after becoming governor, called his first meeting of the assembly in New Bern in 1765. He also took advantage of the goodwill of the colonists to get an appropriation of £15,000 in 1766 for the construction of a magnificent building that would serve as his residence and the permanent seat of the assembly and depository for government records. John Hawks, an English architect, was engaged to build it. "Tryon's Palace," as it was derisively called, was finished in 1770. Now largely rebuilt, it is the major tourist attraction of modern-day New Bern.

Thus New Bern's rise from a German-Swiss colony owned by a feudal nobleman to colonial capital was complete. By 1770 the city was also one of the four principal ports of the colony, a center for the shipment of naval stores, livestock, and lumber in exchange for manufactured goods and foodstuffs from the West Indies.

The colonial government in New Bern was soon overtaken by events that it could not control. First there was the Regulator Rebellion, an uprising of the small farmers of piedmont North Carolina against the high taxes levied to build the palace and the political abuses of the royal regime. Governor Tryon crushed this opposition, but only after a bloody clash at Great Alamance Creek, a few miles west of Hillsborough. In 1771 Tryon left North Carolina to assume new duties as governor of New York.

The new governor, Josiah Martin, got into trouble by trying to implement the new British taxation policy. The hated 1765 Stamp Act, which required that a government stamp be affixed to all papers used in business transactions, was repealed in 1766, but the British Declaratory Act established the principle that the Crown could tax the colonies any way it saw fit. This angered the colonists, who refused to recognize any taxes not voted by the colonial assemblies. To make matters worse, the Stamp Act was followed up with a tax on tea and a grant to the British East India Company of a monopoly on the tea trade.

In 1774 the colony of Massachusetts called for each colony to send delegates to a Continental Congress in Philadelphia. Governor Martin refused to summon the North Carolina colonial assembly, but John Harvey, the speaker, in open defiance called a meeting of a provincial congress in New Bern on August 25. William Hooper, Richard Caswell, and Joseph Hewes were chosen as North Carolina delegates to the Continental Congress.

From this time on, the colonial assembly refused to pay attention to Governor Martin, and revolutionary "committees of correspondence" and "committees of public safety" were formed. The royal government was collapsing, and on May 25, 1775, Governor Martin fled from the palace and took refuge on a British cruiser in the Cape Fear River. The colonial administration was over in North Carolina.

New Bern today is still marked by Graffenried's founding ideas and the colonial era. Union Point, the spit of land at the confluence of the Trent and Neuse rivers where Lawson lived among the Indians and where Graffenried later resided, is now a small park. Lawson's original street plan still survives as the embryo of the modern town. Broad Street and Middle Street intersect at right angles in the way intended by Lawson when he said, "I divided the village like a cross." He also laid out and marked the two "principal streets along and on the banks of the two rivers," today Front Street and Tryon Palace Drive. Lawson also tells us that "since in America they do not like to live crowded, in order to enjoy the purer air, I accordingly ordered the streets to be very broad and the houses well separated one from the other." The historian Janet Seapker has pointed out that this conception, the result of the original city plan, has survived today, defining the character of New Bern as a coastal town with freestanding buildings and spacious gardens in contrast to the crowded aspect of most coastal cities.

After the Declaration of Independence and during the following years of war, New Bern served as the capital of the new state of North Carolina. Richard Caswell, the first governor, received a joyous welcome when he arrived in New Bern in 1776, shortly after his election by the Provincial Congress in Halifax. The first sessions of the state General Assembly met in the palace in April, 1777. The area was, happily, not a scene of fighting during the war, although North Carolina's participation was directed from New Bern. After 1778, however, the assembly no longer met there but convened in other towns closer to the population centers to the west. Finally, in 1794, a permanent capital was established in Raleigh.

The loss of the seat of government was a severe blow to New Bern, but its growing port business more than compensated for the loss. The principal entry into the state was through Ocracoke Inlet, which benefited New Bern. With the cutting of the ties with England, the New England states and the West Indies were the principal trade destinations.

Trade and population both grew dramatically in the postwar era. State tariff laws were abolished, and New England became the major market for the naval stores and lumber produced in the North Carolina backwoods. Tobacco exports also became important, growing from 360,000 pounds in 1768 to about 6,000,000 pounds by 1788. Travel and communication were also improved by the construction of plank roads in the early nineteenth century, and in 1858 the railroad linked New Bern to Beaufort and to Goldsboro and the markets to the west.

The prosperity of this period, based upon the abundant food and raw materials produced by the farms, forests, and waters of the region, is reflected in the exquisite quality of the architecture of New Bern. Scores of attractive buildings from the late eighteenth and nineteenth century enrich the town. Two of these, the John Wright Stanly House, a fine Georgian mansion, and the Stevenson House, a side-hall-plan, Federal-style town house, are open to the public.

Especially beautiful are the churches. Perhaps the finest is the First Presbyterian Church on New Street, a perfect building in the light classicism of the Federal style. The four-stage steeple rises with a dignity and rhythm that gives the illusion of a skyward motion. The Roman Catholic church on Middle Street has a more modest Federal-style design of simple elegance.

Federal-style brick or frame residences of antebellum vintage are found on almost every street in New Bern. Particularly noteworthy are the houses on Front Street and Pollock Street. These exhibit a variety of plans and motifs, with the graceful classical columns, pediments, fans, and sunburst ornamentation that characterize this truly American architecture. The houses of New Bern were almost all executed by local carpenters and artisans. It is today one of the greatest assemblages of Federal-style buildings in the country.

Outside New Bern, along the Neuse and its tributaries, some of the planters grew wealthy enough to build stylish mansion homes. China Grove near Janeiro in Pamlico County is perhaps the finest still remaining; it is a Federal structure with a double porch that has a commanding view of the Neuse River.

This mercantile and planter economy ended with the Civil War, when the Neuse became a battlefield and New Bern a prize of war.

With the fall of Roanoke Island on February 8, 1862, the North Carolina sounds came under Union domination. General Ambrose Burnside, commander of the Federal forces, was not resting on his laurels. He had orders to attack New Bern, the second-largest city on the North Carolina coast.

The defense of New Bern was in the hands of four thousand troops under General Lawrence O'Bryan Branch, a North Carolina native who was a lawyer and a graduate of Princeton University. Two lines of defense were constructed on the south shore of the Neuse, downriver from the city. The first, called the Croatan Works, was ten miles away. It extended from Fort Dixie on the Neuse westward for three-quarters of a mile across the New Bern–Beaufort road. The second was six miles away, from Fort Thompson on the Neuse westward across the Beaufort road and the railroad line to Beaufort. General Branch decided he did not

The Stevenson House, New Bern; note the captain's walk. (*Courtesy of Division of Archives and History, Raleigh, N.C.*)

The John Wright Stanly House, New Bern. (*Courtesy of Division of Archives and History, Raleigh, N.C.*)

have enough men to defend the Croatan Works, so he made preparations to defend the Fort Thompson line.

On March 13, 1862, Burnside and the Federal fleet under Commander S. C. Rowan entered the twelve-mile-wide mouth of the Neuse River. It was a clear spring day. At Slocum Creek, twelve miles from New Bern, Burnside landed his troops and marched overland toward the city. They were surprised at being able to pass unhindered over the undefended Croatan Works and camped for the night just below the Fort Thompson line.

On the next day Burnside attacked, but he encountered stiff resistance from Branch's men. The Federals made little progress until a Massachusetts regiment discovered a break in the Confederate line at the railroad. This weak spot was due to the fact that Branch, short of men, had not extended the Fort Thompson line of fortifications across the railroad but had dropped his men back a hundred and fifty yards at this point.

This opened the way for the Federals to flank the line between the railroad and the river, and a gaping hole was opened in the center of the Confederate defenses. Branch ordered the main body of his troops to retreat to New Bern across the Trent River bridge. When the last of his men were inside the city, the bridge was set on fire to leave the Federals on the other side of the river.

The retreat was to no avail. Commander Rowan with the Federal fleet had come up the Neuse and trained his guns upon the city. It was impossible to hold New Bern, so Branch's army was evacuated by rail to Kinston. Fires broke out as the bitter soldiers took their leave from the old city on the Neuse. Burnside ferried his troops across the Trent and, by the evening of March 14, New Bern was in his hands. Most of the white inhabitants had also fled, and the fine houses were pillaged by Union troops and the remaining black residents.

New Bern remained under Federal control for the rest of the war. Although no link was forged with the main body of the Union Army until General Sherman drove up from the south in 1865, the Federal base at New Bern was a constant thorn in the side of the Confederate armies. From New Bern the Federals mounted raids inland on Kinston, Goldsboro, Tarboro, and Rocky Mount and dominated the North Carolina sounds. Con-

First Presbyterian Church, New Bern. (*Courtesy of N.C. Travel and Tourism Division*)

The estuary of the Neuse River is ideal for sailing. (*Courtesy of N.C. Travel and Tourism Division*)

federate attempts to retake New Bern, under General D. H. Hill in 1863 and General George E. Pickett in 1864, were unsuccessful in penetrating the strong line of fortifications built above the city between the Trent and the Neuse and Forts Anderson and Stevenson that guarded both banks of the Neuse. Happily, the city was spared major physical destruction during the war.

After the Civil War, New Bern was no longer important as a port, and the coastal plantations were in ruins. In the latter years of the century, the lumber industry spurred the economic revival of the town. Fishing settlements such as Bayboro, Vandemere, Pamlico, and Oriental on the lower Neuse shore gave the region a thriving fishing industry in addition to the traditional small-farm agricultural economy.

Since World War II, New Bern and the Neuse region have expanded greatly in population, and small industries have been established in textiles, wood processing, chemicals, meat packing, and tobacco processing. When U.S. 70 was improved and routed through New Bern on Broad Street, communications were improved with the rest of the state, but at the cost of the destruction of many stately old homes and buildings. The population of Craven County, about 75,000, has doubled in the last forty years. Most new construction and development has occurred in the suburban areas around New Bern. The Cherry Point Marine Air Station on the south bank of the Neuse has caused the urbanization of the area around Havelock. To the east, Pamlico County, by contrast, has remained a largely rural area with a stable or declining population. The only industry is seafood processing, and many people commute to the New Bern area for better job opportunities.

The major resources of the region today are the historic buildings of New Bern that give the town a unique and sophisticated atmosphere, enhancing the lives of its people and attracting visitors to the city; the Neuse River estuary—with its fringing marshes and wetlands—that gives beauty, provides recreation opportunity, and is indispensable to wildlife and the fishing industry; and the productive agricultural and forestry lands that have long provided the basis of the area's economy. Development and industrial expansion should not be allowed to destroy these resources.

To help preserve their architectural heritage, New Bernians have designated the city center a historic district, and almost two score buildings are individually listed on the National Register of Historic Places. The consciousness of the citizens of the value of historic preservation will—it is to be hoped—prevent mistakes like those of the recent past, two examples of which are, first, the building of an unsightly motel on the city's waterfront, and, second, the bulldozing of old homes on Broad Street to make room for gas stations and fast-food restaurants. It would be a tragedy if further new construction were allowed to destroy the city's historic past and the feeling of spaciousness given to us by Lawson and Graffenried.

The Neuse River estuary extends about forty-two miles from a point six miles west of New Bern to the mouth of the river in Pamlico Sound. Increasing numbers of sail- and powerboats use the river. Shoreland lots sell at a premium as more and more people demand houses with a view of the water. The river is biologically very productive; fish are abundant at most seasons of the year, and crabs and shrimp are common. Thousands of ducks winter on the river. Since every important species of commercial fish is estuarine-dependent at some stage of its life cycle, the river has direct economic value, providing the basis of a multi-million-dollar commercial fishing industry.

In order to remain productive, the estuary must not be overloaded with man's wastes, and its fringing wetlands must be preserved. The major threat to the viability of the estuary is excessively high concentrations of nutrients—phosphorus and nitrogen—which can cause algae blooms and oxygen depletion. When this happens, fish die, and in extreme cases, hydrogen sulfide gas is produced, making life near the river very unpleasant.

Scientists are not in agreement as to the point to which an estuary can be allowed to degenerate without suffering major adverse consequences. It is clear, however, that an increasing volume of wastes are reaching the Neuse estuary and that minor algae blooms have already occurred. There are numerous contributors to this increase. Runoff from tobacco and hog farms is rich in nutrients. Industrial and municipal pollution comes down the river from above New Bern. Second-home subdivisions are rapidly increasing, especially on the Pamlico County shore; lax practices in the location and the density of septic tanks cause great amounts of waste to filter into the river. Excessive nutrient concentrations occur in South River, a tributary of the Neuse, as a result of drainage and runoff from the several-thousand-acre Open Grounds Farm.

These problems can be solved through coordinated action by local and state government with the support of the people who enjoy and benefit from these resources. If the issues are ignored, the irreplaceable values bequeathed to us from the past will be lost.

10

Carteret and the Cape Lookout Seashore

ON EARLY MAPS OF THE NORTH CAROLINA COAST, AN IS-land headland with trailing shoals juts out into the Atlantic. It is named "Promontorium tremendum" (dreadful promontory), the modern Cape Lookout. On the mainland there is an Indian village, Cwareuuoc, probably belonging to the Coree, an Iroquoian tribe then inhabiting the area. The Indians apparently did not inhabit the islands but used them as places for hunting, fishing, and feasting.

Cape Lookout is the second cusp of the North Carolina Outer Banks. Thereafter the coast bends west to an inlet which is generally regarded as the terminus of the banks. This is now called Beaufort Inlet, although in colonial times it was known as Topsail or Old Topsail Inlet. John Lawson, in his 1709 *A New Voyage to Carolina*, perceptively observed that "Topsail Inlet is about two leagues to the Westward of Cape Lookout. You have a fair Channel over the Bar, and Two Fathom thereon, and a good Harbour in five or six Fathom to come to an Anchor."

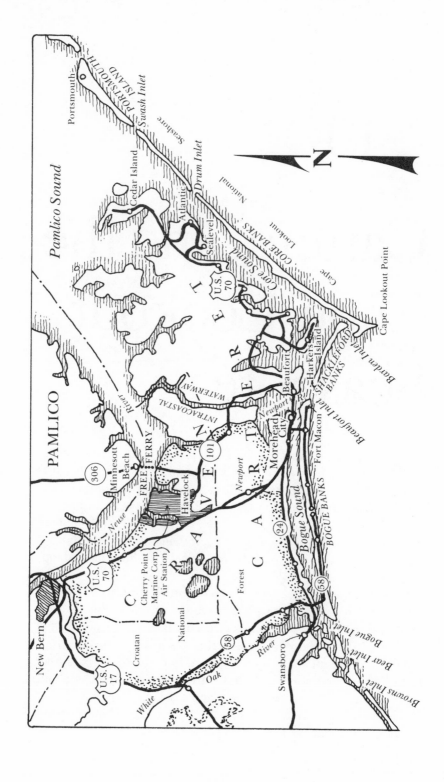

It was not long before a town was founded to take advantage of the "good Harbour." One of the earliest settlers, Robert Turner, laid out and sold twenty-eight lots on land between the North and Newport rivers. This became Beaufort Town. The colonial government, anxious to establish port cities in every section of the colony, formally designated it a "seaport," with the right to collect customs, in 1722. A new precinct, named Carteret after one of the Lords Proprietors, was also established, and in 1723 Beaufort was incorporated as Carteret's seat of government.

Beaufort grew very slowly; John Brickell in his *Natural History of North Carolina*, published in 1737, described it as "small and thinly inhabited." Nevertheless, Spanish privateers from Florida harassed shipping through the inlet, and on August 26, 1747, a Spanish fleet sailed into the harbor and occupied the town for several days.

On the eve of the American Revolution, Beaufort was the third-largest port in North Carolina. The plantations of the Newport River area exploited the rich forests of red and white cedar, cypress, oak, and pine. Lumber products, shingles, and naval stores were shipped to the West Indies in exchange for glassware, cloth, furniture, coffee, and rum. A shipbuilding works was also established. With the coming of war with the British after the Declaration of Independence, Carteret citizens were active in the Revolutionary cause, joining the local militia and Washington's army. The inlet became an important supply line for goods brought by Spanish and French sailing ships destined for the colonial army. Salt was a critical commodity as well, and several operations were established near Beaufort to boil seawater to assure a steady source of supply.

Throughout the war, Beaufort and Old Topsail Inlet were virtually undefended and in constant danger of British attack. But only after Cornwallis's surrender at Yorktown did a British force harass the town. On April 3, 1782, several British ships under Major Isaac Stuart sailed through the inlet, landed, and stayed several days, plundering the town. In the fighting that followed, the schoolhouse and a plantation were burned and several prisoners were taken, but the British, meeting with stiff resistance,

The old Carteret County Courthouse at Beaufort. (*Courtesy of N.C. Travel and Tourism Division*)

sailed back to Charlestown on April 17 without doing further damage.

During the War of 1812, the port of Beaufort and Old Topsail Inlet again took on military importance. Several shipowners received letters of marque and reprisal from the United States government to carry on privateering operations against enemy shipping. This was a kind of licensed piracy, and the privateers and their financial backers were allowed to keep much of the spoils of war. The most successful and famous of the privateers was Captain Otway Burns, whose ship, the *Snap Dragon*, ranged from Greenland to Brazil, capturing cargoes worth millions of dollars during the period from 1812 to 1814. The career of the *Snap Dragon* was ended on June 29, 1814, when she was captured by the British man-of-war *Leopard*. By a lucky chance, Burns was not on this voyage, so he lived to become a successful shipbuilder, politician, and merchant in Beaufort after the war was over.

In the nineteenth century, Beaufort continued to prosper as a port and as an agricultural, commercial, and governmental center. Wealthy planters visited there during the summer to enjoy the cool sea breezes and gay town life. Many Beaufort homes were turned into boarding houses for the summer months, and in 1851 a three-story hotel called the Atlantic was constructed out into the harbor between Marsh and Pollock streets. A railroad was built to Shepherd's Point, across the Newport River from Beaufort, in 1858.

With the outbreak of the Civil War, Beaufort became an important center for ships running the Union blockade of southern ports. After Union General Ambrose Burnside occupied New Bern on March 14, 1862, Beaufort was cut off from the rest of the state, however. Burnside was anxious to capture Beaufort Inlet, the only inlet through the Outer Banks still under Confederate control. He sent General John G. Parke down the Atlantic and North Carolina Railroad toward the coast. Parke took Havelock, Carolina City, and Morehead City unopposed. On the night of March 24, two companies of Federal soldiers were rowed across the Newport River by some black fishermen, and the next morning Beaufort residents awoke to find the Federals in control.

Beaufort or Old Topsail Inlet was guarded by Fort Macon, a large, casemated, brick fortress on the east end of Bogue Banks, completed in 1832. Robert E. Lee had been stationed here as a young army officer. This was the third fort on this site. Fort Dobbs, a wooden structure built in 1756, was never manned and soon was washed away by the sea. Fort Hampton, built in 1808–9, met a similar fate. Fort Macon had been in Confederate hands since April, 1861, when Captain Josiah Pender, the leader of a volunteer group known as the "Old Topsail Riflemen," obtained the surrender of the Federal commander.

Colonel Moses J. White, the Confederate commander of Fort Macon, refused General Parke's demands for surrender, so both sides prepared for a decisive battle. Burnside had the Federal fleet stand at anchor just offshore. General Parke transported men, guns, and supplies from his base of operations at Carolina City, just west of Morehead City, to Bogue Banks, where he es-

Fort Macon on Bogue Banks stood guard over Old Topsail (Beaufort) Inlet. It is now a state park. (*Courtesy of N.C. Travel and Tourism Division*)

tablished a beachhead eight miles from the fort. The troops moved east up Bogue Banks to within a few thousand feet of the fort, where fortified batteries were constructed and rifle pits dug. On April 25 the bombardment of Fort Macon began with a coordinated assault by the Union fleet and land forces. The Confederate guns repelled the sea bombardment, but the land-based guns lobbed shells into the fort with great accuracy. By afternoon White decided his position was untenable and flew a white flag from the ramparts of the fort. The Union was victorious and was then in complete control of the Outer Banks.

The Union army occupied Beaufort for the rest of the war. A house on Queen Street served as General Burnside's headquarters, and the port was used for Northern shipping.

The port declined after the Civil War, and fishing, especially the catching and processing of menhaden, became the principal business. Beaufort continued to be a major summer resort, although the Atlantic Hotel was destroyed in a hurricane in 1879. The town remained relatively isolated; only one road, present Highway 101, led into Beaufort until 1908. In that year a railroad bridge was constructed across the Newport River, followed in 1926 by a highway bridge. Duke University and the federal government both established marine research laboratories near Beaufort.

By the 1960s, however, Beaufort was in serious trouble. Businesses were moving out of the town to shopping centers, the waterfront was decaying, and the once-flourishing fishing industry was in decline because of pollution and overfishing. There was little prospect for new industry to revitalize the town.

This trend was dramatically reversed in the 1970s by town leaders who employed a unique blend of urban renewal and historic preservation to refurbish the old port town without destroying its past. The dilapidated buildings on the harbor side of Front Street were torn down, exposing the beautiful and distinctive double-porch, white frame houses that face the sound. A park and boardwalk now add to the beauty of the waterfront. This has attracted new businesses and tourists to the town.

Through the efforts of the Beaufort Historical Society, the town actively fostered the preservation of its architectural past. It has great resources to draw upon. The atmosphere of the sea still permeates the town. About 120 structures are more than 100 years old, and many date from the eighteenth century. The houses on Front Street, most of which are in fine condition, make a magnificent ensemble. With their gable or pedimented roofs over pillared double porches and their massive brick end-chimneys, they impart a stately dignity to the town. On the east end of the waterfront is the Hammock House, thought to be the landmark "White House" noted in many early mariners' maps of Beaufort. On Ann Street, one block north, there are also many fine homes and churches.

The Old Burying Ground on Ann Street, almost surrounded by three fine churches, is one of the most interesting cemeteries in the state. In use since the founding of the town in 1709, it has an atmosphere of peace and melancholy, lent by its ancient oaks and lichen-covered, crumbling tombstones. Many persons important in local or state history are buried in the cemetery, including Captain Otway Burns and Josiah Pender. Revolutionary and Civil War soldiers as well as victims of the early Indian wars

The grave of Otway Burns, Old Burying Ground, Beaufort. (*Courtesy of Division of Archives and History, Raleigh, N.C.*)

were also laid to rest here. Interesting inscriptions abound, such as that which graces the tomb of Captain John Hill:

> The form that fills this silent grave,
> Once tossed on Ocean's rolling wave,
> But in a port securely fast,
> He's dropped his anchor here at last.

The most poignant story in the Old Burying Ground is the legend of Nancy Manney. This Beaufort girl fell in love with her tutor, Charles French. Her family opposed the romance, and Charles left town, vowing to send for her when he had established himself. The two corresponded faithfully, but the Beaufort postmaster, at the request of Nancy's father, intercepted the letters that each wrote, so that none was ever delivered. Charles eventually rose in the world, becoming Associate Justice of the Supreme Court of the Arizona Territory. He never forgot Nancy, however, and when he retired, he returned to Beaufort and found her. Although Nancy was now ill with consumption, she had never wavered in her love, and she and Charles were finally married. But their time together was brief; a few days after the wedding Nancy died. Charles returned to Arizona heartbroken, and Nancy lies alone in the Old Burying Ground.

Beaufort today is clearly a special town and is so regarded by her inhabitants. Yet some problems remain. Substandard housing units still exist, for instance, especially in predominantly black areas. The town is moving to correct this through the construction of low-cost housing and the enforcement of a housing code.

Beaufort is confronting the issue of growth with caution. The town would like to attract development and industry, but not at the expense of the established natural and historical values of the area. When a developer from the city of High Point recently acquired Carrot Island, a small island in the sound across from the Beaufort waterfront, and threatened to develop it, donations were obtained from three town businesses, Duke University, and The Nature Conservancy to buy the developer out. On another occasion, a Houston-based firm wanted to locate a propane terminal and storage facility on Radio Island in the Newport River. Despite the economic boon the facility would have meant, most of the people in Beaufort opposed it because of the danger of explosion and fire, and the extra expenditure that would have been necessary for additional fire-fighting equipment.

Perhaps the most difficult problem the people of Beaufort face is how to maintain the viability of the commercial fishing industry. Since just after the Civil War, Beaufort has been a center for menhaden fishing and processing. These small fish enter the North Carolina sounds and estuaries in large schools. Prized for making fish meal and industrial oils for paint and margarine, they are caught with a purse seine or a pound net by fishermen using distinctive boats with high crow's nests to spot the schools. Once incredibly abundant, menhaden have suffered a dramatic decline. Other species of fin and shellfish have also been reduced in numbers. The Newport River was once the center of a flourishing oyster industry. The most important factors in the decline of commercial fishing are pollution, overfishing, and the dredging and filling of estuarine marshlands. Pollution is an especially serious problem. Runoff from agricultural lands and discharge from municipal sewage plants and from industrial and commercial facilities all contribute to the creation of excessive levels of pollution. This process is continuing; a new 30,000-barrel-a-day oil refinery has been proposed for the Newport River area.

The governmental response to excessive pollution has been simply to declare the area unsuitable for the taking of shellfish. This not only has failed to solve the problem but has caused the demise of the oyster-gathering industry in most areas. A concerted program is needed to restore the quality of the Newport River and other estuarine waters. Strict enforcement of water quality standards and limitations on the number of pollution discharge permits are necessary to reverse the deterioration of the Newport River and the Beaufort fisheries. Building industrial or oil refinery facilities on the river should not be permitted at the expense of the estuary.

East of Beaufort, several small fishing and farming villages are located on the higher ground of the marshy peninsula known as "down east" Carteret. These towns were settled in the early eighteenth century, and many residents are descendants of the original settlers. Until the present century, these towns were accessible only by boat. They still retain an atmosphere of isolation and solitude.

Marshallberg, which is located on a spit of land between Sleepy Creek and Core Sound, used to be known as Deep Hole Creek because heavy swamp soil was excavated and barged to Bogue Banks during the construction of Fort Macon from 1828 to 1834. Smyrna, Davis, Stacy, and Atlantic are small fishing villages facing Core Sound. Otway is a crossroads community named after Otway Burns. At Sealevel a modern hospital has been established as the result of a gift of the Taylor brothers, local men who did not forget their neighbors after they moved away to seek success in the business world. Atlantic, formerly known as Hunting Quarters, is the home base of many Core Sound watermen. At Cedar Island, on the tip of the Carteret peninsula, the federal government has established a national wildlife refuge, and a state-operated ferry makes regular runs to Ocracoke. The isolation of these fishing communities is diminishing as more and more land along Core Sound is being sold for vacation home sites.

At the southern end of Core Sound is Harkers Island, a five-mile-long sand island with about 1,600 inhabitants. Settled in 1714, when it was granted to Thomas Sparrow, the island ac-

Boats are still built in the traditional way on Harkers Island. (*Courtesy of N.C. Travel and Tourism Division*)

The Beaufort waterfront. (*Courtesy of N.C. Travel and Tourism Division*)

quired its name from Ebenezer Harker, who bought it in 1730. Harkers Island remained thinly settled until 1900, when people from Shackleford Banks arrived after a disastrous hurricane. Electricity was not installed until 1939, and a bridge was not built from the mainland until 1941. The island remained very much isolated until the 1950s. The people here are still fishermen and farmers, and boat building is the most important industry. The traditional Core Sound "sharpie," a shallow-draft boat with sails on either side that looks like a bird in flight when under way, is still made here. In recent years recreational marinas, vacation homes, and motels have been established, and the marine forest that covered the area has been cut down. The National Park Service is developing a Visitors' Center for Cape Lookout National Seashore on the eastern end of the island. From here boats carry passengers to the national seashore. During the summer, the population of Harkers Island goes up by about 2,000 people, and this is expected to increase when the seashore park is fully developed.

Cape Lookout National Seashore was established by Congress in 1966. It includes the wildest and most isolated portions of the North Carolina Outer Banks. Shaped like a gigantic check mark, the seashore extends for fifty-eight miles from Portsmouth Island on the north to Core Banks and Cape Lookout point on the south; Shackleford Banks stretches to the west, ending at Beaufort Inlet.

Unlike the Cape Hatteras seashore, there has never been any major attempt to build an artificial dune system to stop erosion on the islands of the Cape Lookout seashore. Nor has any road been constructed on these islands or any bridge from the mainland. Yet Cape Lookout has a history of occupation and use by Indians and early settlers. At the time the seashore was created, about 340 structures existed on the islands. Most of these were tar-paper shacks used by fishermen. They are being removed by the National Park Service, as are more than 2,500 abandoned vehicles once used as dune buggies by fishermen on the banks.

The Park Service plans to keep most of the seashore in its undeveloped state, constructing only limited camping and day-use facilities. Visitors are to be ferried from Harkers Island to three access points: at Shingle Point in the middle of Core Banks, at the Cape Lookout Lighthouse complex, and in the middle of Shackleford Banks. A ferry will also be maintained between Ocracoke and Portsmouth Island.

The studies of Paul and Melinda Godfrey as well as old maps tell us that dramatic changes have occurred in the shoreline of the Cape Lookout National Seashore. Core Banks is directly exposed to the full force of the winds and storm tides. It is an excellent example of how an undeveloped barrier island works. The dune line is very low and is regularly overwashed by the storm tides, which deposit great flats, called overwash fans, over the dunes. As a result, there is little in the way of stable vegetation or trees; the marsh on the sound side of the island is very extensive. The island is eroding on the oceanfront at the rate of about 165 feet per century. Because of the overwash, however, it is retaining its shape and form, retreating naturally in response to the gradually rising sea level. In 1964, the Army Corps of Engineers proposed a project to control this erosion and stabilize the island. It is now recognized that this would be expensive and ultimately futile.

Inlets have opened at several points on Core Banks. Whalebone Inlet separated Portsmouth Island from Core Banks until it closed in the 1930s. Swash Inlet now serves this function; it has shoaled up so that it is awash only at high tide. Cedar Inlet is shown at the center of Core Banks on maps of the early nineteenth century. Old Drum Inlet was open through here in the eighteenth century, and again from 1933 to 1971. Opened by storms, inlets naturally migrate, because the littoral drift and tidal action cause one side to build up faster than the other, and then ultimately close, as marsh grasses colonize and stabilize the sediment deposited.

In 1971 the Army Corps of Engineers decided to cut New Drum Inlet through Core Banks opposite the town of Atlantic in order to provide a passage for fishing trawlers and other boats from Core Sound into the ocean. Dynamite was used to blast through the sand bank at a narrow point on the island near Old Drum Inlet. Once open, the inlet behaved in ways the Corps did not anticipate. The drift of sand down the banks was interrupted, and the inlet unexpectedly widened to almost 4,000 feet. At the same time, it shoaled up so that nothing larger than a shallow-draft skiff can cross over the bar. The Corps tried dredging to keep a channel open, but gave up in frustration. Now residents of Atlantic are afraid that in the event of a hurricane, their small town will be unprotected from a storm surge through the inlet. They want the Corps to build breakwaters in the inlet! This episode is a case study of the problems caused by man's attempts to control inlet mechanics.

North of Core Banks lies Portsmouth Island, the widest part of the national seashore. In the nineteenth century a chain of islands extended between Portsmouth and Cedar islands, but these have virtually eroded away. At the northern part of Portsmouth, near Ocracoke Inlet, the island is more than two miles wide. This area is large enough to support an extensive marine forest. The town of Portsmouth was located here from its founding in 1753 until the last residents moved away in 1971. It will be discussed in more detail below. Portsmouth Island is eroding as Ocracoke Inlet migrates to the south.

Great change has occurred at Cape Lookout point as well. According to nineteenth-century maps, the cape was much longer and narrower than at present. Accretions of sand on the ocean side widened the beach to the east, and a rock jetty built in 1915 was a factor in extending the hook of the cape several hundred yards to the west. The high dunes now in the middle of Cape Lookout point are the vestiges of the cape of a hundred years ago.

Separating Core Banks from Shackleford Banks is Barden Inlet or, as it is sometimes called, "the Drain." Old maps show that an inlet existed here during the first half of the nineteenth century; then, about the time of the Civil War, it closed, but was reopened in the hurricane of 1933. Barden Inlet provides a passage from Back and Core sounds to the Cape Lookout Bight, the enclosed area behind the fishhook of the cape. The Corps of Engineers has maintained a deep channel through annual dredging, from the east end of Harkers Island through this inlet, retarding its natural tendency to close.

Ironically, this channel has caused erosion to increase on the sound side of the Cape Lookout Lighthouse, since the outgoing tides driven by storm winds from the northeast are cutting away the land. This natural tendency was exacerbated by the Corps' dredging activities, which guide the channel directly in front of the lighthouse. The land in front of the lighthouse is receding at the rate of several feet per year, and in 1978 it was predicted that the lighthouse and the keeper's quarters might fall into the sea as early as 1981.

Cape Lookout Lighthouse, with its distinctive black-and-white diamond pattern, is the most famous landmark on Core Banks. Constructed in the 1850s on the site of an earlier light-house built in 1812, it is still in operation, signaling the where-abouts of the treacherous Cape Lookout shoals. Although the lighthouse is no longer necessary for navigation, plans to save it were devised because of its historic and esthetic value. The con-struction of a stone rip-rap revetment to contain the erosion would cost between three and five million dollars, however, and require a maintenance cost of about a half million dollars per year; this would also change the appearance of the natural shore-line. The National Park Service has, as of the present writing, decided not to take special action to save the lighthouse.

Coastal engineering projects that attempt to stem the natural forces are expensive and often lead to unforeseen side effects, creating the need for even more costly "improvements." And in the end, the forces of the sea, winds, and tides will have their way.

Shackleford Banks, named for the man who first purchased land here in 1714, extends nine miles west from Barden Inlet to Beaufort Inlet and exhibits a geologic and vegetative character very different from that of Core Banks because of its east-west orientation. The dominant sea winds and currents, instead of coming across the island from ocean to sound, tend to carry sand obliquely toward the west. As a result, the island is building to the west into Beaufort Inlet in a series of "recurved spits." This means that the leading edge of the accreting spit tends to curve back into the sound forming a shallow bay. This bay is eventu-ally cut off completely by the building shoals to form a shallow

Cape Lookout Lighthouse. (*Courtesy of N.C. Travel and Tourism Division*)

freshwater marsh. Mullet Pond on the western end of Shackleford is an example of this process; in the nineteenth century, it
was a part of Back Sound, but now it is a freshwater pond.

In the nineteenth century marine forest covered almost the
entire area of Shackleford Banks because of the protection afforded by Cape Lookout. In 1899 a hurricane struck the island,
submerging and killing most of this forest. Additional storms
drove sand across the unprotected bar. In many areas of Shackleford the remains of this forest are visible as a "ghost forest" of
cedar and oak, gnarled and barren amid the still-moving dunes.

Today the entire eastern two-thirds of the island is vegetated
only by marsh and dune grasses, which are cropped short by the
herds of abandoned horses, cows, sheep, and goats. Only the
western portion of Shackleford contains remnants of the oak,
pine, holly, and cedar marine forest and the myrtle-shrub
thicket.

More than just the forces of nature are of interest at Cape
Lookout National Seashore. Reminders abound of the human
culture that flourished here for more than two hundred years.
Hardy men and women lived out their lives on these sand banks,
attracted and benefited by the bounty of the sea, but locked in a
struggle to survive in a hostile environment dominated by the
power of that sea.

Now they are all gone. The sea is unforgiving, and the conditions that fostered life on the remote banks are no more. But
these people did not leave in disgrace; their departure is a reminder of the pervasiveness of change in the coastal area.

The most visible remnant of an Outer Banks community is on
Portsmouth Island. This was the seaport town of Portsmouth,
founded in 1753 by the North Carolina Colonial Assembly to
develop harbor facilities at Ocracoke Inlet. This was necessary
because many of the oceangoing sailing ships could not cross the
bar of the inlet fully loaded. They had to be "lightered"; their
cargoes were either partially or totally unloaded and placed on
smaller ships capable of navigating the shallow sounds (as we
noted in Chapter 8). Fort Dobbs was constructed here in 1757,
but was abandoned after the French and Indian War.

Portsmouth had its greatest prosperity in the nineteenth century. Busy wharves and warehouses were located at Haulover Point. The town contained a marine hospital and a customs house. Just before the Civil War, there were 105 dwelling houses and 13 slave buildings at Portsmouth, and the population was approximately 700, including about 100 slaves.

In 1861, Federal forces landed on Hatteras Island and took Forts Hatteras and Clark. Confederate forces guarding Ocracoke Inlet in the fort on Beacon Island left, and the Portsmouth people began evacuating their town. As the story goes, everyone left except one woman who was too fat to get through the door of her house.

After the war, only about half the population returned. Shipping declined as boats began using the newly opened Hatteras Inlet to the north. Portsmouth was no longer needed; lightering was a thing of the past. A lifesaving station was opened in 1894, but this did not provide enough employment to prevent further decline in the population. The marine hospital burned very mysteriously in 1894.

A few people continued to live in Portsmouth until 1971, when Henry Pigott, the last male resident, died. Marian Babb, the last person left, moved to Beaufort. A few of the houses are leased as summer vacation homes, but the town is now part of the Cape Lookout National Seashore, which is responsible for maintaining the site for its historic value.

Today the visitor can walk the streets of old Portsmouth, deserted but filled with memories of more than two hundred years of Outer Banks history. Houses are in various conditions; some look recently lived in, while others are vine-covered ruins. At the center of town, called the Crossroads, the old U.S. Post Office building stands next to the community cemetery. The old schoolhouse is up the road. Toward the ocean, across the marsh known as Doctor's Creek, is a well-kept pink house that was owned by Henry Pigott. The Methodist Church, built in 1914 on the site of an earlier church that had burned down, is a frame, neo-Gothic structure with a shingled bell tower. It is still used occasionally for weddings. The 1894 lifesaving station dominates a clearing in front of a bay of the inlet, and the cistern of the nineteenth-century marine hospital is nearby.

Portsmouth Island, now a part of the Cape Lookout National Seashore, is the site of an abandoned town. (*Courtesy of N.C. Travel and Tourism Division*)

A second area of long-standing human use and occupation was in the vicinity of the Cape Lookout Lighthouse and the eastern end of Shackleford Banks. For hundreds of years vessels have taken shelter or rendezvoused at the Cape Lookout Bight. This was a harbor of refuge, available without the necessity of navigating through a treacherous inlet to gain shelter from storms. Pirates gathered here in the early eighteenth century. In the 1740s Spanish galleons used the Bight. In 1755 Arthur Dobbs, the royal governor of North Carolina, recommended that the Bight be fortified against the Spanish and French, but nothing was ever done to implement his proposal. During the Revolution, Captain de Cottineau, a Frenchman, built Fort Hancock on the site, with the cooperation of the newly independent State of North Carolina. About eighty men were stationed at the fort until it was decommissioned in 1780. Today, fishing craft and recreational vessels of all kinds still use the Bight's protected harbor.

The first settlers in the Cape Lookout area seem to have been attracted by the discovery in the eighteenth century that whales appeared in considerable numbers off the cape from February to April during their spring migration northward. Whales were often found beached on the shore, and people went out to harpoon them from small boats. Small communities of those whalers grew up in the woods on the eastern end of Shackleford Banks and on Core Banks in the vicinity of the lighthouse.

After the Civil War, the whale gun was introduced, and porpoise and mullet fishing were also carried on. Settlements extended from the lighthouse almost to the western end of Shackleford. No inlet separated Shackleford from Core Banks, and the Bight provided a fine harbor for ships to anchor. In the 1880s the east end of Shackleford was dubbed Diamond City, named after the diamond pattern of the Cape Lookout Lighthouse. Toward the middle of Shackleford was another community named Wade's Shore.

Lifesaving stations were also established on Core Banks—at Cape Lookout in 1888, and in the middle of the banks opposite Hunting Quarters (Atlantic), near present Drum Inlet, in 1897. The surfmen of these stations were often called on to rescue people on ships stranded on the Cape Lookout shoals. In 1904 the Cape Lookout Lightship was stationed out on the shoals to warn ships away from this dangerous area. It was retired from service in 1933.

Today little evidence remains of the nineteenth-century communities at the cape and on Shackleford; there are only the cemeteries and the descendants of the bankers' animals. People left Shackleford after the hurricane of 1899 and went to Harkers Island or Bogue Banks. The lifesaving stations were abandoned; the Hunting Quarters unit burned in 1968, and the Cape Lookout station was moved and converted into a private summer home. The structures at the cape are the lighthouse, its outbuildings—consisting of the keeper's quarters, a coal and wood shed, a generator house, and a small cement-block oil house—and several vacation homes, now in the ownership of the National Park Service.

The emphasis on preservation and conservation that is dominant in both Beaufort and on Cape Lookout National Seashore is in sharp contrast to what is happening in the rest of Carteret County. Real estate and banking interests have encouraged an all-out development approach, resisting efforts by the state government to control unplanned growth. Real estate salesmen bristle at the suggestion that a landowner's decision to do what he wants with his own property should be limited by governmental regulation.

The development tradition started early in Carteret County. In the 1850s, when the area's economy was based on small plantations, farms, and fishing, John Motley Morehead, a former governor of North Carolina, got the idea of founding a "great commercial center" on the shores of Bogue Sound west of the Newport River. He and his associates bought land and brought in the railroad from its eastern terminus at Goldsboro. In 1857, they sold off lots, founding Morehead City and, to the west of it, Carolina City.

Morehead's plans were frustrated by the Civil War. Nevertheless, in the late nineteenth and early twentieth centuries, Morehead City became a summer resort for wealthy vacationers arriving by rail from Raleigh and other cities to the west. Development was concentrated along Bogue Sound, where vacation cottages and several hotels were built. Fish caught in the area were shipped west to market via the railroad, which was nicknamed the "Old Mullet Line." Since World War II, development interest has shifted to Bogue Banks and the surrounding areas of Carteret County.

Today, the old residential and commercial buildings of Morehead City have been largely replaced by modern strip development with convenience stores, fast-food restaurants, and motels along Arendell Street, the principal thoroughfare. A few interesting buildings remain, notably the 1926 Municipal Building, a grandiose Florentine Renaissance structure. An impressive group of the old residences remain along Bogue Sound across from Bogue Banks.

The Morehead City waterfront is still picturesque, with its deep-sea charter boat fleet, fish houses, gift shops, and seafood restaurants. The renowned Sanitary Fishmarket and Restaurant is a huge, high-ceilinged hall overlooking the sound. Patrons dine in an ostentatiously wholesome atmosphere with bright lights and prominent "Absolutely No Drinking" signs on the wall. In the entrance vestibule there is an injunction which reads:

> We appreciate your business BUT . . .
> IF you are drunk or acting drunk stay out.
> It will save you embarrassment because
> we will ask you out if you are in that condition.

Morehead City achieved the dream of its founder, Governor Morehead, when, in 1952, a deep-sea port was established there. Large oceangoing ships enter through Beaufort Inlet, which is dredged by the Army Corps of Engineers. Until the recent boom in coal exports, the port was a chronic money-loser for the State Ports Authority, however. Phosphate has been shipped in large quantities, but many shippers find the location inconvenient, and larger vessels cannot navigate easily through the inlet.

Despite this, because of political considerations, Morehead City gets virtually the same equipment that Wilmington, the other North Carolina port city, gets. In 1977 a huge 2.6-million-dollar crane was installed at the Morehead City port to provide a capability for unloading container cargo ships. No container ships use the port, and the crane sat idle. In 1979, the Ports Authority voted to move the crane to Wilmington at a cost of several hundred thousand dollars. The lesson of this incident is that development of the port should proceed only with the recognition of the natural constraints of geography and navigation. There are now proposals to dredge the Morehead channel to fifty-five feet to accommodate large coal ships. A great increase in shipments may cause complications, however, because the rail line that brings the coal to port runs down the middle of Arendell Street, Morehead's main thoroughfare.

Carteret County west and north of Morehead City is to a great extent part of the Croatan National Forest, which is managed for timber production and wildlife preservation. The town of Newport, an enclave within the national forest, was originally a small agricultural town, but its character has been changed by the proximity of U.S. Highway 70 and the nearby Cherry Point Marine Air Station. Traces of the antebellum plantation culture still remain. Along State Highway 101 in the vicinity of Harlowe, there are several nineteenth-century homes and churches, including the Rufus Bell House, a good example of a frame coastal cottage of the period.

State Highway 24, which leads west from Morehead City parallel to Bogue Sound, gives access to many new sound-side subdivisions and residences. The Cape Carteret area, bounded by Bogue Sound and the White Oak River, is a rapidly expanding residential community. In the nineteenth century this was the site of several small plantations, and some of the old homes remain. The most interesting is the Octagon House, built as a plantation house for Edward Hill in the 1850s. Nearby is the Cedar Point Campground, maintained by the U.S. Forest Service, and the Cedar Point Wildlife Trail leads the visitor through the pine forest and the marshes of the White Oak estuary.

The most rapidly developing area of Carteret County is Bogue Banks, the twenty-five-mile-long barrier island that stretches be-

The Rufus Bell House, Carteret County. (*Courtesy of Division of Archives and History, Raleigh, N.C.*)

tween Beaufort Inlet on the east and Bogue Inlet to the west. This is one of the largest and most interesting of all the islands of the North Carolina coast. Because of its east-west orientation and the shelter from the high-energy ocean waves afforded by Cape Lookout, it originally had a virtually unbroken marine forest—a dense canopy of live oak, cedar, yaupon, and holly. The diversity of plant and wildlife species found here exceeds that of any other North Carolina coastal island.

Until the 1950s Bogue Banks was virtually undeveloped. The eastern end, site of the Civil War's Fort Macon, was given to the State of North Carolina for the establishment of a state park. A few hotels and beach houses were built at Atlantic Beach. The lands between Atlantic Beach and Salter Path were owned by Alice Hoffman, a distant relative of Theodore Roosevelt. Salter Path was a community of outer bankers, descendants of the shipwrecked sailors and others who had first settled the island in the eighteenth century. Like most of the early bankers, they had no deeds to the land, and Mrs. Hoffman brought suit in court to have them ejected from her lands. A court settlement in 1918 specified that Mrs. Hoffman had title to the land but that the bankers had squatters' rights under the legal doctrine of adverse possession, and could remain on the land. An effect of this was that the people of Salter Path avoided paying taxes on the property. In 1974 Carteret County brought suit against the squatters to "quiet" their titles to the land, and the squatters were forced to pay the county property taxes. The rest of the island, west of the present town of Emerald Isle, was owned by a Philadelphia businessman named Henry Fort.

In the 1950s and '60s, Atlantic Beach was developed as a major resort. Alice Hoffman died, and her heirs, the Roosevelt family, sold off land for development, including Pine Knoll Shores, which was incorporated as a town in 1973. Fortunately, 322 acres were donated to the State of North Carolina, including 2,700 feet of beachfront property; this is now the site of the Roosevelt State Park Natural Area and the North Carolina Marine Resources Center, a public aquarium and meeting place. Emerald Isle was intensively developed in the late 1960s and '70s.

By the middle 1970s, Bogue Banks was the most rapidly developing barrier island on the North Carolina coast. As land prices skyrocketed, high-rise condominiums and motels were built to increase the density and squeeze a greater monetary return out of the land. Fishing piers extending hundreds of feet into the ocean sprouted out from the shore, interfering with commercial fishing and attracting more and more people. This process shows no signs of abating. Much of the marine forest has now been cut down, and new bridges and roads are being built to alleviate the inevitable traffic congestion and to improve access to the island.

Geologist Orrin Pilkey, Jr., in his book *How to Live with an Island*, has pointed out that Bogue Banks, because of its width and extensive marine forest, is an island suitable for small-scale development; yet examples of unwise and dangerous developmental practices abound. Dense development has occurred in erosion-prone areas and in places where the island is narrow with few protective dunes. Bogue Banks is experiencing severe erosion at both ends because of migration of the inlets. The most protected and therefore "safe" areas are Pine Knoll Shores and the middle section of Emerald Isle. Few developers have, like the

Atlantis and John Yancey motels, taken the precaution of leaving the protective frontal dunes intact, most opting instead to remove them in order to be closer to the water. At Salter Path and several other points on the island, roads perpendicular to the ocean shore have been cut, unwittingly providing perfect conduits for storm waves over the island. Soon there will be an outcry about "erosion" and "hurricane protection" on Bogue Banks. At Atlantic Beach a seawall has already been constructed, paradoxically resulting in increased beach erosion as the storm waves hit the seawall and reflect back, scouring away the beach sands.

The development of the western part of Bogue Banks and the town of Emerald Isle provides an illustration of the politics of beach development. Shortly after a group of politically well-connected businessmen bought up most of this area in the late 1960s, the state Board of Transportation approved the construction of a new bridge from the mainland, although the area was then largely undeveloped. After the bridge was completed in 1971, development began in earnest. The area was subdivided right up to Bogue Inlet at the western tip of the island. Here the developers ran into trouble because the inlet is migrating to the east. More than a quarter of a mile of the subdivided land washed into the sea. The owners' response to this was, first, to call for federal and state aid to stop the erosion and, second, to make a "charitable contribution" of the now-submerged land to a private school!*

At the same time property owners were asking for public money for erosion control, they were taking steps to bar the public from "their" beach. The inlet area for years has been used by fishermen, shell collectors, and picnickers. In the 1970s the property along the road was posted and a barrier was placed at the end of the road, with a sign reading "Towing Laws Enforced." The town council voted three to two to restrict access to the inlet and turned down an offer by the state to fund a beach access plan for the area. (The owner of the house nearest the inlet was an influential member of the General Assembly.)

Bogue Banks today is an example of how not to manage a bar-

---

*The deduction was later disallowed by the Internal Revenue Service.

rier island. The unwise developmental practices of the present will be the management problems of the future. There will be increasing demands for federal and state money to correct the mistakes that have been made, mistakes that were avoidable with proper attention to the natural processes affecting the island environment.

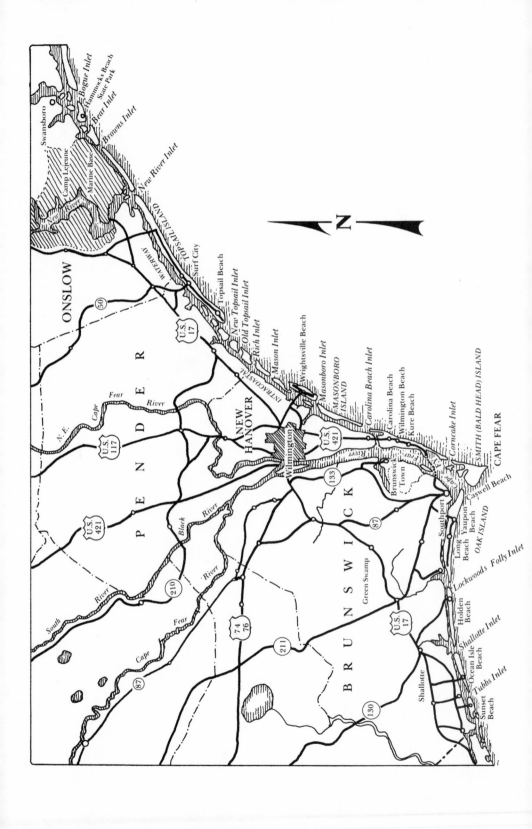

11

The Cape
of Fear

FROM THE WHITE OAK RIVER ON THE NORTH, TO LITTLE River on the south at the present state line, the North Carolina coast is a flat plain edged with barrier islands immediately adjacent to the mainland shore. Numerous inlets cut the offshore bar, signaling the mouths of rivers meandering southeastward to the sea. In contrast to the large, open sounds to the north, the estuaries here are small, with extensive salt marshes.

The Onslow and Pender County beaches in the arc of Onslow Bay to the north of Cape Fear have a more varied history than the beaches farther south. Bear Island lies off the coast at the mouth of the White Oak River between Bogue and Bear inlets. The entire three-mile-long island now constitutes Hammocks Beach State Park, undeveloped except for a beach pavilion and a few unobtrusive dwellings. A free ferry that runs several times a day from a landing on the mainland is the only access to the park. The beach is wide and beautiful, and there is an extensive dune field interspersed with shrub forest in protected spots. Little marine forest can exist on the moving sands except on the border of the sound. The ferry ride passes through a beautiful marsh that is normally alive with herons, egrets, gulls, and terns. Because of the limited access and the absence of roads, a sense of timelessness and solitude permeates the area.

Ironically, the reason this island was preserved is the racial discrimination of the past. Bear Island was part of a coastal plantation in the nineteenth century. After the Civil War, the cotton and peanut lands reverted to pine forest, and smaller farming operations were the rule. In the 1920s, the land, including Bear Island, was bought by a New York physician named William Sharpe, who relates his experiences with it in an autobiography entitled *Brain Surgeon*. Sharpe, who had learned about the area from a black hunting guide named John L. Hurst, moved a large house to the shore of the sound and spent his vacations there. He called the estate "the Hammocks" from the Spanish *la hamaca*, meaning an arable tract of dry land. Hurst and his wife, Gertrude, were the caretakers.

Many people objected to Sharpe's decision to put a black man in charge of the Hammocks. They told him, "A white man must be boss here in the South," and some sent anonymous letters threatening trouble if he didn't make a change. But Sharpe refused to be intimidated. He put an ad in the local newspaper offering a reward of $5,000 for information leading to the arrest and conviction of anyone damaging the Hammocks or injuring its personnel. After this, as Sharpe smugly observes, "There was no further trouble."

In 1949, after many pleasant years in his "paradise," Sharpe agreed with Hurst that there was a need for a recreational area for the black community, which was prohibited from using the white beaches. Upset by the racial discrimination he encountered, he gave the entire estate to the North Carolina Negro Teachers' Association.

During the years Bear Island was owned by the Negro Teachers' Association, excursions by boat were organized, but no money was available for a bridge, and the state refused to appropriate money to improve a black recreation area. The expense of managing the Hammocks grew, so the association eventually decided to give the land to the state for a state park. On May 3, 1961, Hammocks Beach State Park came into being, but because most of the visitors were black, the area remained undeveloped. Today, as a result, it is one of the few islands accessible only by boat, saved from development by historical accident.

Bear Island, Hammocks Beach State Park. (*Courtesy of N.C. Travel and Tourism Division*)

The endangered loggerhead turtle comes ashore to lay its eggs on isolated Bear Island, Hammocks Beach State Park. The young, immediately after hatching, seek the relative safety of the sea. (*Courtesy of N.C. Travel and Tourism Division*)

The trumpet plant (*Saracenia flava* L.) is one of the many rare and unusual species of plants in the Holly Shelter Game Management Area. (*Courtesy of N.C. Travel and Tourism Division*)

Sharpe would probably be pleased with the present condition of his former estate, especially the lack of roads on Bear Island. In his autobiography, he recounts that in 1937 the state had plans to build a road right across his beloved Hammocks. He appealed to authorities in Raleigh, but without avail. Not easily thwarted, Sharpe then obtained a three-minute personal meeting with President Franklin Roosevelt through the intervention of the President's personal physician. Roosevelt told Sharpe to leave the details of the problem to the presidential secretary. Within a few days, Sharpe relates, "Work on the road had ceased."

Across Bear Inlet are two islands separated by Browns Inlet that are part of the Camp Lejeune Marine Corps base. Brown's Island is used for target practice by the military, and Onslow Beach is a training site for amphibious landings. These islands will remain largely undeveloped, however, and the Marine Corps is implementing a program of beach management to preserve their natural character. Sanctuaries, for instance, have been established to protect the nesting sites of the sea turtles that come ashore on summer nights to lay their eggs.

South of New River Inlet is the largest barrier island on Onslow Bay, Topsail Island. Once a beautiful place, Topsail received its name in the early years of the eighteenth century, when pirate ships hid out in the marshes, visible only to the sharp-eyed by the tops of their sails, and waited for a chance to attack passing merchant vessels. During World War II, the U.S. Army bought Topsail for troop training and as part of the coastal defense system. After the war, Topsail was considered for a time as a possible site for the nation's missile launching program, but it was decided that a warmer area would be better, and Cape Canaveral was chosen instead.

So Topsail was sold to real estate developers and two towns, Surf City and Topsail Beach, were incorporated in the 1950s. The fate of the island since gives cause for regretting the sale, for Topsail has the distinction of being the most carelessly and unwisely developed island on the North Carolina coast and is, in fact, a disaster waiting to happen. Development has run wild, and here may be seen mobile home parks very close to the water without protection, finger canals linked with homes cut almost up to the ocean front, and large condominiums constructed dangerously close to an unstable inlet. A huge percentage of the existing buildings on Topsail, including the entire town of Topsail Beach, is located in known flood hazard areas. In 1982, a Corps of Engineers study predicted that during a hurricane, Topsail could expect $35 million in damages from flooding alone, with uncalculated additional damages from high winds, wave action, and erosion.

In the interior of Onslow and Pender counties are large tracts of lands happily owned by the state and managed as wildlife areas and hunting grounds. Hofmann Forest is a 78,000-acre swamp forest managed by the North Carolina Wildlife Commission. The Angola Bay Refuge and the Holly Shelter State Game Management Area are vast wildernesses, valuable resource lands that are preserved remnants of the original lowland swamp ecosystem.

The Onslow Bay coast today presents a contrast between its newer function as a military center and vacation resort and its older traditions. Jacksonville, the largest town in the region, is the creation of the Marine Corps base nearby. The military is the major employer and has brought a measure of prosperity and population growth to an otherwise poor county. But Jacksonville, with its ubiquitous bars, pawnshops, and pleasure houses, has little distinction. The other principal coastal town of the area, Swansboro, presents a marked contrast. Originally settled in the 1720s and incorporated in 1783, Swansboro retains some of the flavor of a pre-Civil War port town with its white-painted houses built on a bluff overlooking the White Oak River. And on the sound overlooking the motels and vacation homes of Surf City, spring plowing is still carried on at Sloop Point, one of the first estates in the area. The house was built in 1726, on a hill that looks across to the ocean, by John Baptista Ashe, whose son John was a leader of the lower Cape Fear area's opposition to the Stamp Act in 1765 and later served as a general in the Revolution.

Farther south is the principal river of the region, the only one large enough to roll boldly into the sea. This is the legendary

Cape Fear, which drains much of the North Carolina piedmont and whose estuary extends for thirty miles below the old seaport town of Wilmington. At the mouth of the river is an island headland called Smith Island. Its large dunes, visible for miles out to sea, caused early sailors to name this end of the island "Bald Head" or "Old Baldy." A line of dangerous shallows called Frying Pan Shoals extends for several miles seaward. These struck dread into the hearts of early mariners, who named the point Cape Fear.

The cape was known to the earliest European explorers of the North Carolina coast. Verrazzano saw it in 1524. Grenville says that his ship, the *Tiger*, was nearly "wrecked at the Cape of Fear," although this was more likely at Cape Lookout. John White, in his account of the 1587 return voyage to the Roanoke colony, recounts that he was "nearly cast away upon the beache, called the Cape of Fear." This was also probably Cape Lookout, but White's maps show that he was certainly aware of Cape Fear. In any case, it is clearly named the Cape of Feare on the Molyneaux globe of 1592.

No account of the origin of the name Cape Fear has ever surpassed that of George Davis, who wrote "An Episode in Cape Fear History" for the *South Atlantic Magazine* in January, 1879:

Looking then to the Cape for the idea and reason of its name, we find that it is the southernmost point of Smith's Island, a naked bleak elbow of sand jutting far out into the ocean. Immediately in its front are Frying Pan Shoals pushing out still farther 20 miles to sea. Together they stand for warning and woe; and together they catch the long majestic roll of the Atlantic as it sweeps through a thousand miles of grandeur and power from the Arctic towards the Gulf. It is the playground of billows and tempests, the kingdom of silence and awe, disturbed by no sound save the sea gull's shriek and the breakers' roar. Its whole aspect is suggestive, not of repose and beauty, but of desolation and terror. Imagination cannot adorn it. Romance cannot hallow it. Local pride cannot soften it. There it stands today, bleak and threatening and pitiless, as it stood three hundred years ago when Grenville and White came near unto death upon its sands. And there it will stand bleak and threatening and pitiless until the earth and sea give up their dead. And as its nature, so its name, is now, always has been, and always will be the Cape of Fear.

The estuary of the Cape Fear River has always been the focal point of human activity on the state's southern coast. The Indians called it Chicora. The Spaniard Lucas Vásquez de Ayllón, who in 1526 tried unsuccessfully to plant a colony on its shores, named the river Jordán and the cape San Romano. In 1662 a group of Puritans from the overcrowded Massachusetts colony were led by William Hilton down to "Clarendon County" (as the region was then called) to settle on the Cape Fear, which was known as the Charles River. They left almost immediately, apparently because the English Crown granted the lands to the Lords Proprietors. In 1664 Englishmen from Barbados, at Hilton's urging, established a settlement called Charles Town on the west bank of the river. They retired in failure in 1667, having alienated the local Indians. Events in London, the Great Plague and the Fire of 1666, prevented any official action to help the colonists.

The Cape Fear River also was the scene of the undoing of Stede Bonnet, one of the most famous pirates of the eighteenth century. A prosperous sugar plantation owner in Barbados, Bonnet went out one day and outfitted a sloop, which he mockingly called the *Royal James*, and began a new life of piracy on the high seas. Legend has it that he chose this life to get away from a nagging wife. In his short career, Bonnet was successful in terrorizing shipping from the Virginia capes to the West Indies.

Bonnet frequently used the Cape Fear River as a harbor of refuge. On September 26, 1718, Colonel William Rhett, with two sloops armed with eight mounted guns each, caught Bonnet at anchor in the Cape Fear. After a fierce exchange of cannon fire, the pirates surrendered. Bonnet was taken to Charleston, where Governor Robert Johnson had him hanged, ignoring his pleas for mercy.

The first permanent settlement in the Cape Fear region grew out of a dispute between North Carolina and her sister colony to the south. In the early eighteenth century, South Carolina claimed ownership of the region and was planning to establish a settlement there. When George Burrington arrived at Edenton, after being appointed governor of North Carolina in 1724, he was quick to realize that the Cape Fear area was a potentially prosperous port and plantation settlement. At the urging of Maurice Moore, a South Carolinian who had fought in the Tuscarora War under his brother James Moore and had stayed in North Carolina, Burrington spent several months at Cape Fear in the winter of 1724–25. He then beat South Carolina to the punch and made grants of land on the river to Moore and his friends. Ignoring South Carolina's claims, Maurice Moore, his brother Roger Moore, and two friends, Eleazer Allen and John Porter, received a total of nine thousand acres. Governor Burrington also acquired large holdings.

Maurice Moore and Burrington (who was removed from office by the Proprietors in July, 1725) dreamed of being recognized as the founders of a new province between North and South Carolina or at least obtaining designation of the Cape Fear as an official port of entry for shipping and trade. In 1727 Moore laid off on the west bank of the Cape Fear a new town, called Brunswick. The choice of this name was an attempt to flatter the reigning monarch, George I, a member of the German House of Brunswick-Hanover. No new colony was created, but in 1729 the North Carolina Assembly established a new county, New Hanover Precinct, also named after the king's family. The boundaries of New Hanover Precinct were not defined, but it extended from a point near the White Oak River south to the boundary with South Carolina, which was still in dispute.

The dispute continued for several years but was finally settled, and a portion of the line was run in 1735. Royal Governor Gabriel Johnston, after a six-week-long conference with South Carolina authorities, agreed that the line should begin at a point thirty miles below the mouth of the Cape Fear River, should run northwest to the 35th parallel, then "due west to the South Seas." The surveying party marched northwest "through Desert and uninhabited Woods in many places impassable." It was apparently very rough going because the party stopped the line several miles short of the 35th parallel. From this point the

Orton Plantation, 1725, on the Cape Fear River. (*Courtesy of N.C. Travel and Tourism Division*)

Poplar Grove Plantation near Wilmington, built during the 1850's. (*Courtesy of N.C. Travel and Tourism Division*)

line was run due west later (in 1764). By this agreement the claim of the North Carolinians was secure.

In the meantime, after the establishment of Brunswick Town in the 1720s, the region was being settled very rapidly. In this, too, colonists from South Carolina were playing an active part. Planters from that colony, especially from Goose Creek, upriver from Charleston, came in, hungry for cheap land and anxious to escape debts they had acquired by buying large numbers of slaves on credit. The cultivation of rice and indigo was introduced. This required river plantations worked by large numbers of black slaves. The Cape Fear quickly became dominated by large plantations; the prototype was Orton Plantation, established near Brunswick Town by "King" Roger Moore.

The growing power of the South Carolina planters concerned the various royal governors of North Carolina. In 1733 Governor George Burrington (who had been appointed by the Crown after it bought out the Proprietors), having broken with his former friends, made a grant of land to John Watson and had James Wimble lay out a town on the site. This was first known as New Town or Newton, but in 1739 it was incorporated as Wilmington and designated the county seat of New Hanover County. This gave Wilmington the all-important courthouse, and Governor Johnston, who succeeded Burrington in 1735, saw to it that the colonial assembly met there from time to time. Brunswick was still the chief port of the region, but its status grew more and more tenuous.

Another blow came in 1748 when the Spanish landed and plundered Brunswick. They were finally driven off by the colonial militia after a fierce fight, during which one of the Spanish ships, the *Fortuna*, exploded and burned. The *Fortuna* was loaded with treasure, much of which was retrieved by the colonists. A painting—the *Ecce Homo*—taken from the ship now hangs in the church house of St. James Episcopal Church in Wilmington. The Spanish attack made clear the exposed position of Brunswick Town on the lower Cape Fear and the more protected position of Wilmington upriver.

Brunswick's last period of prosperity occurred just before the Revolution. Governor Arthur Dobbs liked the climate of the

Cape Fear region and chose to make Brunswick his residence in 1758. He acquired an elegant house named Russellborough, thereafter called "Castle Dobbs," and encouraged the building of St. Phillips Church in the town. In 1762 he shocked the colony by marrying a fifteen-year-old girl, Justina Davis. In 1765 Dobbs died and William Tryon became governor. Tryon lived at Russellborough, which he renamed Bellfont, until his palace at New Bern was completed.

The political unrest that preceded the Revolution began along the Cape Fear after the passage of the Stamp Act in 1765. This law, which subjected documents to a tax, was protested in both Wilmington, where an effigy of Liberty was burned in the streets, and Brunswick, where angry people surrounded the residence of Governor Tryon. In 1775, after Governor Josiah Martin fled his palace at New Bern and took refuge at Fort Johnston at the mouth of the Cape Fear, a group of Whigs led by Cornelius Harnett attacked and burned the fort. This forced Governor Martin to take refuge on the *Cruizer*, a British ship lying offshore.

Governor Martin made one last attempt to regain control of his rebellious colony. He called upon Scottish Highlander settlers loyal to the Crown to assemble at Cross Creek (present Fayetteville) and march down to Wilmington to meet British troops to be brought in by ship up the Cape Fear. Wilmington braced for possible occupation.

Two regiments of American troops under Robert Howe and James Moore marched out to meet the Highlanders at Moore's Creek Bridge, twenty-five miles north of Wilmington. After a short battle, the Tory force was routed, and Wilmington was saved. British troops under Lord Cornwallis sacked Brunswick Town, which had been deserted, but sailed away without attempting to take Wilmington.

Wilmington was spared the rigors of war until 1781. On January 9, Major James Craig and a British force sailed up the Cape Fear and took the city to provide a base for Cornwallis, who was marching up through the Carolinas in an attempt to cut off the southern colonies. After the Battle of Guilford Courthouse on March 15, Cornwallis came to Wilmington to rest and obtain supplies for his troops. After a two-week stay, from April 12 to

25, the British general marched out of Wilmington and headed for Virginia. When news came of Cornwallis's surrender at Yorktown on October 19, Major Craig and his men departed Wilmington for good and sailed out of the Cape Fear.

The period between the Revolution and the Civil War brought prosperity to Wilmington, which became the regional center for the farms and plantations along the Cape Fear. Ships called at the busy port, and in 1840 the Wilmington-Weldon Railroad was completed, providing a transportation link to Virginia and the north. Brunswick Town never regained its former status, however, and by 1830 it had been completely abandoned.

To the north, in Onslow County (created out of New Hanover in 1734), Swansboro served as a minor port during this period, exporting naval stores primarily. Onslow's plantations produced cotton, peanuts, and corn, and three-fifths of the county's population were Negro slaves. The present county seat, Jacksonville, was authorized in 1843 and actually settled about 1849. Richlands, named for the area's fertile soil, has been a farming settlement since 1775. South of Onslow, in the area known as Pender County since 1875, a number of large plantations graced the banks of the Cape Fear: Mosely Hall, Lillington Hall, the Hermitage, Swann Point, and Clayton Hall. They did not survive the Civil War.

At the outbreak of that war, Wilmington was the principal city in North Carolina and one of the most important to the Southern cause. Its geographical location was ideal. Located thirty miles from the sea, it could not be taken easily by Northern troops. The Wilmington-Weldon Railroad provided direct access to Richmond. Two inlets were navigable to the open sea. The main channel of the Cape Fear River, Old Inlet, led out to the west of Smith Island. Another inlet, called New Inlet, which had opened in 1761, allowed access across the bar north of Smith Island.

A system of strong fortifications was erected at the beginning of the war to protect Wilmington. At the entrance to Old Inlet, Forts Caswell and Campbell were built on Oak Island, and Fort Holmes was put up on Smith Island. At Smithville (present Southport), Fort Johnston (also called Fort Pender) was restored. Upriver at Old Brunswick Town, Fort Anderson was constructed. Guarding New Inlet was the strongest fortification of all, Fort Fisher, built in the form of an upside-down "L" with walls twenty-five feet thick and defended with twenty-four guns. Contemporary accounts refer to it as the "Gibraltar of the South."

The Federal fleet blockaded the port of Wilmington throughout the war, but the task was difficult. The two inlets had to be covered by a limited number of ships, and the dangerous Frying Pan Shoals stretched in between. Confederate blockade runners, painted gray with hinged masts lowered close to the deck, slipped in and out of the inlets under the protection of the guns of the shore batteries.

The blockade runners did a profitable business. Cotton, which sold for three cents a pound in the South, could be sold abroad for up to a dollar a pound. On the return voyage, the ships carried guns and supplies for the Confederate armies. Up to a quarter of a million dollars could be made on a single voyage by these ships. As more and more Southern ports fell to the Federals, Wilmington's function grew increasingly indispensable to Lee's army in Virginia. By 1864 Wilmington provided half the supplies and most of the munitions for troops defending Richmond.

In 1864 the Federal authorities in Washington decided something had to be done to close down the port of Wilmington. In December a Federal fleet commanded by Admiral David Porter appeared in the waters off Fort Fisher and prepared to try an assault on the fortress.

The first plan, conceived by General Benjamin Butler, who led the accompanying Union troops, was to explode a ship loaded with powder on the beach in front of the fort. The *Louisiana*, a well-worn old steamer, was selected and prepared. On December 23 the *Louisiana* was towed to within three hundred yards of the beach and the explosion was triggered. Admiral Porter withdrew twelve miles, for it was predicted that buildings as far away as Wilmington would crash to the ground under the shock of the explosion. As it turned out, when the powder boat went up, Colonel William Lamb, commanding at Fort Fisher, merely thought that a Federal blockade vessel had run aground on an offshore bar.

Admiral Porter lost no time in making a second attempt to subdue the fort. On the morning of December 24, he arranged his vessels in a semicircle and began a bombardment. A total of 672 projectiles were fired, but with very little effect. More Union sailors were killed when faulty guns exploded aboard ship than the Confederates lost inside the fort.

On December 25 General Butler landed his troops on the beach above Fort Fisher to try a land-based assault. Admiral Porter continued his offshore bombardment. Butler marched to within fifty yards of the fort but then lost courage and retreated. Butler was in such a hurry to get off the beach that he left a large number of men stranded behind him. Admiral Porter was furious, and the Confederates were jubilant at Butler's failure.

But Porter and the Federals were not about to give up. Reinforcements were sent down from Beaufort, and General Alfred Terry replaced Butler as commander of the Union troops. On January 13, 1865, another assault commenced, with General Terry's troops landing on the beach unopposed while Porter bombarded the fort. The Federal bombardment continued day and night for three days, with up to 100 shells a minute bursting in and around Fort Fisher. On the fifteenth, Terry's troops, with close support from the naval vessels' guns, overwhelmed the fort in hard hand-to-hand fighting. Lamb was wounded and Major James Reilly surrendered the fort, which amazingly had withstood about 50,000 exploding shells without significant damage. Ironically, General Braxton Bragg was camped near Wilmington with 6,000 men, but no effort was made to help the embattled fortress.

After the fall of Fort Fisher, Forts Holmes, Caswell, and Johnston were destroyed and evacuated by their Confederate defenders. One last stand was made at Fort Anderson, on the site of Old Brunswick Town, but it, too, was soon overwhelmed. By February 22 Wilmington was in Federal hands, sealing the doom of Richmond, which was to fall two months later.

Wilmington languished after the war. Lumber and wood products continued to be exported, iron works and fertilizer and textile manufacturing plants were begun, but the city did not keep pace with the cities of the North Carolina piedmont. The railroad was bypassed as a major transportation artery, and racial problems plagued the town. As late as 1910, Wilmington was the largest town in the state; by 1970, it had dropped to ninth in population.

Yet this long period of somnolence had its benefits. Wilmington did not experience the explosive growth of many American cities and avoided the more severe impacts of urban sprawl, renewal, and unimaginative subdivisions. The natural beauty and rural character of the surrounding area was also, to a great degree, unaltered.

Since the late 1960s Wilmington has been enjoying an economic and cultural renaissance that has made it a very pleasant place in which to visit or to live. A significant aspect of this rebirth has been the movement to preserve and restore the architectural and historical monuments of the old city. In 1974 a twenty-block area was listed in the National Register of Historic Places, and the Historic Wilmington Foundation began to purchase and restore many of the important buildings of the past that had fallen into desuetude. New shops and stores were established downtown, many taking over and refurbishing older buildings. The old Cotton Exchange on Water Street now houses restaurants and specialty shops. Chandler's Wharf, at the foot of Ann Street, houses a nautical museum containing historic sailing and fishing vessels that once plied the rivers and sounds of the state. Walking through the streets of Wilmington today, over the grid pattern according to which it was laid out before the American Revolution, is a rewarding experience. An amazing number of commercial, governmental, religious, and residential buildings have survived from the time Wilmington was the state's leading city.

Wilmington is now one of the fastest-growing areas of coastal North Carolina. Its population is projected to increase fifty percent by the year 2000. It is the leading deep-water port in the state, and the volume of business will further increase when the planned Interstate Highway 40 improves its access to the cities of the North Carolina piedmont and the east coast population centers. Major new industrial facilities will be located here.

This new growth presents both opportunities and problems for the city. New commercial, industrial, and housing develop-

This rare picture of old Wilmington shows aspects of the city that can still be recognized today. (*Courtesy of Division of Archives and History, Raleigh, N.C.*)

Chandler's Wharf at Wilmington. (*Courtesy of N.C. Travel and Tourism Division*)

ments will have to be accommodated within the constraints of existing financial and environmental resources. New urban development should be anticipated and guided by planning and legal tools so that municipal services can be extended as economically as possible and natural areas can be preserved. A major constraint to future development will be problems of water supply and quality. Present groundwater supplies are overtaxed, and only the city of Wilmington has a central water system. Most residences and businesses in the county discharge wastes into septic tanks. The lower Cape Fear River as well as the sound areas are experiencing major pollution problems. A countywide water policy is needed to assure adequate future supplies and to alleviate the increasing pollution. It will be a difficult challenge for Wilmington to handle future development in such a way as not to sacrifice the unique character of the city.

Along the ocean side of New Hanover County, a short distance from Wilmington, the barrier islands of the coast provide twenty-seven miles of beautiful sand beaches; on the sound side of the islands there are thousands of acres of marshlands extending in most places to the Intracoastal Waterway channel, which is kept open by constant dredging. Some of these areas are heavily used resorts; others are still practically undisturbed by man. These fragile and attractive areas are among the region's greatest resources. Future policies to guide their use and development will be an important determinant of the character of this part of the coast.

Figure Eight Island, which extends from Rich Inlet to Mason Inlet, is five miles long; access over a private bridge is not allowed without special permission. Beautiful homes have been constructed well back from the beach and in forested areas. The density of development is low, and the natural character of the island has been preserved for the most part. But the price for low-level development has been exacted by excluding everyone but the owners from the area.

South of Mason Inlet, the island of Wrightsville Beach, a playground for the masses, has been extensively developed. The natural dunes and the marine forest have long since disappeared. Government, especially the U.S. Army Corps of Engineers, as

Thalian Hall, Wilmington, as it appeared in 1895. (*Courtesy of Thalian Hall Archives*)

Burgwin-Wright House, Wilmington. (*Courtesy of Division of Archives and History, Raleigh, N.C.*)

well as private owners of beach property, has spent large sums to control beach erosion here, and it is likely to continue to be called upon to do so.

Wrightsville is one of the oldest beach resorts in North Carolina. In 1888 the Wilmington Sea Coast Railway was constructed between Wilmington and the Hammocks, an island in Wrightsville Sound.* A footbridge was built across Banks Channel to the barrier island beach. In 1902 an electric railway line was built across the channel and extended up and down the strand. Hotels and pavilions as well as private cottages were constructed on the island. The best-known hotel was the legendary Lumina, which became famous all over the South as a summer resort. Soft dance music in a glittering pavilion, walks on the moonlit beach, and the smell and sound of the ocean surf in front of Lumina are forever etched in thousands of memories.

Today you cross the sound in a car over a major highway; the railroad is no more. The Hammocks—Harbor Island as it is now called—has been diked and filled. The live oak trees are remnants of a much larger marine forest. The highway continues over Banks Channel to the beach, now filled completely with the works of man. The route of the former electric railway has been paved over and is now Lumina Avenue. Just to the south of the point where the highway meets Lumina Avenue, there is a place by the side of the road still called Station One, the first stop of the old railroad. The Blockade Runner Hotel is at old Station Three. It is the third hotel on this site. At Station Seven is the site of the triple-decked Lumina, torn down in 1973.

Wrightsville Beach is a good example of what a commitment to counteracting the natural shoreward migration of a barrier island means. Wrightsville was densely developed by the 1920s. By the 1950s erosion had become a major problem; the dunes had disappeared or had been removed, and storms and hurricanes devastated the island.

Instead of taking advantage of the opportunity to plan the future development of the island with natural forces in mind, the Army Corps of Engineers decided to fight erosion and return the island to its original profile insofar as possible. In 1965 they con-

*This should not be confused with Hammocks Beach State Park, discussed earlier in the chapter.

The old Lumina, Wrightsville Beach. (*Courtesy of Division of Archives and History, Raleigh, N.C.*)

structed a 2.7-mile-long berm to create an artificial dune line. Then more than 3 million cubic yards of sand and dredge spoil were pumped onto the beach in front of the berm in a process engineers call "beach nourishment." In 1970 another 1.5 million cubic yards of dredge spoil were added.

The result is an artificial beach of coarse, rough material unpleasant to the touch. Along paths leading to the beach there are signs that warn "Danger Dune Eroded Sharp Drop." The action of the waves reflecting against the artificial berm has created a sharp escarpment. Even this unsatisfactory situation can be maintained only by periodic expenditures of ever-greater sums of public tax money; but the ocean will have its way in the end.

It is not hard to spot other examples of development mistakes on Wrightsville Beach. In several places streets have been bulldozed down to and perpendicular to the beach. These are convenient channels for storm waves crashing over the island.

At the north end of the island, a high-rise Holiday Inn has been built on the oceanfront. This is on the site of Moore's Inlet, which formerly separated Wrightsville Beach from Shell Island to the north. In 1965 the Corps of Engineers filled in the inlet, using dredged material from the flood-tide delta in the sound, making Shell Island merely the northern extension of Wrightsville Beach. The Holiday Inn is not only on an artificially filled inlet; it has been built right out on the beach, protected only by a seawall from the storm waves.

Just south of Wrightsville Beach, across Masonboro Inlet, is a narrow, overwashed sand bank called Masonboro Island. It is still in its natural state, the nesting place for many shorebirds. Because of its low elevation and narrow width, it cannot be easily developed and has been acquired by the state for use as an estuarine reserve, a natural area that can be visited for study and recreation.

South of Masonboro Island, the shore is once again heavily developed down to the Fort Fisher State Historic Site. Three towns—Carolina Beach, Wilmington Beach, and Kure Beach—run together in a continuous strip of motels, stores, and beach apartments. Carolina Beach is the most vulnerable to erosion, and the town has been lobbying for state and federal funds to protect the shoreline. Ironically, much of the erosion problem is due to the opening of Carolina Beach Inlet by artificial means in 1952. This cuts off the supply of sand coming from the south on the longshore currents. Since the opening of the inlet, a seawall has been constructed, and an artificial berm with beach nourishment has been used to try to stabilize the beach. Thirty-five years of shoreline engineering has only produced demands for additional and more costly projects.

The Fort Fisher Historic Site terminates at Federal Point, which was called Confederate Point until 1865. More than half of the old fort has eroded into the sea. Until the 1880s New Inlet existed here between the mainland and Smith Island to the south. At that time a dam was constructed to close the inlet and to protect the main channel which extends all the way to Smith Island. Nevertheless, this was constructed in an inlet-prone area, and a much smaller version of New Inlet reopened here in 1938. It is still open and is migrating south along this very unstable edge of beach.

Smith Island, the headland of Cape Fear and part of Brunswick County, is considered by many to be the most beautiful of all the islands of the North Carolina coast. Shaped like an irregular triangle, it comprises more than 12,000 acres, 3,000 of which

The beautiful marine forest on Smith (Bald Head) Island is a priceless asset of the North Carolina coast. (*Courtesy of Division of Archives and History, Raleigh, N.C.*)

A view of the surf from a fishing pier at Carolina Beach. (*Courtesy of N.C. Travel and Tourism Division*)

are high land. The island is a series of relict beach ridges facing the sea. The largest and southernmost of these is Bald Head, named for the rounded high dune at its southwest tip.

The south face of Bald Head is a beautiful sandy beach with well-developed high dunes experiencing relatively little erosion. At the western end are the remains of Fort Holmes and the now abandoned Bald Head Lighthouse, constructed in 1817. Most of the Bald Head high land is covered with a lush maritime forest, the only extensive barrier island forest now remaining on the North Carolina coast. Live oaks three to four feet in diameter are common, and large sabal palmettos give the forest a subtropical appearance. The forest canopy reaches a height of forty feet in many areas.

North of the forested area and east of the channel of the Cape Fear River are extensive marshes intersected by tidal creeks and interspersed with wooded hammocks of high ground. Many of these islands are nesting sites for herons and ibises. Battery and Striking islands in the Cape Fear River are noted bird nesting areas. Bluff Island is large enough to contain a freshwater pond frequented by many species of ducks and shorebirds.

The north-south beach of Smith Island is, by contrast, severely eroding at the rate of up to five feet per year. Open to the full fury of the waves of the Atlantic, it has been the site of numerous inlets. Corncake Inlet was open for many years, and Hazel's Inlet opened in 1954 and has since closed.

Smith Island was first patented to Thomas Smith of South Carolina in 1690, but it has never been extensively settled. In the nineteenth century, it was used primarily as a Coast Guard outpost, and lighthouses existed at both ends of Bald Head. By the early twentieth century, it was considered practically worthless and was twice taken over by the county for nonpayment of taxes.

Various proposals to develop the island have been made. The most ambitious was the plan of a firm known as Rader and Associates in 1963. This involved bulldozing the entire area to a flat, uniform elevation of 8 feet above mean low tide and constructing 125 miles of canals and a resort for 60,000 permanent residents and 15,000 summer visitors and conventioners. Another proposal for development was made in 1969 by Charles Fraser, who wanted to create an exclusive resort similar to Hilton Head, South Carolina. These plans were abandoned after the State of North Carolina expressed its opposition. State authorities expressed the view that the island should be acquired as a state park, but no action was ever taken on this proposal.

In 1970 Smith Island was acquired by the Carolina Cape Fear Corporation, which had a new development plan. An exclusive vacation resort community for 10,000 people would be created in three stages. In the first stage the western end of Bald Head would be developed with a golf course, clubhouse, and the sale of 1,141 residential building lots. The eastern half of the island would be developed in the second stage with the construction of another golf course and the sale of 600 lots. In the third stage, Middle Island, immediately north of Bald Head, would be developed at a density of 1.9 units per acre.

Access to the island was the major problem in implementing this plan. State and federal officials at first opposed the development plan, turning down requests for a bridge and even a permit for docking facilities. The reasons given at the time, in 1972, were that the development of the island would "disrupt a vast fish and wildlife habitat of unique value," create a serious risk to public safety by locating a large population on a remote island, and impose a burden on the public treasury of future demands for hurricane protection. Then, in 1974, a deal was struck between the state and the developers. A marina permit was granted in exchange for a quitclaim deed to the state of the 10,000 acres of marshlands and outlying islands.

Two conservation organizations, the Sierra Club and the Conservation Council of North Carolina, brought suit, charging that the permit had been illegally issued, and a protracted and bitter court battle took place. During the long fight, Carolina Cape Fear Corporation went bankrupt, and the island was taken over by its principal creditor, Business Investment Group (BIG) of Valley Forge, Pennsylvania. In 1976 the conservationists' lawsuit was ended when the courts failed to stop the project, even though it was found that federal officials as well as the developer had violated several legal provisions.

Bald Head Island Corporation, a subsidiary of BIG, is now selling lots and plans to develop the island according to Carolina Cape Fear's three-stage plan. A golf course and several homes have already been built, and lot sales for Stage One are continuing. Some of the marine forest has been cut.

But many people think Smith Island has not been completely tamed yet. Lot sales are going rather slowly, and the success of the latest development plan is not yet assured. Much of the island is still the same as it was when the first explorers arrived at Cape Fear. Unforeseen quirks of fate may yet determine the island's destiny as they have so many times in the past.

Across the Cape Fear Inlet to the west of Smith Island on historic Long Bay are the Brunswick County barrier island beaches. The largest, Oak Island, includes the three communities of Caswell Beach, Yaupon Beach, and Long Beach. At the eastern end of Caswell Beach are the ruins of the Civil War Fort Caswell, destroyed by retreating Confederate troops in 1865, and the Coast Guard lighthouse, newer and less picturesque than others of its genre. Across Lockwoods Folly Inlet is the six-mile-long island of Holden Beach, extensively developed except at the western end near Shallotte Inlet, which has a history of migration. Next is Ocean Isle Beach, where a building boom has taken place. Across Tubbs Inlet to the west is Sunset Beach, a small island relatively undeveloped but catching up fast. Mad Inlet to the west is aptly named, since its channel meanders but can be walked across at low tide to Bird Island, a small uninhabited and beautiful place on the South Carolina border.

These islands have the warmest climate and are among the most beautiful in the state, with broad sandy beaches and, for the most part, natural dunes. On the sound side, thick marsh grass is bathed in the tides. Patches of the live oak marine forest still exist in protected and unbuilt areas. Access from the mainland is by causeway, which intersects a sand roadway running parallel to the beach.

Virtually all the development of these islands has occurred within the last twenty-five years. In 1954, Hurricane Hazel made a direct hit on these beaches, sweeping them clean. For some time thereafter land prices were depressed and houses were built behind the dunes. In the late 1960s and early '70s land prices soared, and the density of development increased dramatically. Beach houses were built on tiny lots crowded together to fulfill the demand for a place near the ocean shore. The shrub-forest vegetation was cut, and subdivisions were plotted from sea to sound. Finger canals were created in some places on the sound side to give greater access to water.

The process of development is continuing apace on the islands. There is apparently unlimited demand for use of a very fragile and limited resource. The situation should be controlled, taking into consideration the natural constraints of the barrier island system. Some of the natural realities that need to be considered are the fact that erosion is occurring on the oceanfront and near the inlets, except for certain well-vegetated areas in the middle of Sunset Beach and Ocean Isle Beach. Even these would be overwashed in a major storm or hurricane. In addition, groundwater supplies are limited, and the density of development and the use of septic tanks have created the necessity of importing fresh water from the mainland to supply the current level of development. But the complete urbanization of these islands is not what most of the people who use them want. The result would be the elimination of the natural, "family beach" atmosphere, increased pollution of the marshes and sounds, increased traffic, roadways, and commercial development, and the need to engage in expensive erosion control projects. Recently a longtime owner of beach property, Rhoda Holden McMillan, wrote in a letter to the Raleigh *News and Observer*:

I own a cottage and other real estate at Holden Beach which is on land that has been in my family since 1756. More development has taken place there since 1956 than in all the previous 200 years. The island can simply not stand another 20 years of uncontrolled development, else it will be sliced into narrow asphalt covered strips lying between silt-filled canals.

Yet every year more houses and condominiums are built, with no end in sight.

The mainland area of Brunswick County is still rural in character. The major towns are support centers for the recreational

Oak Island Lighthouse stands at the eastern end of Caswell Beach. (*Courtesy of N.C. Travel and Tourism Division*)

Shrimp boats are a familiar sight near Southport. (*Courtesy of N.C. Travel and Tourism Division*)

beaches and the farming and forestry operations. The town of Calabash near the South Carolina border is famous for the more than twenty seafood restaurants which are crowded with visitors each summer season. Shallotte is a center of commercial activity. Southport is the supply source for Oak Island and caters to boaters using the Intracoastal Waterway. It is a quiet town with beautiful frame houses along its waterfront. The Brunswick Nuclear Power Plant has been constructed just north of Southport by the Carolina Power and Light Company in order to take advantage of the abundant flow of the Cape Fear River to cool its condensers. An intake canal has been dug from the river to the plant, and a discharge canal conveys the heated effluent to a pumping station on Oak Island, where two pipes, 13 feet in diameter, convey the water 2,000 feet into the ocean. The Environmental Protection Agency has expressed concern over the possible impact of the heated effluent on marine life.

North of Shallotte and just east of N.C. 211 is one of the most important and interesting areas of coastal North Carolina. The Green Swamp covers almost 25,000 acres of wild wetland pine savannahs and the dense evergreen shrub bogs called pocosins. Here grow the largest variety of carnivorous plants in the nation. Pitcher plants, sundews, Venus flytraps, and other plants have developed the amazing ability to attract and entrap small insects, which are slowly digested by enzymes the plants produce. This is a biological adaptation that enables them to thrive in nutrient-poor soil. Fourteen varieties of these plants are found here.

Other interesting plant communities are present also. The pine savannahs contain at least ten species of wild orchids as well as sedges, ferns, cane, and wild huckleberry. There are at least two distinct types of pocosins, identified and mapped by ecologist Russell Kologiski. The pine-ericalean pocosin consists of stunted, gnarled pond pine trees and, underneath, a thicket of evergreen shrubs, titi, zenobia, fetterbush, and gallberry. Thorny vines grow entwined among the shrubs, and the ground is covered with thick, spongy sphagnum moss. In the second variety of pocosin, the pine trees are better developed, and red maple and black gum also grow in the evergreen shrub thicket. The sphagnum groundcover is not as thick. This is a transitional plant community whose next stage is the bay forest, which is found in higher and drier areas of the swamp and is made up of red maple, pond cypress, black gum trees, and, rarely, Atlantic white cedar. This wilderness is the home and last refuge for many animals and birds. The eastern cougar roams here, as do alligators, bears, bobcats, deer, minks, and otters. Rare birds include the Bachman's warbler, bald eagle, peregrine falcon, and red-cockaded woodpecker. The people of the region are interesting too; they live in the backwoods, regarding outsiders with suspicion, and no one is sure of their origin. Some of them are thought to be descended from Portuguese pirates cast away on the coast in the seventeenth century.

The Green Swamp is named for John Green, who was granted the area by the English Crown before the Revolution. The swamp originally extended over 200,000 acres, but most of it has been ditched and drained and is now used for farming and timber production. The roughly 25,000 acres that are left were designated by the Department of the Interior as a National Natural Landmark in 1974. This was owned by the Federal Paper Board Company of New York, which recently donated the southern half—13,850 acres—to The Nature Conservancy. If at all possible, the remainder of this unique place should be permanently preserved in its natural state.

The Cape Fear region presents a varied panorama of wilderness and highly developed beaches, urban centers, and impenetrable lowland swamps. With care, it can continue to serve these varied functions in the future.

III

Protecting the Coastal Heritage

12

Coastal Legal Battles

FEW PEOPLE, WHEN THEY VISIT THEIR FAVORITE BEACH OR guide their boat through a marsh channel, worry about whose property they are using. But it is important who owns these areas. The laws of private property operate on the coastal margin as well as farther inland. If a beach, a marsh, or the bottom of a sound is privately owned, it can theoretically be developed, and the owner can exclude the rest of the world from using it.

Fortunately, those who assume they have a right to swim, boat, and fish in coastal waters are right. The legal theory upon which this right depends goes back to medieval England. In medieval times—about the thirteenth century—it became established that the king, then the personal proprietor of all England, held those lands over which the tides ebbed and flowed in trust for his subjects. This guaranteed the people the right to navigate and fish without royal interference.

This "public trust" doctrine, as it is called, was carried over and refined by American law. Judges in this country decided that the important thing was to protect the right to navigate in ocean water, sounds, rivers, and lakes. If a body of water was navigable, its bottom could not be privately owned, and it was held by the state in trust for the people. The dividing line between private ownership of the shoreline and public trust lands was held to be the mean of all the high tides over a lunar cycle of 18.6 years, in the case of tidal waters, or the ordinary high-water mark, in the case of non-tidal waters.

In North Carolina this high-water boundary line has always been the applicable legal rule. The bottomlands of coastal sounds and rivers thus belong to the state. The tidelands along the oceanfront and coastal marshlands below mean high water also may be claimed under this legal doctrine. Offshore shoals and islands that are raised are likewise the property of the state. Private property rights stop at the water's edge.

Still, this does not end controversy over the boundary between private and public areas. The mean-high-water line cannot be located on a beach. There is no physical mark, nor can there be. Mean high water changes constantly over time because the sea itself is variable. The beach sands also change in response to the natural forces of littoral drift, overwash, and island migration—what people commonly call erosion and accretion.

The law is inadequate for formulating a legal rule to express these shoreline changes and resolve the difficulties over property rights. The best it has been able to do is to devise the rule that the shore owner gets the benefit of any accretion and must bear the loss of any erosion of his property. In the case of a sudden change in the shoreline—called an *avulsion*—the owner has the right to take remedial action to restore the loss.

In addition to natural changes in the shoreline, to complicate the situation there are also man-made changes. A shoreline owner cannot take action to raise land above the high-water mark without obtaining an "easement to fill" from the state; if he does so without such an easement, the new land belongs to the state. There is a big loophole in this law, however. If the purpose of the fill is to reclaim land lost by natural processes, no easement is required. This has meant that a great deal of filling is done without a permit. Even where a permit is required, it has up to now been automatically granted by the state property office. State officials have too often simply refused to recognize any responsibility to protect public trust rights against fills by shoreline owners. They have mistakenly assumed that the rights of private owners outweigh public ownership rights.

Yet another problem about using the high-water mark as a significant boundary is that, until 1959, the State of North Carolina officially allowed coastal marsh and swamplands to be purchased by individuals. These areas were considered wastelands, and the state was only too glad to see them transferred to private owners who might find some profitable use for them. Many of the lands granted were below the mean-high-water mark. But no one kept track of which lands were granted and who the owners were. Many people claimed ownership of marshlands in the hope that they would someday become valuable. It was impossible to tell whether or not the claims were valid.

In 1965 the state took action to try to sort out the real claims from the false ones. A law was passed requiring all persons claiming ownership of land below mean high water to register with the state. The idea was that government officials would bring legal challenges against questionable claims. The courts gave them some ammunition by saying no claim to marshlands was valid unless the owner could show an unbroken chain of title back to the original state grant. But few challenges were ever brought, and the data compiled lies gathering dust in Raleigh. No political official wanted to risk the consequences of alienating the claim-holders.

Even after 1959, when the sale of state lands was prohibited by law, grants continued to be made by the state. One of the largest involved a 1962 conveyance of navigable waters at Figure Eight Island. In 1971 a young law student working as a summer intern for the state attorney general came to me. He told me he was researching the question of whether the state could bring suit to reclaim the 156 acres illegally granted at Figure Eight Island. He told me he had concluded that the state would be successful and had recommended that the suit be brought. A few months later I asked him what had become of the Figure Eight lawsuit. He told me that the matter had been dropped because of the potential political consequences of the lawsuit.

Fortunately, the public has some rights even where private owners claim control over offshore areas. In one litigated case

(*State* v. *Twiford*), the private owner, a woman from New Jersey, blocked off Jean Guite Creek in Currituck Sound, claiming ownership of the creek bottom. The court examined the evidence of past use of the creek as a harbor of protection from storms and a thoroughfare for the public. It said that the grant of land under navigable water was void, but that even if the land were privately owned, the public would have an easement to pass by boat over the area. This means that even private owners of small creeks and marshland cannot prevent public access by boat.

Another case arose out of a rather curious publicity stunt. In the summer of 1965, Larry Capune began a trip from Coney Island, New York, to Florida, using an eighteen-foot-long paddleboard. "I would paddle it with my hands and steer with my feet," he explained. "Paddling, I placed my arms in front of me and pulled down alongside the board." Capune had already made a similar trip down the west coast.

This unusual voyage was rudely interrupted when Capune got to the Morehead Ocean Pier, which extends a thousand feet out into the ocean from Bogue Banks. Space on the pier was rented out to sport fishermen, and to protect his business, the owner, John Robbins, did not allow any boating, surfing, or swimming within 150 feet of the pier. On August 15, Capune, innocent of any knowledge of the restrictions, blithely paddled toward the pier, intending to go under it to the other side. Incensed at this behavior, Robbins ran out on the pier, yelling, "Go back where you came from!" Before Capune had a chance to react, Robbins began throwing soft-drink bottles at him. The third bottle found its mark, and Capune received a head wound requiring twenty-four stitches to close.

In the ensuing lawsuit, the principal question was whether Capune had any right to paddle under the pier. The court answered by saying that the shoreline owner may be able to build a pier into the water from his property, but this does not affect the right of the public to pass under the pier without being molested. So, while Capune had to give up his venture and never reached Florida, he gained the distinction of having helped to create an important point of coastal law.

But despite the long history of these legal doctrines that give the public important rights in the coastal zone—the public trust, navigability, and the mean-high-water line—it is obvious that they are inadequate to the management of coastal resources and the environment. They are not respected either by nature or by man. They are the products of an age when people did not understand the natural and physical processes of the coast and did not use the area as we do today.

When people go to the North Carolina beaches for fishing or recreation, they do not stay seaward of the high-water mark. They consider the area to be open at least up to the frontal dunes. The high-water mark is not relevant. Nor is it relevant to the ecosystems of the coastal area. The barrier island system cannot be managed at the water's edge; all the component parts have a function that must be preserved. The dunes store sand necessary for the maintenance of the island, absorb storm waves, and shelter onshore areas. They are constantly shifting in response to wave and wind action. There is also a constant interchange of sand and sediment between sea and shore, so that the whole system is in a state of dynamic equilibrium with respect to the multiple forces of its environment. The maritime forests and other vegetation play a key role in maintaining this equilibrium and in retaining the thin lens of fresh groundwater floating on top of the heavier salt water beneath the sands.

The mean-high-water mark is likewise inadequate in defining the other major coastal ecosystem—the estuary, where large flows of fresh water meet salt water. Integral parts of the estuarine ecosystems are the salt marshes found behind barrier islands, along the fringes of bays and sounds, and along tidal streams and creeks. The marsh serves as a buffer between the shore and estuary and is the habitat for many plants and animals. The decaying organic material produced by the marsh (*detritus*) is the basis of the marine food chain for many animals, including most commercially valuable finfish and shellfish and thus for man himself. Marsh grasses grow not only below the ordinary high-water line but also on higher, irregularly flooded areas. Also essential to the functioning of the estuarine system are the million-and-a-half acres of swamp forests of the North Carolina coast, which grow on river floodplains and in moist, peaty soil, as well as the more than 2.2 million acres of pocosins of the coastal plain. These habitats interact with the estuary by retaining excessive fresh-water flows that would upset the salinity balance, purifying water runoff, and maintaining the groundwater table. They are also used by man for fishing, hunting, and forestry, and they are some of the most important wildlife areas in the southeast.

Despite all this, the law has gone beyond the relatively safe confines of the "ordinary high water" boundary only with the greatest of difficulty. The first battles were fought over the beaches and the supposed right of the owner to close off the dry-sand area above mean high tide. Courts in Oregon and California responded by saying even privately owned beach property could not be blocked off if the public had obtained an implied easement through custom or by long years of uninterrupted recreational use. In addition, some states passed laws allowing people to use the beach to the first line of visible vegetation. North Carolina has not yet accepted these doctrines, but in 1969 the General Assembly passed legislation that at least established beach preservation lines and regulated development on the beach and frontal dunes.

The real fight in North Carolina has been over the wetlands and marshes. In the early 1960s ecologists such as Art Cooper of North Carolina State University called attention to the value and beauty of the estuary and coastal wetlands. In 1967 Dave Adams, the state commissioner of fisheries, called for a "unified effort" by government to protect these resources. These ideas were presented to the interagency Council on Natural Resources, and on November 21, 1967, an Estuarine Study Committee was formed to "develop a comprehensive state program for multiple use of the state's estuaries and to present this program in time for implementation by the 1969 General Assembly."

The Estuarine Study Committee was skillfully managed by Adams and Milton Heath, a lawyer on the staff of the University of North Carolina Institute of Government. Their report called for a new approach to estuarine resources consisting of four parts: (1) a continuing inventory of the state's wetlands was to be maintained; (2) all public projects affecting the estuaries were to be reviewed; (3) the state was to begin a program of marshland acquisition; and (4) private development in wetlands was to be controlled.

These recommendations were acted upon by the 1969 General Assembly, which passed the Dredge and Fill Permit Act. This law required that any person desiring to carry out any excavation or filling in of tidelands or marshlands must first obtain a permit from the state. The application for a permit could be denied if there was a "significant adverse effect" on use by the public, or on wildlife or marine resources. The particularly interesting thing about this legislation is the way "marshland" was legally defined. The "ordinary high water mark" principle is nowhere to be found. Instead, marshland—and thus the area to be regulated—is defined in terms of the species of vegetation commonly found in coastal wetland habitats: saltwater cordgrass, black needlerush, cattail, salt-meadow grass, and the like. The law had finally discovered ecology and had entered the environmental era. In 1971 the legislation was strengthened to allow still more protection for wetlands. The Department of Natural and Economic Resources was empowered to issue orders protecting specifically designated areas of coastal wetland. This meant that the state could act to preserve marshland *before* it was threatened by development. A protective order would put potential developers on notice that certain lands were not to be disturbed.

But it soon became apparent that passing legislation is one thing and implementing it quite another. Although many people observed the law and became conscious of the necessity of preserving wetlands, difficulties arose. Because of political opposition, the Department of Natural and Economic Resources never issued any protective orders, and that part of the law became a dead letter. Applications for permits were almost never denied. In addition, illegal dredging and filling activities took place, and the small enforcement staff was inadequate to deal with them. After a permit was granted, it was often impossible to tell whether the conditions of the permit were observed or even whether the developer viewed it as a license to fill additional wetlands beyond the scope of the permit. Violations of the law were treated benignly by the courts. In one case the judge in a coastal county fined a convicted violator one cent, declaring that he intended to do a lot of dredging himself.

In the face of weak enforcement and implementation by the state, environmentalists next sought help from federal authorities. Two laws, Section 10 of the 1899 Rivers and Harbors Act and Section 404 of the Federal Water Pollution Control Act, set federal standards for developmental activities in navigable waters. Unfortunately, these laws were administered by the U.S. Army Corps of Engineers, the federal agency most involved in coastal development through its massive shoreline engineering and navigation projects. This fox-in-the-hen-house was not about to take an active role in regulating private development. It considered the mean-high-water line the limit of its jurisdiction.

Environmental groups finally sued to force the Corps to recognize its responsibility to protect the nation's wetlands. One of these lawsuits involved the construction of a marina on Smith Island at the mouth of the Cape Fear. I served as the attorney for the plaintiffs, the Conservation Council of North Carolina and the Sierra Club.

The developers of the marina were clever enough to construct the marina above the mean-high-water line. They simply dug a big hole on the high ground and a connecting channel to the Cape Fear River. They obtained a permit to dig the channel but followed the Corps' advice that they did not need a permit to destroy the wetlands above mean high water.

One of our main contentions and objectives in bringing suit against the marina project was to get a court ruling that the Corps had jurisdiction to regulate wetlands growing above mean high tide. We thought that the court should require the Corps to prepare an environmental impact statement before allowing destruction of the wetlands and the development of Smith Island.

When we filed suit, in June, 1974, we had no idea what we were getting into. Within a few days, I was receiving anonymous phone calls from employees of the U.S. Department of the Interior in Washington. They told me a story of political influence and intrigue involved in getting the permit to build the marina. I was soon being sent secretly copied documents from Interior's files. From these documents it became clear that high officials at

Interior had ordered all lower-level departmental offices to rec-
ommend to the Corps that the permit be allowed. These included the Raleigh field office, the Atlanta regional office, and
the Washington staffers of Interior, all of whom thought the permit application should be denied.

The lawsuit had disrupted these carefully laid plans. The atmosphere was tense and bitter, and feelings ran strong on both
sides. We were opposed by lawyers for the developers and the
Corps as well as by the Department of Justice in Washington and
the North Carolina attorney general. The developers and the
Corps thought they could end things quickly by contesting
the right of the plaintiffs to bring suit; that way they could avoid
the merits of the case. This tactic backfired. Although Federal
District Court Judge John Larkins ruled in their favor, the environmentalists appealed, and Judge Braxton Craven of the U.S.
Court of Appeals for the Fourth Circuit issued an order prohib-
iting the construction of the marina pending appeal. Now the
project was stopped, and time was on the side of the environmentalists.

The appeal to the Fourth Circuit proved inconclusive since
the court said that further proceedings were necessary to determine whether the plaintiffs could bring suit. On November 7,
1974, the day after the appeal was decided, the lawyers for the
developers went before Judge Larkins to ask him to dissolve the
injunction. The plaintiffs countered this motion by pointing out
that the case was still before the Fourth Circuit and they were
preparing a petition for rehearing by that court. Judge Larkins
agreed that the injunction could not be lifted.

But the attorneys for the developers were not easily thwarted;
they left the hearing, chartered a private plane for Richmond,
and obtained an order from Judge Clement Haynesworth sending the case down to Judge Larkins in the District Court. Despite the fact that we were not given any notice of this unusual
procedure, Judge Larkins quickly lifted the injunction, once
again allowing work on the marina to proceed. But Larkins also
ruled that the environmentalists should be allowed to bring suit,
so more court battles were to follow before the wetlands issue
could be resolved.

Another hearing was held before Judge Larkins on May 15, 1975. Another new and unexpected development occurred. It was found that the developers had not complied with the condition of the permit that required them to give a quitclaim deed of the 10,000 acres of wetlands at Smith Island to the State of North Carolina. Instead of giving the deed to an independent escrow agent, as they had promised, they had simply given the deed to their own attorney. An angry Judge Larkins issued a new injunction against the marina, and he announced he would hand down a written opinion on the other legal issues involved.

This triggered additional unusual events. The most bizarre was a handwritten note about the case that someone anonymously provided us, which cryptically referred to "$50,000 under the table." We never discovered the meaning of this. In addition, my superior, Dean Robert Byrd of the University of North Carolina School of Law, received several phone calls and letters complaining about my involvement in the case. Steve Berg, then a reporter for the Raleigh *News and Observer*, was given a VIP tour of the island. On his return he called me and said that people were saying it was wrong for me as a state employee to become involved in the litigation. He asked me whether my work on the case was "on the university's time." I replied that I worked on the case at night and on weekends, and as long as university professors were allowed to consult for oil companies and private industry, I would work for environmental organizations. His story that appeared the next day on the Smith Island development did not mention the issue.

On July 24, 1975, Judge Larkins finally released his decision on the case. He ruled that coastal wetlands shoreward of the mean-high-water mark contribute to the productivity of the estuary and thus were within the jurisdiction of the Corps of Engineers. Although the judge refused to further enjoin the construction of the marina, saying the violation of law was a minimal, technical one, the important principle had been won: the Corps could no longer refuse to regulate development in wetlands above the mean-high-water line.

By the time the Corps of Engineers was forced by environmentalists and the courts to become concerned about the consequences of shoreland development, the federal government had initiated new action to manage coastal resources. In 1966 the Congress established the Commission on Marine Science, Engineering and Resources to prepare a report on "the preservation of our coastal shores and estuaries." Another study commissioned in 1966 was a report on pollution in estuarine areas of the country. These efforts culminated in the passage of the Federal Coastal Zone Management Act of 1972. This law provided money and other incentives to coastal states to encourage them to establish a comprehensive plan for management of coastal lands and waters. Participation was voluntary, however; no state was forced to respond. But if a state accepted federal money, its program had to conform to minimum federal standards.

In North Carolina by the late 1960s, the future of the coast was a hot political issue. North Carolinians were accustomed to thinking of their state's coastal area as their own proprietary preserve. Because of the relative isolation of the North Carolina coast and the pattern of east-west highways, the coastal area received relatively few visitors from other states. Most of the people who enjoyed the traditional pursuits on the North Carolina coast were coastal residents themselves or people who drove in from the piedmont or the mountains of North Carolina on a regular basis.

At this time there were virtually no restrictions on what could or could not be done on the wild and beautiful lands and waters of the coast. To many it became clear that the North Carolina coast was quite literally being loved to death. Residential, commercial, and agricultural development were proceeding to the point of threatening the very natural resources on which they depended. As the integrity of the natural systems was drawn into question, so too was the traditional way of life of the people of the coastal area. From one season to the next there were perceptible changes: pollution of coastal waters, declines in fishery production, overbuilding, and the disappearance of the marine forests and wildlife.

By the early 1970s a consensus was reached that something fundamental had to be done to ameliorate this situation. As a law professor at the University of North Carolina at Chapel Hill, I participated in an effort, joined by hundreds of other people, to formulate a comprehensive plan to deal with the issues that would arise in the future on the North Carolina coast. It was a time when the environmental movement was at its height, and there was political support for environmentally protective legislation. Yet, as expected, there was great opposition to any governmental measure that would restrict the right of any landowner on the coast to do what he wished with his property.

Fortunately we started out with the fact that a significant portion of the coast of North Carolina was already in public ownership. The two national seashores, Cape Hatteras and Cape Lookout, together comprise 127 miles of public shoreline. Add the other islands that are located in areas owned by the federal and state governments and one finds that about 48 percent of coastal North Carolina is in public ownership. These public lands could be managed in a way so as to benefit the general public. Our aim was to concentrate on the lands and waters which were not in public ownership in order to protect the resources involved. Our purpose was not to destroy private ownership rights but rather to enhance them by assuring the right balance of development and conservation of resources in order to preserve the undoubted charms of the coast and the historical, social, cultural, and economic balance of the coastal area.

In 1972, I found myself in charge of an effort to draft a new law for the comprehensive management of the North Carolina coast. What we came up with is now known as CAMA, which stands for the Coastal Area Management Act. It took two long years of public debate and political action for this measure to be enacted into law. Finally in 1974 the General Assembly of the state adopted this legislation after one of the most bitter political fights in the history of the state. But the enactment of the law hardly finished matters. It took four long and hard years of additional work to mount a program and to get it to the point where it merited approval by the federal government. In addition, the law was attacked in the courts as unconstitutional. But 1978 was a banner year; not only was CAMA approved and accepted by the federal government, but it was also declared constitutional by the North Carolina Supreme Court.*

CAMA has made a huge difference in the way the North Car-

*Adams v. North Carolina, 249 S.E. 2d 402 (N.C. Sup. Ct. 1978).

olina coast has been developed in the last ten years. Although mistakes have been made, the administration of the law has been extremely wise. A balance has been struck between the paths of unlimited development on the one hand and total environmental protection on the other. Most experts regard North Carolina's program of coastal management as the most successful and well rounded of any state.

CAMA established both a planning program and a regulatory program for the coast. The policy decisions for both programs are in the hands of a unique state body, the Coastal Resources Commission (CRC), which is made up of fifteen persons appointed by the governor, the majority of whom are residents of the coastal counties themselves. It is important to note that the CRC members are not government bureaucrats. They are citizens and coastal residents who are asked to resolve the conflicts and to set out action guidelines for their coastal neighbors. The CRC is assisted by a Coastal Resources Advisory Council, which has forty-seven members who are primarily elected representatives of local governments on the coast. This structure has happily been largely responsible for the public and political acceptance of the CAMA program.

A first element of the CAMA program is that for the first time all twenty coastal counties as well as fifty-five municipalities were required to adopt land-use plans for their geographic areas. These plans are flexible instruments and must be updated every five years. They serve as a guide for public development decisions as well as for individual subdivision and zoning decisions. The object of the planning process is to get the people of each jurisdiction to take a long-term perspective on their community. They are forced to ask questions such as: What do we want our town to look like in the next five years or beyond? Will we have enough open space, including water supplies and community centers? Where do we want industry to locate, and which areas do we want to keep open for recreation and other public uses?

A second element of CAMA is a regulatory program that requires a permit for land development in certain areas of the coast. The areas that are subject to regulation are actually quite limited; they are called Areas of Environmental Concern (AECs). The AECs are defined carefully in the law and in the regulations. They include oceanfront areas subject to erosion, storm flooding, and inlet movement; estuarine and public trust waters; coastal wetlands; a seventy-five-foot-wide buffer area around estuaries; public fresh water supplies; and fragile coastal, natural, and cultural resource areas. Within these specially designated and mapped areas, any devleopment requires a permit from the Coastal Resources Commission and must comply with the standards in the act and land-use planning guidelines. Administration of this permit program is a massive job, despite the fact that outside of coastal wetlands and waters only 3 percent of the planned area of the coastal counties is within an AEC. There are several thousand permit applications each year. Major permits are handled at the state level, while minor permits are generally handled at the local level. The most significant standard enforced by the regulations for AECs is the requirement of a minimum oceanfront setback in order to reduce public costs from siting development in erodible areas, to protect the public's use of the beach, and to protect dunelands and aesthetic values. The minimum setback distance, which is based on historic erosion rates, is measured from the edge of the beach or from behind the protective frontal dune. The minimum ocean setback requirement also reduces the need for erosion control devices such as sea walls that would permanently harden the oceanfront area.

To ensure the future enjoyment of the beauty of the coast, North Carolina has also worked to acquire strategically located parcels of land and to assure access to her miles of wide ocean beaches. In 1982 the state established the North Carolina National Estuarine Research Reserve, which is an outdoor laboratory where scientists, students, and the public can study firsthand the various types of estuarine habitat and wildlife in a relatively undisturbed state. So far, four sites have been added to the system in various parts of the coast. Currituck Banks, on the northern part of the Outer Banks, is an interesting transition zone exhibiting a mixture of northern flora and fauna as well as that associated with the southern part of the coast, which is influenced by the Gulf Stream. Farther south, the Rachel Carson Area near Beaufort Inlet is located at the confluence of the New-

Four areas have been designated as Estuarine Reserves in North Carolina.

port and North rivers and exhibits a typical sheltered tidal river estuarine system. A third reserve, Masonboro Island, located near Wilmington, is an excellent example of an undisturbed barrier island complex located on a river mouth estuary. The fourth area, Zeke's Island, near the mouth of the Cape Fear River, is typical of an estuary that is dominated by ocean and inlet processes.

North Carolina's beach access program is one of the most active of any state. Established by law in 1981, the purpose of the beach access program is to assure that development will not block off citizen access to any part of North Carolina's fine oceanfront beaches. Beach access corridors have been established in virtually every part of the coast. They can be recognized by their colorful signs, orange and blue on a white background. The beach access program has been integrated with the Coastal Area Management Program in several ways. The CRC has responsibility for acquiring beach access, and priority for acquisition is given to lands that are unsuitable for permanent substantial structures.

In many areas, land acquisition and the designation of coastal areas as estuarine sanctuaries, wildlife refuges, or parks is the only way to protect the rights of the public to these resources. North Carolina is also moving to resolve claims to private ownership of lands that are submerged or part of coastal marshes. Under legislation passed in 1985, the state is examining these private claims one by one in order to either validate or reject them and to assert public trust rights over such lands if necessary and appropriate.

The early years of CAMA in the 1970s were a struggle to survive. Coastal management was politically unpopular in many quarters, and we had to show that the program could actually preserve coastal resources without inhibiting economic development. I believe that these early years were crucial and that through the efforts of many people we succeeded in these goals. As a result, CAMA has attained a certain degree of acceptance, even in coastal North Carolina. The program has also matured to the point where the future will be much different than the past.

The first benefit of CAMA is that, by and large, people on the coast now have an understanding of why coastal management is needed and what the program is trying to accomplish. It is not a question of stopping economic development but rather of working with the natural forces on the coast in order to attain the right type of economic development in the right places and to maintain a balance between preservation and development for the enjoyment of the people of the region as well as the many visitors who come to enjoy the coast. Largely through CAMA, people have become aware of the value of the marshlands to fisheries and of the fact that there are geological and other forces going on that cannot be denied or controlled by man.

This realization has, to a great degree, muted the bitterness between environmentalists and developers. Both groups now realize to a greater extent than ever before that they must work together and that coastal management will not succeed in an atmosphere of confrontation. Thus, in the future I see a greater willingness to compromise and a greater degree of cooperation than in the past.

Another healthy trend is a lessening of reliance on regulation and an increasing reliance on incentives and other tools to preserve coastal resources. At the inception of the CAMA program, regulation was the primary means of coastal management. Regulation proved unpopular and was, to a large degree, unsuccessful. Regulation is still important, but through the efforts of many people the bureaucratic barriers have been reduced and there is less confrontation between the regulators and the people. For example, the Corps of Engineers Section 404 program is now working in harmony with the CAMA program to largely eliminate duplicative federal and state regulations.

Another development on the federal level was the enactment of a law establishing the Coastal Barrier Resources System, which consists of undeveloped coastal barriers on the Atlantic and Gulf coasts. This new law prohibits any new federal expenditures or financial assistance for development of this system, and it amends the National Flood Insurance Act to prohibit the issuance of new federal flood insurance for any new construction or substantial improvement of structures located within the system. This act is premised not on regulation, but on removing the incentives to develop areas that should be preserved. This is a healthy alternative to regulation. This incentive approach can be combined with an acquisition approach to preserve areas of the coast with minimal resort to heavy-handed regulation.

Finally, CAMA has contributed to giving the people of coastal North Carolina a renewed sense of pride in the beauty and resources of their region. This new sense of pride has helped them realize the uniqueness of the area and how their lifestyles are related to the characteristics of coastal North Carolina. The realization that the lifestyle of those living in the region depends to a certain degree on the preservation of these resources as well as a healthy balance between development and preservation has contributed to the political acceptance of CAMA and will continue to be the strength of the coastal zone management program in North Carolina in the future.

13

Continuing Controversies and Their Management

THE SEACOAST OF NORTH CAROLINA IS A VERY SPECIAL place, but what makes it so? The wildness of the natural environment? That certainly still exists in many areas and is one of the wonderful assets of the coast. Yet it is no wilderness, although one can still walk alone on an island beach, paddle through a virgin swamp forest, and fish in solitude on the sounds.

But the seacoast is more than that. It is the sandy streets of Ocracoke, the lighthouses on the capes, the ghost town on Portsmouth Island, the Beaufort waterfront, the splendid architecture of New Bern, and the shaded streets of Edenton.

In short, the *human* coast is as important as the natural one.

The key to the fascination of the area is that it is one of the oldest settled areas of the nation, the scene of both high drama and ordinary life for three hundred years and more. During this time man changed it, put his stamp on the land. The natural environment was altered, but the remarkable and special thing was that it was bent, never broken. The beaches were still free, the estuaries were still productive, forests and wetlands remained.

This was never planned or decreed by anyone; it was largely an accident of history and geography. For much of the past, North Carolina has treated her seacoast as an unwanted appendage. The offshore waters were too dangerous. Sounds and harbors were too shallow and inaccessible. The barrier islands were too remote and unstable. The shorelands were too wet for agriculture. Cities and towns were too isolated. While other coastal states were emphasizing their coastlines, North Carolina was ignoring hers.

But since the 1950s, coastal North Carolina has been "discovered." The demand for shoreland recreation has soared, producing a land and building boom as people rush to be near the ocean and sounds. Industry is moving to take advantage of the abundant water resources of coastal locations. The energy "crisis" is leading to the need for more refineries and storage facilities and pressure to exploit potential energy sources, such as peat. New technology and the trend to large corporate farms have allowed new forms of agriculture to be carried on in the coastal region. The federal government has established large military installations in the area.

New political power has come to coastal North Carolina as a result of the emphasis on its resources. No longer content with being the "stepchild" of the rest of the state, tidewater North Carolina is demanding a place in the mainstream of the economic life and new prosperity of the "sun belt." Government developmental agencies have been called upon to build new highways, water and sewer plants, port facilities, and navigation channels in the coastal counties of the state.

All this will produce new economic growth and development of the shorelands, estuaries, beaches, cities, and towns of coastal North Carolina. The population of these areas will increase. The sense of remoteness that it is possible to experience in many areas of the coast today may become a thing of the past.

But as the North Carolina coastal region develops, it would be a mistake if her people were to turn their backs on the human traditions and natural environments that have enriched the lives of the inhabitants for so many years. The challenge of the future will be to assimilate the changes, new development, and population growth that are coming to the region and still preserve the distinctive traditions and natural resources for present and future generations to enjoy and experience. Public opinion surveys have established that coastal residents of the state are fundamentally happy with their present lot; they do not want to see drastic changes in their way of life. But unwelcome changes have occurred and will continue, threatening the heritage of the coast. Continuing problems and controversies will have to be faced and managed. These will not be solved next year or in the next ten years. They will be with us as long as man looks to the North Carolina seacoast to satisfy multiple and often conflicting needs: recreation, solitude, fishing, farming, minerals, energy, industry, shopping centers, and cities.

Up to now in this book we have examined the North Carolina coast, its geology, its history, and some of the problems peculiar to each region. Now, in this chapter, we will look back over what we have covered to attempt to provide a framework for the solution of coastal problems in general. Of these, there are three overriding categories: (1) how to use the barrier islands; (2) how to maintain the productivity of the estuaries and offshore areas; and (3) how to attain the optimal pattern of human use of coastal resources for agricultural, industrial, and urban needs.

How to Use the Barrier Islands

Most of us love to go to "the beach." Our idea of the perfect vacation is to rent or own a house, as close to the ocean as possible, where we can swim, sunbathe, and sit on the porch listening to the waves.

This desire multiplied by several million people adds up to one thing: development pressure. It explains why barrier island real estate is some of the most expensive in North Carolina, and the end of the upward price spiral is not in sight. It also explains why immense change and unprecedented management problems are threatening these islands. If we are not careful, we will destroy those very things about the North Carolina islands that are so attractive to us.

From Currituck on the north to Sunset Beach on the south, subdivision and development are proceeding apace, except in the national seashores, wildlife refuges, and state parks. On the Currituck Outer Banks, more than eight thousand lots have been plotted and many have been developed. The beach will be filled up with motels and homes within ten years if the area is not acquired for a wildlife refuge by the federal government.

South of Currituck, the Dare County beaches are among the most rapidly developing in the state, right up to the entrance of the Cape Hatteras National Seashore, which is federal parkland. But even the national seashore is under great pressure. The privately owned enclave communities—Rodanthe, Salvo, Waves, Buxton, and Hatteras—will be intensely developed. Only Ocracoke at the southern terminus seems safe because of its isolation, traditions, and the lack of available room for growth. The Cape Lookout National Seashore, including Portsmouth Island, Core Banks, and Shackleford Banks, is one of the few places on the coast that will remain relatively untouched by the building boom; there are no enclaves of private land and no roads or bridges to these islands.

Farther south, the beaches stretching all the way to Cape Fear are already blanketed with motels, shopping centers, and beach cottages, and more of the same is planned. In this area only Bear Island (the site of Hammocks Beach State Park), the federally owned beaches of Camp Lejeune, and Masonboro Island (a future state park), are exempt. Smith Island is still largely intact, but large-scale development is planned. The Brunswick County coast—Yaupon Beach, Long Beach, Holden Beach, Ocean Isle Beach, and Sunset Beach—has been subdivided from ocean to sound, and more buildings are added every year.

Why is this a concern, one might ask. Shouldn't we let this happen? An obvious answer is that this scale of development destroys the natural communities of these islands. The dunes are bulldozed, marine forests are cut, birds and other wildlife are driven out. This is a good and sufficient reason for many people to be against this way of using the barrier islands. But to many other people this is not enough. They say there are enough areas on the coast set aside for wildlife, and besides, which is more important—birds or people? They need other reasons before they can be convinced that there is a problem. There are plenty of reasons.

EROSION

Recently a medical doctor looked at his expensive Topsail Beach vacation home perched perilously close to the ocean and shook his head. "I know government can't *stop* erosion, but they sure as hell can do something to *control* it!"

This illustrates the attitude of most beach property owners. They think of erosion as an unexpected catastrophe, a freak accident against which they have the right to look to government for protection. In the past, government has willingly complied, partly because owners of beach property have often had some of the best political connections in the state. Besides, who could object to the worthy goal of preventing perfectly good land and buildings from falling into the sea? Don't we need to stabilize the beaches to preserve them?

But beach protection projects cost millions of dollars of taxpayers' money. The current price tag for the proposed project at Carolina Beach, for example, is $18.4 million. Furthermore, beach erosion is not an accidental occurrence; it is the product of natural forces. Few terrestrial environments are as unstable and dynamic as barrier islands. We know that these islands survive and cope with these forces by moving and changing shape, in a process we have already identified as *island migration*. It becomes *erosion* only when man-made structures get in the way. Few places on these islands have remained stable for even as short a time as one hundred years. We know that in most areas sooner or later the ocean will intervene in some way, just as we know that a train will eventually come rolling down a stretch of empty railroad track.

In many cases innocent people are victimized by developers who build on a hazardous beach and then sell out before the trouble begins. One developer dug canals and sold off lots at the southern end of Topsail Island in 1967. By the early 1970s the state was asked to provide funds to stop erosion and protect the expensive homes that had been built. The state provided $30,000 in taxpayers' money to construct some groins but refused to shell out additional money so that the same developer could sell more lots. That made the developer, who was also the mayor of New Topsail Beach, very angry. "The state doesn't know what the hell they're doing," he was quoted as saying. "They claim I'm too close to the inlet. Hell, it's way over there," he added, waving his arm. "I don't think they have the right to tell me what I can and can't do."

Geologist Orrin Pilkey of Duke University has pointed out that in addition to costing taxpayers' money, there are two other severe problems with shoreline engineering to control erosion. First, once artificial beach protection is begun, it can never be terminated but must be continued indefinitely into the future. Second, although erosion can be controlled for a limited time by artificial means, the remedies will end up destroying the beaches they were meant to protect.

Let's look at the forms of beach protection available. Seawalls can be constructed parallel to the shore at the back of the beach. These may be of wood, cement, or rock, or the dune itself may be built up into a solid, high wall of sand. This protects the landward area for a time, but the sand in front of the wall tends to disappear as the storm waves crash against the wall and reflect back, scouring out the beach. Sooner or later the wall itself will be undercut or broken through by the sea; then the wall must be reconstructed behind the original wall. Meanwhile the sound side of the island will also tend to erode, since it is deprived of the sand and sediment it would receive through the normal action of winds and overwash flows.

This phenomenon can best be observed at older developed resorts in New Jersey and Florida, which have completely lost their beaches. An interim stage can be seen in North Carolina at Wrightsville Beach and Atlantic Beach, where the stabilized frontal dune has been transformed into a solid wall, and the beach has lost much of its sand. The northern Outer Banks from Currituck to Ocracoke also present problems left over from the dune-building done by the Civilian Conservation Corps in the 1930s. The frontal dunes along Cape Hatteras National Seashore were built up to protect the seashore road and the enclave communities on the banks. But now the National Park Service is on the horns of a dilemma. It must either continue to maintain the dune, at the cost of millions of dollars and the loss of the beach, or face the blame for allowing the sea to encroach, cutting the road and possibly destroying the private investment of the Outer Banks' communities. Both are unattractive alternatives. The Park Service has not yet had to face the day of reckoning, however, because the sea has been unusually quiet. But that day cannot be far off, and the management mistakes of the past will continue to be with us.

Groins and jetties are also sometimes used to preserve the beach, the primary difference being that groins are heavier and more substantial. These are structures built at right angles to the beach which trap the sand moving down the beach in the longshore current. They do a fine job of trapping sand and building up the beach on one side. But on the other side the beach erodes rapidly since it is starved of sand. This leads to the building of more jetties, and eventually a whole field of them march down the shore. In the area between the jetties or groins there is still a lack of sand, and it becomes necessary to place sand on the beach to fill it in. Next, the jetties are either destroyed in storms, overtopped, or undermined, and have to be replaced. Groins tend to become denser and heavier, forcing the littoral drift to move offshore along the tips of the groins and the whole beach to erode and become sand-starved. We have now come full circle except that, instead of a natural, migrating (eroding) beach, we now have an engineered eroding shoreline.

Another possible way to "save" a beach and prevent erosion is through what is called "beach nourishment." This is a euphemism for pumping sand onto the beach. It is expensive, although it does not cost as much as groins and seawalls. But the problems are legion. First, it is a very temporary solution: since only the above-water area is "nourished," it results in a steeper beach, more subject to the eroding action of the waves. Second, the sand pumped onto the beach has to come from somewhere. At Cape Hatteras a large hole was dug just behind the dune to nourish the beach in front of the lighthouse. There is now a lake of murky water on the strand. Often the sand is taken from the sound or from channels and inlets. This was tried at Wrightsville Beach. The first material used was too fine-grained; it washed away in the first season. Then coarser material was used. It holds better but is unpleasant to walk on and has a blackened appearance. And eventually it, too, will wash away.

Coastal engineering should be avoided in North Carolina as much as possible. The natural beach preserves itself through complex movement; the artificial beach carries the seeds of its own destruction. Compare Bear Island, where no money has been spent on erosion control, with Wrightsville Beach, where millions of dollars have gone for dune stabilization, beach nourishment, groins, and jetties. The beach at Bear Island is broad, with gleaming white sand; Wrightsville is narrow, blackened, and eroding. Wrightsville is about fifty percent of the way along the path that leads to a seawall and total loss of the beach.

HURRICANES AND NORTHEASTERS

The large storms that originate in the tropical waters of the Caribbean or the Atlantic in the late summer and fall are officially classified as hurricanes when their winds reach a velocity greater than seventy-four miles per hour. Many of them are considerably more powerful. The North Carolina coast is particularly vulnerable to being hit because of the distance it juts out into the Atlantic. In the winter, severe storms called "northeasters" affect the coast as low pressure areas tend to park just offshore, sending powerful winds out of the northeast against the barrier islands.

Like erosion, these storms are certain to continue; we just do not know when or where they will strike. We do know quite a bit about their likely effect, however. The winds are often strong enough to take roofs off houses and to overturn automobiles. Worst of all are the storm waves and tides they produce. The surge of wind-driven water and sand can inundate entire islands, which may become covered with three to four feet of water. The island disappears entirely, and the water is driven up the estuaries, flooding the mainland shore as well. But the major destruction comes after the center of the hurricane has passed, when the winds shift and the tremendous storm tide returns to the sea. It rolls back across the island, often crushing all structures in its path and even cutting new inlets through the bar.

Hurricanes have caused death and destruction on the North Carolina barrier islands and the mainland throughout history. In the nineteenth century, Portsmouth Village was virtually destroyed by a hurricane. A storm in 1899 caused the abandonment of Diamond City on Shackleford Banks. Early resort hotels were destroyed or damaged by hurricanes. A Morehead City man, William B. Duncan, wrote a letter to his son describing the damage caused by the storm of August 19, 1879: "The Atlantic Hotel is entirely gone. Not one brick or plank left on top of each other at the place it formerly stood. . . . Mr. White's shop was washed down. The last store in front of Captain Samuel Dill's washed down and gone all to pieces."

In the 1950s a series of hurricanes devastated many of the islands. The most famous was Hurricane Hazel in 1954, which destroyed most of the structures on the beaches at that time in the Cape Fear area. Wrightsville Beach and Carolina Beach suffered severe damage, and the Brunswick County beaches were virtually swept clean by the storm.

But most of the development of the North Carolina barrier islands has occurred during the 1960s and 1970s, a period which has been unusually quiet. The last major hurricane was Donna in 1960, and the last big northeaster was the Ash Wednesday Storm of March, 1962. Since that time the rate of construction and development has been tremendous, greater than anything in all the previous history of the coast. The number of people and structures that are now in jeopardy has increased dramatically. Ironically, a major reason for this is that the federal government has subsidized development through its flood insurance program, without which private lending institutions would not readily make construction loans for these areas. We know the "killer" hurricanes will return. But next time the damage will be in the hundreds of millions of dollars. There will be the usual helicopter tours by sympathetic politicians and the call for federal disaster relief. But why can't we realize that we are simply victims of our own folly?

WATER AND WASTE

The more densely developed a barrier island becomes, the greater the need for fresh, potable water and efficient, effective disposal of sewage and other wastes. In North Carolina the practice has been to develop the barrier islands using individual or small community wells for water supply and individual septic tanks for sewage disposal.

These methods work well when there are only a few houses on the beach. Underlying most barrier islands is a thin, lens-shaped zone of fresh water, replenished by the rains that soak into the sands. This is quite close to the surface and can be easily tapped by man. A few wells and septic tanks will not cause much of a problem because of the small quantities of water and waste involved. But as the island develops and more and more wells and septic tanks are put in, problems appear. There is only so much fresh water, and if more is taken out than is replenished by rainfall, what is known as "saltwater intrusion" begins. The salt water under the lens of fresh water enters the aquifer. Wells begin to pump brackish water.

The proliferation of septic tanks causes another problem. Septic tanks work by slowly filtering effluent through bacteria-rich soil. Barrier islands have very little actual soil, and their sands are bacteria-poor and very porous. The sewage effluent thus tends to flow swiftly into the aquifer after very little treatment. In short, people start drinking their own and everyone else's untreated sewage.

Since this situation is intolerable, residents begin looking for an additional water supply, a different method of disposal of sewage, or more likely both. What can be done? It is immediately apparent that there are no easy solutions. A barrier island, although surrounded by water, is a freshwater-poor environment. It is more so after having been developed, since the marine forest and other vegetation that naturally help conserve water are probably gone. There are no clear, fresh streams flowing nearby. Some areas, such as Nags Head, are lucky enough to have a few freshwater ponds, but these are rare. The usual alternatives open to residents are (1) water reuse, (2) salt water desalinization, and (3) a water supply source on the mainland. Water reuse is a long way from public acceptance, even though it may prove to be the easiest and least expensive alternative. Another difficulty with reuse is the need for a fail-safe technology for treatment and monitoring when it is done on a continuous basis. Desalinization techniques are used only experimentally on the North Carolina coast. All the known processes employ a great deal of energy for both treatment and transportation since the water must be moved uphill. The most frequent solution, then, is to look to mainland sources of fresh water. But this also is fraught with difficulties. Mainland sources are usually already being used, so that this procedure involves taking someone else's water. Transport is also expensive since a water line must be built and maintained across long stretches of land and water in often extremely fragile areas. The community of Avon on the Outer Banks recently began to obtain water from Buxton through the construction of a water line several miles long through the Cape Hatteras National Seashore. This water line is vulnerable to being cut in the next storm and will be very expensive to maintain.

Waste water disposal presents an even gloomier picture. Other than septic tanks, the alternatives include (1) building treatment plants, (2) land disposal, (3) deep-well disposal, and (4) ocean outfalls. Except for ocean outfalls, each is much more expensive on barrier islands than in noncoastal areas. There is normally very little room on an island for either a conventional treatment plant or a land disposal system, which involves spraying the effluent on a golf course or some other large, open area. Deep-well injection runs the risk of eventual contamination of groundwater supplies. Little is known about where the injected materials will eventually end up.

North Carolina seems to be moving toward the last alternative, ocean outfalls, which are long pipes extending into the ocean. In theory they work by disposing of waste at sea, where it will be harmless to the environment. In some parts of the country they have worked quite well, while in other areas they have been disastrous. The impact of the sewage plume ejected will vary according to the conditions of each particular area, the shallowness of the water, and the characteristics of the prevailing currents, winds, and waves. North Carolina has shallow waters for a greater distance off its coast than the west coast, where some outfalls have been successful. Not only is there danger of creating a "dead area" in the ocean in the immediate area of the pipe, but the effluent may drift back onto the beaches. Scientists are studying the North Carolina coast so that if outfalls are used, these problems will be avoided. But no one really knows what will happen until after the outfalls are built. If one is successful and there is little noticeable effect, it is sure that more will be constructed. Human nature being what it is, there will be a proliferation of outfalls. No one knows what will happen then. And only after raw sewage starts washing up on the beach will a new "problem" suddenly be discovered. By then it will be too late.

Bridges and Roads

Development of the barrier islands means that bridges are constructed from the mainland, and highways and streets criss-cross the islands themselves. This brings speed, convenience, and the comforts of modern civilization; it also brings noise, pollution, and destruction of the natural environment. We are used to this, and few people oppose a road despite the trade-offs involved. But it is not generally realized that additional considerations arise when it comes to building roads and bridges on the barrier islands.

First, in the case of islands, the equation can be turned around; instead of development bringing highways, *highways bring development*. The truth of this axiom can be seen when one considers that before the construction of bridges and roads, there was very little development on North Carolina's barrier islands. Nags Head was a small resort on Albemarle Sound until the bridges and roads were constructed in the 1930s. Other islands "benefited" from the military roads and bridges constructed during World War II. Highway access has increased the value of property on these islands tremendously. A north-south road up Currituck Banks would triple the value of each oceanfront lot. A bridge to Smith Island would be a bonanza to its owners. This is why the pressure for roads and bridges comes not so much from the people who *live* in the area but from those who want to *develop* it.

A second axiom having to do with highways and barrier islands is that initial highway access leads to a cycle of road and bridge building that virtually never ends. A perfect example of this is Bogue Banks. The initial two-lane bridge to Atlantic Beach from Morehead City was followed by the extension of the road west of Salter Path and later west of Emerald Isle. It was quite a poor road, with no shoulders and several sharp curves and doglegs. As soon as the road had been extended the length of the island, development pressure justified the construction of a new bridge at the western end of the island, and one was built, a graceful, modern bridge that spans the sound high above the Intracoastal Waterway.

The result of the second bridge, of course, was to increase traffic on the Bogue Banks road, and highway engineers soon proposed its "improvement." In 1973 a modern two-lane highway complete with paved shoulders and grassy borders was proposed. The doglegs and curves were to be straightened and the community of Salter Path was to be bypassed on the ocean side with a new highway section through the frontal dunes. Plans called for an eventual five-lane highway to be built.

In 1975 a group of local residents of Bogue Banks decided to oppose the new highway, especially the Salter Path Bypass and the later five-lane project. I was their attorney, together with Mike Curtis of Greensboro. An unusual incident occurred before we filed suit in the case. I was in federal district court on another case and making small talk with the judge. I casually remarked, "We're going to have another of these environmental cases for you, Your Honor." He asked, "What about?" "The Bogue Banks road," I replied.

Then the good judge launched into a tirade. "I know all about that one. Isn't it terrible? Ed Willis took me out there the other day and showed me where the road will go. Why, it'll destroy the dunes that protect us all."

Ed Willis, a longtime resident of Salter Path, was one of our clients. He had taken the liberty of educating the judge about the case before it was filed. He wasn't entrusting things to his attorneys alone.

Two months later we had a court hearing to obtain a preliminary injunction against the road. We presented our evidence; witnesses testified and were cross-examined by attorneys for the state Department of Transportation. The judge listened attentively, but I felt very confident. At the end of the hearing, as I expected, the judge issued the injunction. I walked out thinking that maybe Ed Willis knew more about the law than I did.

The Highway Department never gives up, however. After the injunction was granted, we had numerous conversations with highway engineers in the judge's presence about how the highway could be improved in such a way as to minimize destruction of the beautiful marine forest. We tried to get them to adapt the highway to the barrier island environment. But they knew only one way of building a two-lane highway. There was a standard design, whether for piedmont, mountains, or islands. The judge eventually threw up his hands and allowed them to build the highway except for the Salter Path Bypass.

Road building is sure to continue on Bogue Banks. In 1978 the state Department of Transportation proposed a new bridge over Bogue Sound from Morehead City to Pine Knoll Shores. This would relieve the congestion on the old bridge over to Atlantic Beach. When this happens, if not before, there will be irresistible pressure to construct the Salter Path Bypass, and the five-lane highway cannot be far behind.

The third certainty about road and bridge building on barrier islands is that afterward, special anti-erosion measures must always be taken to protect the facility. This is not sufficiently understood. Department of Transportation engineers justified the Salter Path Bypass next to the frontal dune by saying the road would protect against erosion. This is nonsense. As Art Cooper, then deputy director of the Department of Natural and

Economic Resources, pointed out in a letter of comment, "This will not aid erosion prevention but will only require that more stringent erosion control methods be employed because of the highway." It is not hard to see the fate of island road and bridge building in North Carolina. U.S. 421 has been taken by the sea near Fort Fisher. The western end of the Bogue Banks road drops off into the sea as a result of the migrating inlet. The Cape Hatteras Seashore highway has been washed out several times. The Oregon Inlet bridge, built in 1963, was closed for repairs in 1978 because of the shifting of the inlet. The need to "stabilize" the inlet is now partly justified in terms of the necessity of saving this bridge. We are locked into a never-ending cycle of building controls to protect island roads and bridges from the sea.

BEACH ACCESS AND USE

The developed barrier island also presents a difficult problem of beach access and use. There are two aspects to this problem. One is that the members of the public, who have the right to use the "wet sand" area below the mean-high-water line, can no longer get to the beach. When the shoreline is fully developed, there will be a wall of privately owned homes and businesses between the road and the ocean. In many areas of the coast, development has reached the point where beach access is a critical issue. The public may have rights under the legal doctrines of customary use, implied dedication, and prescription, but these are open questions in North Carolina. Government will increasingly be called upon to purchase, at extremely high prices, shorefront parks and parking areas as the only certain way to assure that members of the general public have access to the beach.

The second aspect of the access problem arises from the need, once access to the public is given, to assure that the use of the area by large numbers of people does not damage the dunes and the natural environment. The use of off-road vehicles and even walking on the dunes must be monitored and regulated to protect the resource adequately.

What are the solutions to these problems of island development? How should we manage the barrier islands? As I have stressed throughout this book, we should manage them within the constraints of the natural forces that operate on them. Any other management policy is too costly in both economic and environmental terms. The National Park Service, as we have seen, has recognized this and has adopted a policy which states that "as far as possible" there will be no further attempts to restrain the natural processes of erosion, deposition, dune formation, and inlet formation. The qualifying language is a concession to the fact that past construction must sometimes be protected. But new construction cannot be placed in areas subject to flood or wave erosion hazard unless "it is essential to meet the park's purpose . . . no alternative locations are available, and . . . the facilities will be reasonably assured of surviving for their planned lifespan without shoreline control measures."

Such a policy is difficult to apply even in National Park Service lands, as we have seen in the case of the Cape Hatteras National Seashore. Privately owned barrier islands present a more complicated set of policy choices. Management raises the specter of governmental regulation and interference with property rights.

But ironically, the greatest need for policy change in barrier island management is not more governmental regulation; it is repeal of those governmental policies that subsidize and promote barrier island development. Ending these policies would eliminate millions of dollars in unnecessary government spending and is justified on both economic and environmental grounds. Many particular federal and state policies should be changed. The most important are those dealing with (1) erosion control, (2) flood insurance, (3) transportation, and (4) water, sewer, and electric utility development.

First, neither the Corps of Engineers nor the state should permit or support structural measures of erosion control such as bulkheads, groins, and jetties, unless clearly needed to protect an existing urban area or structure that cannot be moved. Inlets should not be "stabilized" except to permit access to the state ports at Morehead City and Wilmington.

Second, the federal flood insurance program should be

changed to eliminate any financial incentive for barrier island development. Better construction standards should be enforced, and premiums should be raised to reflect the true cost of insurance protection. Particularly hazardous areas should be mapped and designated as areas where new construction is not insurable. If an insured area is damaged beyond repair by a storm or hurricane, the people should be relocated and the property should be acquired instead of providing funds for reconstruction.

Third, the state and federal departments of transportation and the U.S. Coast Guard should declare a moratorium on constructing new bridges to barrier islands. Existing roads should not be widened, and new roads should not be built into undeveloped areas.

Fourth, where federal or state agencies are called upon to make grants or loans to finance electric utility lines, water projects, or sewer projects on barrier islands, the application should be carefully scrutinized to determine whether imprudent development would be fostered by the grant or loan. Federal agencies already have this authority under presidential executive orders and the National Environmental Policy Act. State agencies are required to do this under the North Carolina Environmental Policy Act.

Regulation of barrier island development can be carried out primarily by the "areas of environmental concern" (AEC) provisions of the Coastal Area Management Act. Although North Carolina has declined to designate the entire barrier island system as an AEC, many of the AEC categories apply, such as inlet lands, erodible areas, beaches, frontal dunes, and marshlands. Significant natural areas and historic sites on barrier islands may be nominated and accepted as AEC's. For all AEC areas, the Coastal Resources Commission can apply both use standards and performance standards such as set-back and construction requirements.

Outside the AEC areas themselves, the planning provisions of CAMA can be used to control unwise development. Density limits can be adopted where limited supplies of water make them necessary to preserve the supply and avoid pollution. Controls on the numbers and placement of septic tanks can also be applied. Every beach community should be required to have a hurricane evacuation plan as well as plans for public beach access and limiting the use of off-road vehicles.

How to Manage the Estuaries and Offshore Waters

We have seen that the estuary lagoons behind the barrier islands, the inlets, and the offshore waters have been used for centuries—as navigation channels, for fishing, and for recreation. While they are still important for these purposes, new uses have also been discovered. Vast phosphate deposits underlie the Pamlico River. Tests are being conducted to determine whether oil and gas lie offshore. In the future there may be floating nuclear power plants, deep-water port facilities, and a variety of mining activities. Aquaculture, the controlled raising of fish, may become an important new industry. With all these new activities, it is more important than ever to plan for the intelligent use of the resource.

Pollution

All of the estuaries of North Carolina are experiencing serious pollution problems. The Chowan River is the most endangered; algal "blooms" caused by excessive concentrations of nitrogen and phosphorus have adversely affected fishing, angering residents of the area. Some have sent bottles of black, polluted water to congressmen and state officials. As one resident put it, "Someday soon you'll be able to go down to Oregon Inlet and see the blue waters of the ocean on one side and the green waters of the sound on the other." But the Pamlico and Neuse River estuaries are also threatened. And the Cape Fear estuary suffers from discharges of major industries on its shores.

The causes of pollution are diverse and hard to manage. Industries and towns discharge effluent into coastal rivers. Fertilizer runoff from agriculture is a problem, especially from the vast "superfarms" that have been created with drainage canals flowing into the sounds. The increased flows of fresh water have apparently changed the salinity balance of some areas, adversely affecting fish spawning grounds. The proliferation of development on the shores of the sounds has meant an increase in septic tanks, which often operate improperly because of the high water table or unsuitable soils. With the expected increased traffic in oil tankers along the coast and the construction of energy facilities, oil storage terminals, refineries, and perhaps drilling rigs, oil pollution may soon threaten the beaches and sounds.

Up to now, the main tactics state authorities have used to combat pollution have been (1) to close badly contaminated areas to fishing and shellfishing and (2) to move shellfish from polluted to clean areas. About 680,000 acres of the sound and coastal lagoons have been closed and are now posted with pollution warnings. It is obvious that warnings are an unacceptable way of dealing with the problem. Pollution entering coastal waters should be treated at its source through better enforcement of water quality standards and limitations on the discharge of effluents. But in order to preserve the functioning of the estuarine system and offshore waters, the treating of wastes is not enough; the actual uses to which the land is put must be controlled. Recreational developments, farming, and forestry activities, for instance, are all important sources of pollution to estuarine waters. Finally, a systematic inventory should be made of the present and likely future uses of the estuaries and offshore areas. The initiation of new uses such as mining, waste disposal, and energy production facilities should be preceded by rational planning in order to protect water quality and the traditional uses of fishing, recreation, and wildlife management.

DREDGING AND FILLING

In order for an estuary to function effectively, its contour and circulatory pattern must be maintained. The estuary is a vast transport system allowing marine organisms, including most species of commercially valuable fish, to travel through the inlets to the marshes, tidal rivers, and creeks and then to return to ocean waters. The fringing marshlands and sand flats are also essential to the process, contributing shelter and nutrients and protecting against erosion. Dredging canals and filling in the coastal marshlands and sand flats should not be permitted. These not only change the water circulation pattern and destroy sources of nutrients but also create pollution "traps." Bridges and other structures in the estuarine region should not be allowed to alter the natural pattern of water circulation. The dredging of essential navigation channels and the deposit of dredge spoil should be carried out in such a way that damage to wildlife is minimized. Dredge-spoil islands should be situated and managed as wildlife areas since eighty percent of the colonial nesting birds in coastal North Carolina utilize them as nesting grounds.

COASTAL SWAMP FORESTS AND POCOSINS

Often forgotten is the fact that coastal North Carolina includes more than two million acres of freshwater wetlands—vast and impenetrable swamp forests of cypress and pine as well as the open bogs called pocosins. As we have seen, the unique and mysterious Carolina bays are also part of this natural system. These watery lands are an integral part of the hydrology and ecology of the estuaries; there is a constant exchange of water and a contribution of nutrients to the coastal sounds. From the Dismal Swamp on the north to the Green Swamp on the south, these wetlands are the sources or important contributors to the coastal rivers and creeks that flow into the sounds and lagoons. Without them, the estuaries could not exist; they are also essential to the freshwater aquifer underlying the region, and they protect the surrounding land against flooding and erosion. In addition, they are important natural areas, the source of the unique plant life and rich wildlife heritage of the coast.

In recent years these areas have been clear-cut and drained at an alarming rate. Hundreds of square miles have been transformed into farmlands indistinguishable from the plains of the Midwest. In many cases it has been found that the agricultural lands thus created are of very low productivity. Further transformation of these lands—whether for agriculture, forestry, or the mining of peat deposits—should not be carried out without careful study of the costs and benefits involved. The cost of constant maintenance of the water table should be carefully calculated as well as problems such as soil fertility, water pollution, and the disruption of groundwater circulation. A large portion of such lands must be preserved in their natural state if the healthy estuarine system is to survive.

The Coastal Area Management Act provides the legal authority necessary to protect these estuarine lands against unwise development. All of the coastal sounds and lagoons as well as the marshlands and estuarine shorelands to a distance of seventy-five feet from the water have already been designated AEC's and are subject to permit requirements that set use and performance standards for development in such areas. Similar protection should be given to the swamp forests and pocosins of the coast. These areas should be inventoried and studied for their possible designation as complex natural area AEC's. The richest and most valuable of such lands should be identified and protected.

How to Manage for Urban, Industrial, and Agricultural Needs

The key to providing for urban, industrial, and agricultural needs while still preserving the natural heritage of the coast is rational land-use planning. The Coastal Area Management Act implements this by classifying the lands of the twenty-county coastal area into five categories—developed, transition, community, rural, and conservation. This is intended to provide for a range of different intensities of development reflecting the goals of each particular community. These classifications can provide a system for state and local policies for public roads, schools, utilities, and other public services. They can be used as a framework for private investment as well.

The land classification system should not be arbitrary. Rather, it should be based upon a rational and scientific analysis of the resources, both natural and human, of each area. Prior to classification, the characteristics and natural constraints of coastal lands should be studied. Why is a particular area important? What should happen and not happen there? How does each area fit into the pattern of future community goals and into the coastal region as a whole? The most intense developments should be permitted where there is optimal access to supplies of fresh water, where waste disposal is easiest, and where transportation and energy services can be most economically provided. Agriculture should be allowed on lands with good drainage and adequate soil conditions. Wise plans and policies for urban and industrial development can provide attractive places for human activity while preserving the resources that have made possible the distinctive way of life of the area. We can accommodate the need for development without encroaching upon the vital natural areas of the coast.

The point of departure for development planning should be the conservation of the historic districts and buildings of the coastal area. Almost all the principal towns have historically significant and beautiful homes, stores, and public buildings. Many, such as Edenton, New Bern, Beaufort, and Wilmington, have town centers of national importance. In the countryside throughout coastal North Carolina there are fine old mansions and plantation houses. These should be identified, and future planning should be consistent with their character and preservation.

In order to be effective, planning must be implemented by local and state governments. Zoning, subdivision controls, and other land-use instruments should be used to guide development according to the classifications. Large-scale projects such as peat mining, refineries, and corporate farming should be subjected to an environmental impact analysis before being permitted to proceed. All of the lands and waters of the coastal zone should be comprehensively managed to both foster their productive use and assure their preservation.

Coastal resources management is not just a negativistic governmental program. Restrictions are placed upon the freedom to develop and use resources so as to provide the greatest enjoyment of those resources by all of the people, not just a few. It is important that these programs be perceived by coastal residents as a positive force, designed to provide for development while protecting against change that would destroy the coastal heritage of North Carolina and the value of the natural resources: the productive estuaries, beaches, shorelands, swamplands, and historic towns and buildings upon which that heritage depends.

EPILOGUE

A critical juncture has been reached in the long history of the coastal region of North Carolina. This area now has the opportunity to preserve the best of its history and traditions and to develop in harmony with the natural focus that created and sustained it.

Resiliency is a dominant characteristic of the North Carolina coast. Its past is studded with mistakes and failures, fighting and bloodshed. But somehow the region has always bounced back. The disaster of the Lost Colony was followed by the founding of distinctive colonial towns such as Edenton, Bath, Beaufort, and New Bern. Early sectional differences between coastal areas were overcome during the period of the Revolution and early statehood. The great virgin forests were cut, fish and wildlife were taken without restraint, but the natural resource base remained. Human slavery and the inequality of the plantation system were abolished in the conflagration of the Civil War, but the economy revived, and efforts were made to correct racial discrimination and poverty.

Is further social progress and economic growth inconsistent with the survival of the natural systems and resources of the region? This is the great question that must now be faced. It is shortsighted to answer that natural and cultural resources must always give way to human concerns. Progress is not unlimited use and destruction of resources. It is, rather, learning to live within the constraints that will assure the resources' continued usefulness and productivity. Realization of this fact in the context of management of coastal resources gives the hope that the North Carolina coast in the future will overcome the tendency in recent years toward overuse of these resources that has threatened to destroy it as a special place.

APPENDIX

Practical Hints for Visitors

Aquariums and Museums

Three excellent aquariums are maintained by the state of North Carolina on various parts of the coast: the North Carolina Aquarium at Pine Knoll Shores (near Morehead City); the North Carolina Aquarium at Fort Fisher (near Wilmington); and the North Carolina Aquarium on Roanoke Island (near Manteo). Displays in these facilities concentrate on the marine and coastal environment. They are open to the public from 9 A.M. to 5 P.M. Monday through Friday and from 1 P.M. to 5 P.M. on Saturday and Sunday.

The aquarium at Pine Knoll Shores is part of the interesting Theodore Roosevelt Natural Area, a state park.

In Beaufort, the North Carolina Maritime Museum has fascinating displays about the coastal heritage of North Carolina.

The Museum of the Albemarle in Elizabeth City offers exhibits showing the natural and human history of the Albemarle region.

The Cape Hatteras National Seashore has interesting exhibit centers featuring the ecology, geology, and history of the Outer Banks. The Bodie Island Lighthouse and Visitors' Center is the most extensive, but there are other visitors' centers at Cape Hatteras and at Silver Lake on Ocracoke near the ferry slip. Any of these will provide information on the location of some of the still-visible shipwrecks. The Buxton Woods Nature Trail near Cape Hatteras—just three-quarters of a mile long—is very well laid out. The Sandcastle Discovery Center near Coquina Beach presents a full program of recreational and educational features on the seashore during the summer.

The Cape Lookout National Seashore has a visitors' center and museum on Harkers Island. Also planned are a historic restoration of the Cape Lookout lighthouse area along with camping and visitors' facilities nearby. Similar facilities are also planned for Portsmouth.

In the Wilmington area, the Wilmington-New Hanover Museum has displays on the history of the Cape Fear region. Chandler's Wharf, on the waterfront, is a museum of the type of ships that once plied the Cape Fear estuary.

BEACHES

North Carolina has 301 miles of ocean beaches. The time-honored way of "going to the beach" is to rent a motel room or a cottage (or more recently a condominium) on one of the barrier islands. About half of the coast has facilities for this type of thing, including the enclave communities on the Cape Hatteras National Seashore. You can choose a commercial area, such as Nags Head, Atlantic Beach, Emerald Isle, or Wrightsville Beach, or a "family beach," such as one of the Brunswick County beaches. Information about rentals is available from the local chambers of commerce.

Very few barrier islands are still in a near-natural state. The best of these are Shackleford Banks and Core Banks, both part of the Cape Lookout National Seashore, which can be reached by ferry from Harkers Island. Portsmouth Island, the northern part of the seashore, can be reached by charter boat from Ocracoke. Another wonderful place, accessible only by ferry, is Bear Island, site of Hammocks Beach State Park, near Swansboro. Masonboro Island, near Wilmington, is another state-owned, near-natural island. Ferry access is planned. Smith, or Bald Head, Island is perhaps the most interesting barrier island in North Carolina, and much of it is still undisturbed. Unfortunately, it is privately owned and being developed. It is to be hoped that Currituck will remain another "wild beach," accessible only by ferry. The Cape Hatteras National Seashore is a beautiful, open, public beach; it has, however, been altered somewhat by the road and by erosion control measures. There are campgrounds at intervals of several miles on this seashore.

BEACH ACCESS PROGRAMS

Although much of the land near the ocean is privately owned, the beach itself belongs to everyone, and, in 1981, the North Carolina General Assembly created a beach access program and provided $1 million to get. it started. All coastal communities must provide sites to allow the public access to the beach. Many of these have parking, restrooms, outdoor showers, water fountains, and trash collection facilities. They can be recognized by the orange and blue signs along the roadside. For information, write to the Office of Coastal Management, P.O. Box 27687, Raleigh, NC 27611; (919) 733–2293.

COASTAL MANAGEMENT

North Carolina has one of the most innovative and widely acclaimed coastal management programs in the nation. Under the authority of the Coastal Area Management ACT (CAMA), passed in 1974, all twenty coastal counties must prepare and keep current land-use plans, and development within designated "areas of environmental concern" requires a permit from the state. For information, contact the Office of Coastal Management, P.O. Box 27687, Raleigh, NC 27611; (919) 733–2293.

ESTUARINE RESERVES

Of the hundreds of thousands of acres of richly productive estuaries on the North Carolina coast, four areas totaling twelve thousand acres have been set aside as the North Carolina National Estuarine Reserve, which was established in 1982. These may be visited for recreation, wildlife viewing, and research, although camping is generally forbidden.

The four areas are as follows:

1. Currituck Banks (in Currituck County)
2. Rachel Carson (near Beaufort)
3. Masonboro Island (near Wilmington)
4. Zeke's Island (near Southport)

For information, contact the Reserve Analyst, Office of Coastal Management, P.O. Box 27687, Raleigh, NC 27611; (919) 733–2293.

GEOLOGY FOR THE LAYMAN

The best way to see for yourself some of the natural processes at the seashore is to take the self-guided field trip charted in *How to Live with an Island,* by Orrin Pilkey, Jr., Orrin Pilkey, Sr., and Robb Turner. In the book *From Currituck to Calabash* by the Pilkeys and William Neal, there is much useful information as well. The appendix of the latter contains two field guides to the geology of North Carolina shorelines. The southeastern shore is described by William Cleary and Paul Hosier, and the northern Outer Banks is described by Stan Riggs and Stephen Benton.

HISTORIC LIGHTHOUSES

There are six historic lighthouses on the North Carolina coast: Corolla (brown); Bodie Island (white and black rings); Cape Hatteras (white and black spiral); Ocracoke (white); Cape Lookout (black and white diamond); and Bald Head (white).

HURRICANES AND STORMS

Because of its geographic position, thrust out into the Atlantic, coastal North Carolina is threatened each year by large storms and hurricanes. A storm is called a hurricane when it has sustained winds of seventy-four miles per hour or greater. If a hurricane is approaching, there will be plenty of warning, and you should carefully follow the instructions of civil defense authorities. The last major hurricane to hit the North Carolina coast was Diana in 1984. People on the coast still talk about the legendary hurricane Hazel, the strongest storm on record, which hit in 1954.

INLETS

Twenty-six inlets (gaps between the barrier islands) are open in coastal North Carolina. Inlet areas are notoriously unstable; they open and close with regularity. Inlet areas are very interesting to explore for the purpose of collecting shells and viewing wildlife.

STATE PARKS AND WILDLIFE REFUGES

Dismal Swamp State Park is still being developed for visitors' use. It lies south of the Virginia state line and west of U.S. 17. Access is expected to be provided off State Road (S.R.) 1219.

Merchants Millpond State Park near Gatesville is a good place to see the swamp forest ecology of the region.

Goose Creek State Park preserves a portion of the Pamlico shore between Washington and Bath. It is off S.R. 92.

Swanquarter National Wildlife Refuge is located on the shore of Pamlico Sound near Swan Quarter. Mattamuskeet National Wildlife Refuge is an excellent place to observe wintering swans, ducks, geese, and other wildlife. There is a visitors' center off U.S. 264.

Pea Island National Wildlife Refuge is located in the Cape Hatteras National Seashore. There are bird observation platforms and other vantage points from which to see the outstanding number and variety of birds on the Outer Banks. The visitors' center is just north of Rodanthe.

Jockey's Ridge State Park near Nags Head preserves the highest sand dune on the Outer Banks. It is a popular place to watch and participate in the sport of hang gliding.

Carolina Beach State Park near Wilmington preserves some of the original coastal ecosystems of the Cape Fear region. In its low-lying areas of bog and grassland grow the Venus flytrap, parrot and trumpet pitcher plants, yellow butterwort, red sundew, and terrestrial bladderwort—carnivorous plants which have evolved the capacity of trapping and digesting insects to better survive in the nutrient-poor soil. The prickly pear cactus which favors higher, sandy areas, can also be seen here. Within the park is a large sand dune which William Hilton, on his exploration of the river in 1663, named Sugar Loaf. From here Confederate lookouts observed the Battle of Fort Fisher in 1865. Snows Cut, the northern boundary of the park, is a channel for the Intracoastal Waterway dredged between the river and the sound in the 1930s by the Army Corps of Engineers.

The Croatan National Forest maintains recreation areas and nature and hiking trails for visitors. Information can be obtained at the Ranger Station off U.S. 70 south of New Bern. Near Cape Carteret there is a campground and nature trail.

GARDENS

Those who enjoy formal gardens maintained after the fashion of the eighteenth century should visit the Elizabethan Gardens on Roanoke Island and the Tryon Palace gardens in New Bern. In the Wilmington area there are beautiful garden-parks and cemeteries of a more informal character. Especially interesting are Greenfield Gardens, a municipal park; Airlie Gardens, a former rice plantation; and the Orton Plantation gardens on the west bank of the Cape Fear off N.C. 133.

FERRIES

Several state-operated ferries ply the coastal sounds. A trip on one is an experience in itself. There is regular service across the Cape Fear between Southport and Fort Fisher. Ocracoke is served by ferries from Cedar Island in Carteret County and from Swan Quarter. There is a free ferry between Hatteras and Ocracoke islands across Hatteras Inlet. Other free ferries provide service across Currituck Sound between Currituck and Knotts

Island, across the Pamlico River between Bayview and near Aurora, and across the Neuse River between Minnesott Beach and Cherry Branch. For information and schedules write Director, Ferry Division, North Carolina Department of Transportation, P.O. Drawer P, Morehead City, North Carolina 28557.

FOOD AND LODGING

There are only a few rules to observe here. For good food, order the fresh seafood. It is wonderful, simply prepared, and very inexpensive. Avoid the chains in favor of the "down-home" places. Calabash, near the South Carolina state line, a city of fresh seafood restaurants, should not be missed. Prices are very reasonable for lodging also, except on the beach.

HISTORIC DISTRICTS AND SITES

ROANOKE ISLAND AND THE DARE BEACHES

The leading area here is the Fort Raleigh National Historical Site on U.S. 64–264 north of Manteo. Fort Raleigh itself was reconstructed in the 1950s in accordance with historical and archaeological evidence.

Drinkwater's Folly (also known as the Dough House) is on the north side of S.R. 1167 just west of where it joins U.S. 64–264. Built in 1805 for Ashley Dough, it is the oldest house in the area. It was moved here from its former location at the site of the Elizabethan Gardens. It is a private residence.

Of several interesting houses in Manteo, my favorite is the Pugh-Meekins House on the corner of Sir Walter Raleigh Street and Uppowoc Avenue. This is a house in the late-nineteenth-century Queen Anne style. Note the wraparound porch, shingled gables, and rounded corner tower with a conical roof. It, too, is a private residence.

A section on the beach that is well worth seeing is the Nags Head Beach Cottage Row historic district between U.S. 158 Business and the ocean. The houses evoke the life-style of the early resorts of the 1920s and 1930s. At the same time they are simple, beautiful, and functional. Most were built by the Elizabeth City contractor Samuel J. Twine. Dating from the same era

(1932) is the First Colony Inn, on the east side of U.S. 158 Business two-tenths of a mile south of Hollowell Street in Nags Head.

Some of the old lifesaving stations can still be seen as well. The Caffey's Inlet station is eight-tenths of a mile south of the Currituck County line near Duck on the east side of S.R. 1200. This structure dates from the early twentieth century, although there has been a lifesaving station here since 1874. Kitty Hawk Lifesaving Station is on the east side of U.S. 158 opposite its junction with S.R. 1206. The Kill Devil Hills station and boathouse is on the east side of U.S. 158 at Milepost 9, Kill Devil Hills. These are now privately owned.

In so-called Old Nags Head is the Fearing House, on the east side of Sound Side Road, one mile southwest of U.S. 158 Bypass. It dates from the mid-nineteenth century and is now a private residence.

The Wright Brothers National Memorial is on U.S. 158 Bypass in Kill Devil Hills. Here a museum and a granite pylon commemorate the "first flight."

THE ALBEMARLE

The town of Edenton is the major attraction here, a place of national significance and interest. The visitors' center is in the Barker House (built in 1782) on the waterfront. The outstanding buildings include the Cupola House (1725), the Chowan County Courthouse (1767), St. Paul's Church (begun in 1736), with an interesting burying ground, and the James Iredell House (date uncertain but eighteenth century). All are open to the public.

A free pamphlet available at the Barker House makes a walking tour of Edenton interesting and informative. Such a tour is the best way to get the full flavor of this stately town, which has good examples of the building styles of the past—Georgian, Federal, Greek Revival, and Victorian.

The plantation homes in the countryside around Edenton are private but may be seen from the road. Perhaps the most elegant is Hayes, across Queen Anne's Creek from Edenton. Constructed in 1817, it has a magnificent columned double-porch facade. East of Edenton on Albemarle Sound are other plantation homes: Sycamore, Athol, Mulberry Hill, and Sandy Point. The Yeopim Church, built in 1851, is a beautiful white frame meeting house for the oldest Baptist congregation in the county.

Other tours in the Albemarle are interesting also. The town of Windsor has a courthouse built in 1887, a rose-colored Greek Revival and Italianate structure with a pediment supported by columns. St. Thomas Episcopal Church, built in 1839, is nearby, and white frame houses adorn the other main streets. The Gray-Gillam House, a pre-Revolutionary structure, was built by the Gray family, who gave the land for the town in the eighteenth century. Windsor Castle, with its facade of four white Ionic columns, was built in the 1850s by the Winston family. To the south of town are two plantation houses, Rosefield, the birthplace of William Blount, a signer of the federal Constitution, and Hope Plantation, now open to the public, the birthplace of Governor David Stone (1808–10).

Hertford, the seat of Perquimans County, is a beautiful old town built on the shores of the Perquimans River. The courthouse was built about 1825, and many nineteenth-century homes remain along Front Street. Holy Trinity Episcopal Church dates from 1848. George Fox, the founder of the Quakers, preached in this vicinity in 1672, and small communities in the area, such as Belvidere, were originally settled by Quakers from Pennsylvania in the early eighteenth century. South of Hertford in the Harveys Neck peninsula is the Newbold-White House, possibly the oldest in the state, and several other early plantation homes or sites.

Across the river in the Durants Neck area is the large, brick plantation house called Leigh's Farm. Constructed by slaves, it has a gambrel roof enclosing a third-story ballroom and a double porch framed with six Doric columns. It is perhaps the largest of the old manor houses of the Albemarle. Governor Seth Sothel is said to be buried here.

Elizabeth City, the largest city of the region, is the seat of Pasquotank County. Its antebellum buildings have suffered from twentieth-century demolition, but several dozen nevertheless remain. The waterfront, the site of a busy port in the nineteenth century, has been allowed to deteriorate, and access to the river is blocked by decaying buildings. Attractive neighborhoods of Victorian-era houses are found in the residential sections of the city. The Museum of the Albemarle has been established in Elizabeth City to exhibit the history of the region.

The neck of land south of Elizabeth City is historically interesting. Nixonton, the county seat and chief port until the rise of Elizabeth City, is an area of ramshackle homes and trailers, and the old customs house is a decaying reminder of busier times. At Halls Creek is the site of the first assembly of Carolina settlers in 1665, convened by William Drummond, the first governor of the province. At Cobb Point is the site of the naval battle that resulted in the capture of Elizabeth City by Union forces in 1862. Nearby is Enfield Farm, the site of Culpeper's Rebellion in 1677.

Across the Pasquotank River lies the peninsula of Camden County. This predominantly rural area produces mainly agricultural and forest products. A large second-home development is under way in the south half of the county. Much of the population commutes to either the Elizabeth City or the Norfolk area to work.

SOUTH ALBEMARLE

Plymouth merits more attention than it normally receives. The fine sense of proportion downtown is due to the 1787 street plan by Arthur Rhodes. The most distinctive structure in town is the Latham House at 233 Main Street. This is a two-story Greek Revival building with a central-hall floor plan, which was built in 1850. The oldest house in Plymouth is the Nichols House, built in 1804, on the corner of Washington and Third streets. The Clark House, at 219 Jefferson Street, is a Federal-style frame house built in 1811. The Ausbon House, on the southeast corner of Washington and Third streets, the Armisted House, at 302 West Main Street, and the Stubbs House, a large two-story Greek Revival frame dwelling on Winesett Circle, all date from about 1830. On the south side of S.R. 1112 is Garrett's Island Home, a small frame house built about 1750. Several old churches in the town are also worth noting. Grace Episcopal Church, at the southwest corner of Madison and Water streets, is a brick Gothic Revival structure completed in 1861. The Plymouth United Methodist Church at Third and Adams streets dates from 1832. It was veneered in brick in 1932. Some interesting buildings were constructed after the Civil War as well. The Addie Brinkley House at 201 East Main Street is a handsome Victorian structure. The Hornthall House, 109 West Main Street, has a hip roof intersected by gables. The Spruill House at 326 Washington Street has interesting ornate sawnwork decoration. The Plymouth railroad depots are one-story, gable-roof structures built in the early twentieth century.

In the vicinity, some of the old plantation homes may still be seen. Westover is on the south side of S.R. 1300, three-tenths of a mile west of the junction with S.R. 1329. A private residence, it is a two-story, three-bay house in the Greek Revival style. Blount House nearby, facing Albemarle Sound, one and a half miles north of S.R. 1324, is also in the Greek Revival style.

The town of Roper on U.S. 64 has a small late nineteenth—early twentieth century commercial district with an adjoining area of frame houses, forming a pleasing town ensemble.

The Rehobeth Church on the side of U.S. 64, four-tenths of a mile west of the junction with S.R. 1317 in the vicinity of Skinnersville, was constructed by slaves in 1853. Private.

The commercial district of the town of Creswell contains an uninterrupted series of nineteenth-century store buildings.

Near Creswell is St. David's Chapel at the junction of S.R.'s 1158 and 1159. This was built in 1803 by the Reverend Charles Pettigrew. His home, Belgrade (built about 1800), is on the north side of S.R. 1158, three-tenths of a mile east of the junction. Both private.

Pettigrew State Park, near Creswell, consists of Lake Phelps and a few hundred acres along the north and south shores of the lake. Visitors can picnic or camp among huge cypress trees, and there are boat-launching facilities. Nature trails and a swimming beach are planned. Somerset Place, the old mansion of Josiah Collins, is the major attraction of the park. A splendid line of century-old cypress trees conducts the visitor up the old carriage road to the house on the shore of Lake Phelps. Distinctive for its three sets of double gallery porches and constructed of heart cypress, it is one of the most magnificent coastal plantation houses still surviving in North Carolina. In front of the house, the old 1787 canal still drains the lake, and beyond is a lawn with centuries-old trees. Brick walls enclose the outbuildings of the old plantation, while nearby a path passes through the remains of the old slave residences, chapel, and hospital. In the same vicinity are the sites of the plantation and cemetery of the Pettigrew family, for whom the park is named. Excellent guided tours of the historic sites are conducted daily.

East on U.S. 64, the town of Columbia has an interesting old-time commercial district. Fort Landing is the former point of embarkation for a ferry across the broad mouth of the Alligator River. East Lake has a beautiful white frame Methodist church on the north side of U.S. 64, seven-tenths of a mile east of the junction with S.R. 1102. It was built about 1887. The small communities of Manns Harbor and Mashoes are longtime fishing villages.

CURRITUCK

Near Corolla, the Currituck Lighthouse is one of the oldest on the Atlantic coast (1823). The Jones Hill Lifesaving Station is now partially buried by the drifting sand. The shooting clubs are interesting, especially Whaleshead near Corolla and the Currituck Shooting Club. Other clubs include Monkey Island, Swan Island, and Pine Island.

BATH AND THE PAMLICO SHORE

The town of Bath is the focal point of interest on the Pamlico shore. The historic district comprises the old town. Information and a film are available at the visitors' center.

Two eighteenth-century buildings that remain were constructed at the apogee of Bath Town's colonial-era prosperity. The Palmer-Marsh House (east side of Main Street near Carteret Street), built about 1744 by Michael Coutanche, a French merchant who came to Bath from Boston, is a large two-story frame structure with shutters and a gable roof. Its most interesting feature is a huge double chimney seventeen feet across, so big that two windows have been hung in the center on each floor to provide light for chimney closets. In the 1760s the house was acquired by Colonel Robert Palmer, the surveyor-general of the colony, who remained loyal to the king at the time of the Revolution and returned to England. The house was then acquired by Jonathan and Daniel Marsh, merchants from Rhode Island. The Marsh family owned it for more than a century, until the Historic Bath Commission purchased the house and restored and furnished it with objects from the colonial period. Two outbuildings, the wellhouse and smokehouse, have been reconstructed, and the Palmer-Marsh family cemetery with headstones from the eighteenth and nineteenth centuries may also be seen.

St. Thomas Episcopal Church on Craven Street is another building shown on surveyor Claude Sauthier's 1769 map that may still be seen. Constructed about 1734 as a brick, gable-roofed hall, this is the oldest existing church building in the state. The interior still has the original wooden pews and tile floor. During the middle years of the eighteenth century, St. Thomas's was the center of religious life for Bath County, the Parish of Pampticough. The English church viewed the town as a hardship missionary post, and it was several years before a permanent minister came to Bath. A glebe house (rectory), constructed in the late eighteenth century, stands near the church.

In the nineteenth century several buildings with a different architectural character were constructed in Bath. The Bonner House (Front Street), built about 1830, is a two-story frame building with porches and without shutters, which were considered unfashionable at that time. The interior is well appointed with a chair rail and elegant Federal-style fireplace mantels. The site of the house, overlooking Bath Bay, is the place John Lawson chose for his home in 1704. Buzzard's Hotel (Main Street between Craven and Carteret), dating from about 1840, is a two-story frame building used as an ordinary (inn and tavern). The Van Der Veer House (west side of Harding Street between Carteret and Craven) is a private dwelling built about 1790.

Washington is a larger town, important in earlier times as a center for the West Indies trade and later as a railroad center. Downtown are commercial buildings such as the Havens Warehouse (404 West Main Street) and the Bank of Washington building (216 Main Street, now the North Carolina National Bank), constructed in the style of a classical temple. These are suggestive of the prosperity of the nineteenth-century economy. Religious structures including the First Presbyterian Church and St. Peter's Episcopal Church date from the second half of the nineteenth century. Several frame dwelling houses on Main and Water streets are more than a hundred years old. The Holladay House (706 West 2d St.) and "Elmwood" (731 West Main Street) are interesting nineteenth-century mansions. The oldest houses in Washington are the Telfair and Myers houses on Water Street. The old Washington Railroad Station (Gladden Street at West Main), built in 1904, is a handsome brick structure converted to a community center. In spite of the destruction of the Civil War, Washington retains one of the most important ensembles of architectural beauty in the coastal area of North Carolina.

About halfway between Washington and Bath in the Jessama vicinity is the Zion Episcopal Church (mid-nineteenth century), on the south side of U.S. 264, two-tenths of a mile east of the junction with S.R. 1601. Private.

In Belhaven, there are some interesting homes on Front Street facing the estuary of the Pungo River. The Belhaven Memorial Museum, housing a collection of all manner of things, is in the courthouse on Main Street. The River Forest Manor, a turn-of-the-century mansion, is a pleasant place to eat and spend the night.

Fairfield, on the north shore of Lake Mattamuskeet, is well worth a visit. There are nineteenth-century commercial buildings on the north side of S.R. 1305 just west of the junction with N.C. 94. The Fairfield United Methodist Church on the west side of N.C. 94 remains unchanged since it was built in 1877. The interior retains its original furnishings. There are several nineteenth-century houses in the town.

Swan Quarter has three interesting churches: Calvary Episcopal Church (corner of S.R.'s 1129 and 1130), Providence United Methodist Church (corner of S.R.'s 1129 and 1131), and Swan Quarter Baptist Church (S.R. 1129 one-half mile north of S.R. 1130).

On the Lake Mattamuskeet wildlife refuge, near New Holland, is a large brick structure originally constructed as a pump house in 1926. The 120-foot smokestack is now used as an observation tower.

Between the refuge and Engelhard on both sides of U.S. 264 there are more than a dozen nineteenth-century farmhouses and churches. Amity Methodist Church is on the northwest side of U.S. 264 at the junction with S.R. 1107. Wynne's Folly is on the east side of U.S. 264, a mile south of the junction with S.R. 1311. The name comes from the large windows. The house was built for Richard Wynne of Philadelphia about 1850. St. George's Episcopal Church (1874–75) is on U.S. 264, a half mile east of S.R. 1107.

Stumpy Point is an old fishing village picturesquely located on a bay of Pamlico Sound. It has numerous nineteenth- and early twentieth-century houses.

The town of Aurora, on the south side of Pamlico Sound, has a late nineteenth–early twentieth-century commercial district, especially the north and south sides of Main Street between Fourth and Fifth streets.

CAPE HATTERAS SEASHORE AND OCRACOKE

Most of the old lifesaving stations within the seashore still exist. They are:

Bodie Island (east side of N.C. 12, 5.3 miles south of U.S. 158 junction)

Oregon Inlet (off N.C. 12 just south of Oregon Inlet)

Chicamacomico (N.C. 12 near Rodanthe)

Little Kinnakeet (2.6 miles north of Avon on the west side of N.C. 12)

Creed's Hill (on the east side of N.C. 12, 1.9 miles north of the junction with S.R. 1246 near Frisco)

Durant's (east side of N.C. 12 north of Hatteras)

There are three outstanding lighthouses within the seashore. Bodie Island Lighthouse and Keeper's Quarters is now a visitors' center. The Bodie Island light (1872) has a distinctive parallel-stripe pattern. Cape Hatteras Lighthouse (1870) is a brick structure 208 feet high, the tallest lighthouse in the nation. It has barbershop spiral stripes. Ocracoke Lighthouse, a conical brick structure painted white, was built in 1828.

NEW BERN AND THE NEUSE SHORE

New Bern is a treasury of colonial-era and nineteenth-century buildings of national significance. The most magnificent building in town, Tryon Palace, has been reconstructed (except for one original wing) and painstakingly recreated following John Hawks's original plans and Governor Tryon's inventory of furnishings.

About a dozen pre-Revolutionary New Bern houses can still be seen. Some of these, such as the Hawks House (306 Hancock Street) and the Major James Davies House (313 George Street), are simple story-and-a-half coastal cottages with front porches. Others, such as the Coor-Bishop House (501 East Front Street) and the Smith-Whitford House (506 Craven Street), are two-story Georgian structures. The York-Gordon House (213 Hancock Street) is interesting because of its gambrel roof. Near New Bern in the Craven County countryside stands Bellair Plantation, a magnificent Georgian brick home that attests to the eighteenth-century prosperity of the region. The oldest house in the area, Clear Springs Plantation, is a small story-and-a-half Georgian frame house constructed about 1740.

Scores of attractive buildings from the late eighteenth and nineteenth centuries enrich the town. Two of these, the John Wright Stanly House, a fine Georgian mansion, and the Stevenson House, a side-hall-plan, Federal-style town house, are part of the Tryon Palace complex and open to the public.

Especially beautiful are the churches. Perhaps the finest is the First Presbyterian Church on New Street, a perfect building in the light classicism of the Federal style. The four-stage steeple rises with a dignity and rhythm that gives an illusion of motion skyward. The Roman Catholic church on Middle Street has a more modest Federal-style design of simple elegance.

Federal-style brick or frame residences of antebellum vintage are found on almost every street in New Bern. Particularly noteworthy are the houses on Front Street and on Pollock Street. These exhibit a variety of plans and motifs, with the graceful classical columns, pediments, fans, and sunburst ornamentation that characterize this truly American architecture. The houses of New Bern were almost all executed by local carpenters and artisans. It is today one of the greatest assemblages of Federal-style buildings in the country.

Toward the middle of the nineteenth century, other styles became fashionable in New Bern. The Slover-Bradham House (201 Johnson Street) was built in 1848 in the Renaissance Revival style. It was used by the Union general Ambrose Burnside as headquarters during the Civil War occupation of the city. The Gothic Revival style was used for the First Baptist Church with its massive brick entrance tower.

Outside New Bern, along the Neuse and its tributaries, some of the planters grew wealthy enough to build stylish mansion homes. China Grove near Janeiro in Pamlico County is perhaps the finest still remaining, a Federal structure with a double porch and a commanding view of the Neuse River.

CARTERET AND CAPE LOOKOUT SEASHORE

The architecture and "townscape" of Beaufort reflects its past as a small, isolated maritime village. The historic district and especially the waterfront are extraordinary in their functional beauty and evocation of man's relationship with the sea. The Jacob Henry House (229 Front Street) is the best example of the Federal style in Beaufort. Henry was elected to the North Carolina General Assembly in 1808, but his right to take his seat was challenged in 1809 because he was Jewish and "denied the Divine Authority of the New Testament." He won his fight to be seated with a brilliant speech on religious freedom that was widely reported at the time.

The Old Burying Ground at Beaufort is on the block between Ann, Craven, and Broad streets. The large trees, melancholy atmosphere, and interesting grave markers make this a favorite spot for visitors.

The best building in Morehead City is the Morehead Municipal Building on the southwest corner of Evans and South Eighth streets. Built in 1926, it is in the Florentine Renaissance Revival style.

On the east end of Bogue Banks is Fort Macon, now a state park and museum, begun in 1826.

Near Cape Carteret is an interesting Octagon House (completed 1856) on a dirt lane four-tenths of a mile off the north side of N.C. 24, one-tenth of a mile east of the junction with S.R. 1214. Private.

On Cape Lookout National Seashore is the abandoned town of Portsmouth at the north end of Portsmouth Island (reached by boat from Ocracoke). About twenty buildings remain, including the Coast Guard station and the Portsmouth Methodist Church.

The Cape Lookout Lighthouse, with its distinctive diamond markings, is on Core Banks. It was built betweeen 1857 and 1859.

CAPE FEAR

Wilmington is a distinctive urban center. An amazing number of commercial, governmental, religious, and residential buildings have survived from the time Wilmington was the state's leading city. Five Georgian buildings from the eighteenth century remain, of which the Burgwin-Wright House (Third and Market streets), with its double porches, is the most elaborate. This house was Cornwallis's headquarters during his two-week stay in Wilmington in 1781.

In the nineteenth century a variety of building styles were used in Wilmington. For churches, the preferred mode was Gothic Revival. St. James Episcopal Church (1840) has an exquisite tower pinnacle, and the parish house was built in the shingle style in 1901. St. Thomas Catholic Church is a smaller Gothic Revival structure completed in 1846. The New Hanover County Courthouse, built in 1894, is a flamboyant, High Victorian Gothic building. Thalian Hall, a wing of the City Hall, on Third Street, is an imposing Neoclassical building completed in 1855.

The most distinctive and important Wilmington building style in the nineteenth century was Italian Revival, a Victorian building technique emphasizing elaborate columns, arches, friezes, and ballustrades. The De Rosset House (23 Second Street) is the most grandiose example of this, on a terraced hill overlooking the Cape Fear River. It is being restored by the Historic Wilmington Foundation. The Zebulon Latimer House (126 S.

Third Street) is a brick dwelling in this style, an Italian patrician mansion. Many frame residences in Wilmington exhibit aspects of the Italianate style as well.

An outstanding feature of Wilmington is not only the individual buildings, but the character of the neighborhoods, where the residences form a rhythmic unit set in the beauty of large trees and shrubs. The Nun Street neighborhood exhibits large frame urban houses built in the period 1880–1910. Along Third and Fourth streets there is a beautiful ensemble of houses constructed just before and after the Civil War. On Front and Water streets are several interesting nineteenth-century commercial buildings, including the Front Street Market and the Wilmington Iron Works. Outside of the downtown area, in the 1700 block of Market Street, are some examples of mansions built in a neighborhood that was fashionable in the early twentieth century.

Pleasant open spaces in the city provide rest amid the distinctive southern coastal vegetation dominated by centuries-old live oaks draped with Spanish moss. Greenfield Park is a former millpond with cypress trees growing in the still waters of the lake. Oakdale Cemetery, the nineteenth-century burial ground for the city, is a beautifully landscaped setting for old-fashioned Victorian grave markers of iron and stone.

Outside the city, on the shores of the sound, is an area of nineteenth-century rice plantations, now a neighborhood of exclusive homes. Airlie Gardens estate exhibits a profusion of virgin moss-decked oak and pine, a remnant of the lush forests that once grew near Cape Fear. A nineteenth-century chapel remains as well. Several antebellum sound houses still exist in the vicinity of Masonboro.

South of Wilmington is Fort Fisher, built at the southern tip of the peninsula between the Cape Fear River and the ocean. This was the last major coastal fortification held by the Confederates; it finally fell on January 15, 1865, after an epic battle. The Blockade Runners Museum near Carolina Beach exhibits the Confederate ships that ran the Union blockade.

North of Wilmington, near Currie, is Moores Creek National Military Park, the site of an important Revolutionary War battle on February 27, 1776. The American victory influenced North Carolina to vote for independence at the Continental Congress.

On the west bank of the Cape Fear in Brunswick County there are several attractions of major interest. Off N.C. 133 is Orton Plantation, the most spectacular of the eighteenth-century Cape Fear River houses. Nearby is the site of Brunswick Town, a major port of Cape Fear in the early eighteenth century, which was abandoned after the Revolution. This is now a state historic site. The buildings have been excavated and the ruins of St. Philips Church may be seen. Russelborough, which was later the residence of colonial governors, was the focus of resentment against the Stamp Act in 1776. The Confederate Fort Anderson was built here later to defend Wilmington.

At Southport is the site of the Confederate Fort Johnston. The Frying Pan Lightship, which warned shipping away from Frying Pan Shoals from 1930 to 1964, is now moored at the foot of Howe Street. Today the quiet old houses on Bay Street look out upon the Cape Fear Inlet still marked by the Bald Head Lighthouse to the east and the Oak Island Lighthouse with the ruins of old Fort Caswell to the west.

BIBLIOGRAPHY

CHAPTER ONE

Bellis, V. J.; O'Connor, M. P.; and Riggs, S. R. *Estuarine Shoreline Erosion in the Albemarle-Pamlico Region of North Carolina*. Raleigh: University of North Carolina Sea Grant Program, 1975.

Clay, J. W.; Orr, D. M., Jr.; and Stuart, A. W., eds. *North Carolina Atlas*. Chapel Hill: University of North Carolina Press, 1975.

Dolan, R. G. "Barrier Dune Systems along the Outer Banks of North Carolina: A Reappraisal." *Science* 176 (1972):286–88.

Dolan, R. G.; Godfrey, P. J.; and Odum, W. E. "Man's Impact on the Barrier Islands of North Carolina." *American Scientist* 61 (1973):152–62.

Dune of Dare Garden Club. *Wildflowers of the Outer Banks*. Chapel Hill: University of North Carolina Press, 1980.

Giese, G. L.; Wilder, H. B.; and Parker, G. G., Jr. *Hydrology of Major Estuaries and Sounds in North Carolina*. Raleigh: U.S. Geological Survey, Water Resources Division, 1979.

Godfrey, P. J., and Godfrey, M. M. *Barrier Island Ecology of Cape Lookout and Vicinity, North Carolina*. Washington, D.C.: U.S. Government Printing Office, 1976.

Kaufman, Wallace, and Pilkey, Orrin H. *The Beaches Are Moving: The Drowning of America's Shoreline*. Garden City, N.Y.: Anchor Press/Doubleday, 1979.

Parnell, James F., and Soots, Robert F., Jr. *Atlas of Colonial Water-birds of North Carolina Estuaries*. Raleigh: University of North Carolina Sea Grant Program, 1979.

Pilkey, Orrin H., Jr.; Neal, William J.; and Pilkey, Orrin H., Sr. *From Currituck to Calabash: Living with North Carolina's Barrier Islands*. Research Triangle Park: North Carolina Science and Technology Center, 1978.

CHAPTER TWO

Baker, Simon, ed. *Coastal Development and Areas of Environmental Concern*. Raleigh: University of North Carolina Sea Grant Program, 1975.

Dunbar, Gary S. *Historical Geography of the North Carolina Outer Banks*. Supervised and edited by Fred Kniffen. Baton Rouge: Louisiana State University Press, 1958.

Mook, M. A. "Algonkian Ethnohistory of the Carolina Sound." *Journal of the Washington Academy of Sciences* 35 (1944):Nos. 6–7.

Morison, Samuel E. *The European Discovery of America: The Northern Voyages A.D. 500–1600*. New York: Oxford University Press, 1971.

Phelps, David S. *Archeological Studies of the Coastal Zone of North Carolina*. Raleigh: The North Carolina Archeological Council, 1978.

Powell, William S. *North Carolina: A Bicentennial History*. New York: W. W. Norton and Co., 1977.

Quattlebaum, Paul. *The Land Called Chicora*. Spartanburg: The Reprint Co., 1973.

Quinn, David B. *North America from Earliest Discovery to First Settlements: The Norse Voyage to 1612*. New York: Harper and Row, 1977.

Quinn, David B., ed. *The Roanoke Voyages, 1584–1590*. 2 vols. London: The Hakluyt Society, 1955.

Rights, Douglas L. *The American Indian in North Carolina*. Winston-Salem: John F. Blair, Publisher, 1957.

South, Stanley A. *Indians in North Carolina*. Raleigh: State Department of Archives and History, 1965.

Stick, David. *The Outer Banks of North Carolina, 1584–1958*. Chapel Hill: University of North Carolina Press, 1958.

U.S. Office of Coastal Zone Management, and State of North Carolina Coastal Zone Management Program. *State of North Carolina Coastal Management Program and Final Environmental Impact Statement*. Washington, D.C.: U.S. Department of Commerce, 1978.

Wetmore, Ruth Y. *First on the Land: The North Carolina Indians*. Winston-Salem: John F. Blair, Publisher, 1975.

CHAPTER THREE

Arnaudin, Steven. "North Carolina Coastal Vernacular." In *Carolina Dwelling*, edited by Doug Swaim, pp. 62–69. Raleigh: North Carolina State University School of Design, 1978.

Bisher, Catherine W. "The 'Unpainted Aristocracy': The Beach Cottages of Old Nags Head." *The North Carolina Historical Review* 54 (1977):367–92.

North Carolina Division of Community Planning. *Dare County Land Use Plan*, 1976.

―――. *Jockey's Ridge Master Plan*, 1976.

Outlaw, Edward R., Jr. *Old Nags Head*. Norfolk: Liskey Lithograph Co., 1956.

Stick, David. *Dare County: A History*. Raleigh: State Department of Archives and History, 1970.

Stick, David. *The Outer Banks of North Carolina, 1584–1958*. Chapel Hill: University of North Carolina Press, 1958.

CHAPTER FOUR

Barrett, John G. *The Civil War in North Carolina*. Chapel Hill: University of North Carolina Press, 1963.

Bond, Sharon; Cook, Grover; and Howells, David. *The Chowan River Project: Summary Report*. Raleigh: Water Resources Research Institute, 1978.

Boyd, William K., ed. *William Byrd's Histories of the Dividing Lines Betwixt Virginia and North Carolina*. Raleigh: The North Carolina Historical Commission, 1929.

Brickell, John. *The Natural History of North Carolina*. 1737. Reprint. Murfreesboro: Johnson Publishing Co., 1968.

Lefler, Hugh T. *North Carolina History Told By Contemporaries*. Chapel Hill: University of North Carolina Press, 1948.

Merrens, Harry Roy. *Colonial North Carolina in the Eighteenth Century*. Chapel Hill: University of North Carolina Press, 1964.

North Carolina Division of Community Planning. *Camden County Land Use Plan*, 1976.

―――. *Edenton-Chowan County Land Use Plan*, 1976.

―――. *Elizabeth City Land Use Plan*, 1976.

―――. *Gates County Land Use Plan*, 1976.

―――. *Hertford County–Ahoskie Land Use Plan*, 1976.

―――. *Pasquotank County Land Use Plan*, 1976.

―――. *Perquimans County Land Use Plan*, 1976.

―――. *Town of Winton Land Use Plan*, 1976.

Parramore, Thomas C. *Cradle of the Colony*. Edenton: Edenton Chamber of Commerce, 1967.

Powell, William S. "Carolana and the Incomparable Roanoke: Explorations and Attempted Settlements, 1620–1663." *The North Carolina Historical Review* 51 (1974):1–21.

Rankin, Hugh F. *Upheaval in Albemarle, The Story of Culpeper's Rebellion 1675–1689*. Raleigh: The Carolina Charter Tercentenary Commission, 1962.

Robinson, Blackwell P., ed. *The North Carolina Guide*. Chapel Hill: University of North Carolina Press, 1955.

CHAPTER FIVE

Blake, James G. *Land Potential Study for Currituck County, North Carolina*. Raleigh: North Carolina Department of Conservation and Development, 1966.

Boyd, William K., ed. *William Byrd's Histories of the Dividing Line Betwixt Virginia and North Carolina*. Raleigh: The North Carolina Historical Commission, 1929.

Currituck Historical Society, The. *The Journal of the Currituck Historical Society* I, no. 3, 1976.

Envirotek, Inc. *The Currituck Plan: Outer Banks Development Plan*. Currituck: Currituck County Commission, 1974.

North Carolina Division of Community Planning. *Currituck Land Use Plan*, 1976.

Soucie, G. "Fare Thee Well, Currituck Banks." *Audubon* 78 (1976):22–35.

State v. Narrows Island Club, 100 N.C. 477 (1888).

U.S. Fish and Wildlife Service. *Final Environmental Impact Statement, Proposed Wildlife Refuge On the Currituck Outer Banks*, 1980.

Vigneras, L. A. "A Spanish Discovery in North Carolina in 1566." *The North Carolina Historical Review* 46 (1969):398–414.

CHAPTER SIX

Barrett, John G. *The Civil War in North Carolina*. Chapel Hill: University of North Carolina Press, 1963.

Franklin, John H. *The Free Negro in North Carolina, 1790–1860*. Chapel Hill: University of North Carolina Press, 1943.

Griffin, William A. *Ante-Bellum Elizabeth City: The History of a Canal Town*. Elizabeth City: Roanoke Press, 1970.

North Carolina Department of Cultural Resources. *Historic and Architectural Resources of the Tar-Neuse River Basin*. Appendix for Region Q and R, 1977.

North Carolina Division of Community Planning. *Dare County Land Use Plan*, 1976.

———. *Tyrell County Land Use Plan*, 1976.

———. *Washington County Land Use Plan*, 1976.

Pomeroy, Kenneth B., and Yoho, James G. *North Carolina Lands: Ownership, Use, and Management*. Washington, D.C.: The American Forestry Association, 1964.

Robinson, Blackwell P., ed. *The North Carolina Guide*. Chapel Hill: University of North Carolina Press, 1955.

Wall, Bennett H. "The Founding of the Pettigrew Plantations." *The North Carolina Historical Review* 27 (1950):395–418.

Washington County Historical Society. *Historic Washington County*. 1970 [?].

CHAPTER SEVEN

Allcott, John V. *Colonial Homes in North Carolina*. Raleigh: The Carolina Charter Tercentenary Commission, 1963.

Davidson, Eliza. "North Carolina Churches: Exploration in the Mountains and the Tidewater." In *Carolina Dwelling*, edited by Doug Swaim, pp. 184–95. Raleigh: North Carolina State School of Design, 1978.

Hyde County Historical Society. *Hyde County History, A Hyde County Bicentennial Project*, 1976.

Lee, Enoch Lawrence. *Indian Wars in North Carolina, 1663–1763*. Raleigh: The Carolina Charter Tercentenary Commission, 1963.

Marsh, Kenneth F., and Marsh, Blanche. *Colonial Bath, North Carolina's Oldest Town*. Asheville: Biltmore Press, 1966.

North Carolina Division of Community Planning. *Beaufort County Land Use Plan*, 1976.

———. *Goose Creek State Park Master Plan*, 1976.

———. *Hyde County Land Use Plan*, 1976.

Paschal, Herbert R., Jr. *A History of Colonial Bath*. Raleigh: Edwards and Broughton Co., 1955.

Reed, C. Wingate. *Beaufort County: Two Centuries of Its History*. Raleigh[?], n.p., 1962.

CHAPTER EIGHT

Bragg, Cecil S. *Ocracoke Island: Pearl of the Outer Banks*. Manteo: Times Printing Co., 1973.

Burk, C. John. "The North Carolina Outer Banks: A Floristic Interpretation." *The Journal of the Elisha Mitchell Scientific Society* 78 (1962):21–28.

Cumming, William P. *Captain James Wimble, His Maps, and the Colonial Cartography of the North Carolina Coast*. Raleigh: State Department of Archives and History, 1969.

Dunbar, Gary S. *Historical Geography of the North Carolina Outer Banks*. Baton Rouge: Louisiana State University Press, 1958.

Goerch, Carl. *Ocracoke*. Winston-Salem: John F. Blair, Publisher, 1958.

Godfrey, P. J.; Leatherman, S. P.; and Buckley, P. A. *Impact of Off-Road Vehicles on Coastal Ecosystems*. Proceedings of the Symposium on Technical, Environmental, Socioeconomic and Regulatory Aspects of Coastal Zone Planning and Management, San Francisco, March 14–16, 1978.

Hyde County Historical Society. *Hyde County History, A Hyde County Bicentennial Project*, 1976.

Leatherman, S. P.; Godfrey, P. J.; and Buckley, P. A. *Management Strategies for National Seashores*. Proceedings of the Symposium on Technical, Environmental, Socioeconomic and Regulatory Aspects of Coastal Zone Planning and Management, San Francisco, March 14–16, 1978.

MacNeill, Ben Dixon. *The Hatterasman*. Winston-Salem: John F. Blair, Publisher, 1958.

National Park Service. *Environmental Assessment, Cape Hatteras National Seashore, North Carolina*, 1974.

North Carolina Department of Cultural Resources. *Historical and Architectural Resources of the Tar-Neuse River Basin*. Appendix for Region Q and R, 1977.

North Carolina Division of Community Planning. *Dare County Land Use Plan*, 1976.

———. *Hyde County Land Use Plan*, 1976.

Pilkey, Orrin H., Jr.; Neal, William J.; and Pilkey, Orrin H., Sr. *From Currituck to Calabash: Living with North Carolina's Barrier Islands*. Research Triangle Park: North Carolina Science and Technology Center, 1978.

Riggs, Stanley, and Benton, Stephen B. *The Northern Outer Banks of North Carolina*. Raleigh: University of North Carolina Sea Grant Program, 1979.

Stick, David. *The Outer Banks of North Carolina, 1584–1958*. Chapel Hill: University of North Carolina Press, 1958.

U.S. Army Corps of Engineers. *Manteo (Shallowbag) Bay, North Carolina: Final Environmental Impact Statement*, 1977.

Wechter, Nell Wise. *The Mighty Midgetts of Chicamacomico*. Manteo: Times Printing Co., 1974.

CHAPTER NINE

Dill, Alonzo T. *Governor Tryon and His Palace*. Chapel Hill: University of North Carolina Press, 1955.

Hobbie, John E., and Smith, Nathaniel W. *Nutrients in the Neuse River*

Estuary. Raleigh: University of North Carolina Sea Grant Program, 1975.

Lawson, John. *History of North Carolina*. 1714. Reprint. Richmond: Garrett and Massie, 1937.

North Carolina Division of Community Planning. *Craven County Land Use Plan*, 1976.

———. *New Bern Land Development Plan*, 1976.

———. *Pamlico Coastal Area Management Plan*, 1976.

Robinson, Blackwell P. *The Five Royal Governors of North Carolina, 1729–1775*. Raleigh: The Carolina Charter Tercentenary Commission, 1963.

Seapker, Janet K. "The Architecture of New Bern." In *Guide to Historic New Bern, North Carolina*, edited by H. B. Taylor. New Bern: Craven County American Revolution Bicentennial Commission, 1974.

Todd, Vincent H., ed. *Christoph von Graffenried's Account of the Founding of New Bern*. Raleigh: Edwards and Broughton Printing Co., 1920.

CHAPTER TEN

Burke, Kenneth E., Jr. *The History of Portsmouth, North Carolina*. Washington, D.C.: Insta-Print, 1976.

Godfrey, Paul J., and Godfrey, Melinda M. *Barrier Island Ecology of Cape Lookout National Seashore and Vicinity, North Carolina*. Washington, D.C.: U.S. Printing Office, 1976.

Godschalk, David R.; Parker, Francis H.; and Knoche, John R. *Carrying Capacity: A Basis for Coastal Planning*. Chapel Hill: Department of City and Regional Planning, University of North Carolina, 1974.

Hill, Mrs. Fred, ed. *Historic Carteret County, North Carolina, 1663–1975*. Beaufort: Carteret Historical Research Association, 1975.

Holland, F. Ross, Jr. *A Survey History of Cape Lookout National Seashore*. National Park Service, 1968.

Kell, Jean Bruyere. *Historic Beaufort, North Carolina*. Greenville: National Printing Co., 1977.

Kell, Jean Bruyere, ed. *North Carolina's Coastal Carteret County During the American Revolution, 1765–1785*. Greenville: Carteret County Bicentennial Commission, 1975.

Moon, Travis W., and Trott, William M. "Estuarine Pollution: The Deterioration of the Oyster Industry in North Carolina." *The North Carolina Law Review* 49 (1971):921–43.

National Park Service. *Environmental Assessment, Cape Lookout National Seashore, North Carolina*, 1978.

North Carolina Department of Cultural Resources. *Historic and Cul-*

tural Resources of the Tar-Neuse River Basin. Appendix O and P, 1977.

North Carolina Division of Community Planning. *Beaufort Land Use Plan,* 1976.

———. *Carteret County Land Development Plan,* 1976.

Paul, Charles L. "Beaufort, North Carolina: Its Development as a Colonial Town." *The North Carolina Historical Review* 47 (1970):370–87.

Paul, Charles L. "Factors in the Economy of Colonial Beaufort." *The North Carolina Historical Review* 44 (1967):111–34.

Pilkey, Orrin H., Jr.; Neal, William J.; and Pilkey, Orrin H., Sr. *From Currituck to Calabash: Living with North Carolina's Barrier Islands.* Research Triangle Park: North Carolina Science and Technology Center, 1978.

Pilkey, Orrin H., Jr.; Pilkey, Orrin H., Sr.; and Turner, Robb. *How To Live With An Island.* Raleigh: North Carolina Department of Natural and Economic Resources, 1975.

Salter, Ben B. *Portsmouth Island, Short Stories and History.* Portsmouth Island: Privately published, 1972.

Shu-Fun-Au. *Vegetation and Ecological Processes on Shackleford Bank, North Carolina.* National Park Service, 1968.

Stick, David. *The Outer Banks of North Carolina, 1584–1958.* Chapel Hill: University of North Carolina, 1958.

U.S. Army Corps of Engineers. *Erosion Study of Cape Lookout Lighthouse.*

CHAPTER ELEVEN

Barrett, John G. *The Civil War in North Carolina.* Chapel Hill: University of North Carolina Press, 1963.

Cleary, William J., and Hosier, Paul E. *The New Hanover Banks: Then and Now.* Raleigh: University of North Carolina Sea Grant Program, 1977.

Clifton, James M. "Golden Grains of White: Rice Planting in the Lower Cape Fear." *The North Carolina Historical Review* 50 (1973):365–93.

Cooper, Arthur W., and Satterthwaite, Sheafe. *Smith Island and the Cape Fear Peninsula, A Comprehensive Report on an Outstanding Natural Area.* Raleigh: North Carolina Wildlife Preserves, 1964.

Evans, Willima McKee. *Ballots and Fencerails: Reconstruction on the Lower Cape Fear.* Chapel Hill: University of North Carolina Press, 1967.

Howell, Andrew J. *The Book of Wilmington.* Wilmington[?]: n.p., 1930[?].

Lee, Lawrence. *The Lower Cape Fear in Colonial Days.* Chapel Hill: University of North Carolina Press, 1965.

Lee, Lawrence. *New Hanover County: A Brief History*. Raleigh: Department of Cultural Resources, 1977.

North Carolina Department of Cultural Resources. *Historic and Architectural Resources of the Tar-Neuse River Basin*. Appendix for region Q and R, 1977.

North Carolina Division of Community Planning. *Coastal Area Management Land Use Plan, City of Wilmington–New Hanover County*, 1976.

————. *Coastal Area Management Land Use Plan, Onslow County*, 1976.

————. *Coastal Area Management Land Use Plan, Pender County*, 1976.

————. *Coastal Area Management Land Use Plan, Town of Sunset Beach*, 1976.

Pilkey, Orrin H., Jr.; Neal, William J.; and Pilkey, Orrin H., Sr. *From Currituck to Calabash: Living with North Carolina's Barrier Islands*. Research Triangle Park: North Carolina Science and Technology Center, 1978.

Price, Charles L., and Sturgill, Claude C. "Shock and Assault in the First Battle of Fort Fisher." *The North Carolina Historical Review* 47 (1970):24–39.

Ross, Malcolm H. *The Cape Fear*. Seven Rivers of America series. New York: Holt, Rinehart and Winston, 1965.

Sharpe, William. *Brain Surgeon: The Autobiography of William Sharpe*. New York: Viking Press, 1952.

Soble, Carol; French, Steven P.; and Godschalk, David R., eds. *Regional Land Planning for Coastal Counties: North Carolina's Cape Fear COG*. Chapel Hill: Department of City and Regional Planning, 1977.

South, Stanley A. "'Russellborough': Two Royal Governors' Mansion of Brunswick Town." *The North Carolina Historical Review* 44 (1967):360–72.

Sprunt, James. *Chronicles of the Cape Fear River, 1660–1916*. 2d ed. Raleigh: Edwards and Broughton Printing Co., 1916.

U.S. Army Corps of Engineers. *Final Environmental Impact Statement, Bald Head Island, North Carolina*, 1977.

Waddell, Alfred Moore. *A History of New Hanover County and the Lower Cape Fear Region, 1723–1800*. Wilmington: Privately printed, 1916.

CHAPTER TWELVE

Bode, Robert V., and Farthing, William P. *Coastal Area Management in North Carolina: Problems and Alternatives*. Chapel Hill: North Carolina Institute of Civic Education, 1974.

Brower, David J.; Frankenburg, Dirk; and Parker, Francis H. *Ecological*

Determinants of Coastal Area Management. 2 vols. Raleigh: University of North Carolina Sea Grant Program, 1976.

Capune v *Robbins*, 160 SE 2d 891 (N.C. 1968).

Conservation of North Carolina v *Costanzo*, 398 F. Supp. 653 (E.D. N.C. 1975).

Hawley, Arthur J. *The Present and Future Status of North Carolina Wetlands.* Raleigh: Water Resources Research Institute, 1974.

Heath, Milton S., Jr. "A Legislative History of the Coastal Area Management Act." *North Carolina Law Review* 53 (1974):345–98.

Schoenbaum, Thomas J. "The Management of Land and Water Use in the Coastal Zone: A New Law Is Enacted in North Carolina." *North Carolina Law Review* 53 (1974):275–302.

Schoenbaum, Thomas J. "Public Rights and Coastal Zone Management." *North Carolina Law Review* 51 (1972):1–41.

State v *Twiford*, 48 SE 586 (N.C. 1904).

State ex rel Thornton v *Hay*, 462 P2d 671 (Ore. 1969).

U.S. Office of Coastal Zone Management, and State of North Carolina Coastal Zone Management Program. *State of North Carolina Coastal Management Program and Final Environmental Impact Statement.* Washington, D.C.: U.S. Department of Commerce, 1978.

CHAPTER THIRTEEN

McElyea, William D.; Brower, David J.; and Godschalk, David R., *Before the Storm: Managing Development to Reduce Hurricane Damages.* Raleigh: Office of Coastal Management, 1987.

Pilkey, Orrin H., Jr.; Neal, William J.; and Pilkey, Orrin H., Sr. *From Currituck to Calabash: Living with North Carolina's Barrier Islands.* Research Triangle Park: North Carolina Science and Technology Center, 1978.

Rankin v. *Coleman*, 394 F. Supp. 697 (E.D. N.C. 1975).

Schoenbaum, Thomas J., and Silliman, Kenneth G. *Coastal Planning: The Designation and Management of Areas of Critical Environmental Concern.* Raleigh: University of North Carolina Sea Grant Program, 1976.

Schoenbaum, Thomas J., and Rosenberg. "The Legal Implementation of Coastal Zone Management." *Duke Law Journal* 1 (1976).

Stewart, James M., ed. *Water Supply and Wastewater in Coastal Areas.* Raleigh: Water Resources Research Institute, 1975.

INDEX

The Appendix is not indexed.